Case Histories in Community Organization

HARPER'S SOCIAL SCIENCE SERIES

Under the Editorship of

F. STUART CHAPIN

Case Histories
in
Community
Organization

MURRAY G. ROSS

PROFESSOR OF SOCIAL WORK
UNIVERSITY OF TORONTO

HARPER & BROTHERS PUBLISHERS NEW YORK

Contents

PART FOUR
THE COMMUNITY WORKER AND THE COMMUNITY

Foreword

A S MOST of those engaged in teaching or studying community organization are aware, there is a paucity of case records which report the activities of professional workers in the community. This book is designed to fill this vacuum, at least in part.

The episodes reported here have been collected over many years and used in teaching classes in Community Organization at the University of Toronto. Very few of them are complete and detailed records, and the term "episode" is perhaps a more accurate descriptive term than "case history." There are, however, advantages to the brevity of some of the records. They are sufficiently brief to be read quickly, yet of adequate length to illustrate a number of important points and to stimulate discussion. On the whole, while the records are of uneven quality, I have found them extremely useful and provocative in discussions of community organization principles and methods.

It is futile, of course, to attempt to analyze these or any other records without some frame of reference. Thus the first chapter of this book is devoted to theory. It carries further and makes more explicit some of the ideas expressed in my *Community Organization: Theory and Principles* and is designed to encourage the student to consider differences in objectives and methods in community work. When the student has these different conceptions clearly in mind he has some basis for analyzing a particular episode. He may then determine which approach is used, appraise its consistency, evaluate its effectiveness, and consider whether some other approach may have been more useful in the particular situation described.

The community worker is not a psychiatrist, a case worker, nor a personnel officer. Nevertheless, he works with individuals in face-to-face situations and in small and large committees. The nature of the responsibility and role of the community worker in his relationships with individuals is a matter that has eluded precise definition. The episodes in Part Two are included to suggest a few of the varied situations which confront the community worker as he deals with individuals in the community. Discussion of these episodes may well clarify the role of the worker, although it needs to be emphasized that this role is related to a philosophy, and that to take a position in respect to the virtues or defects of what the worker does, requires consistency in one's conception of community work.

Part Three of this book presents a number of episodes which relate to groups that are involved directly or indirectly in community projects. It is frequently said that any community is composed of a network of groups and that the essence of community organization is to engage these groups in common tasks. However this may be, it is unquestionably of the greatest importance for the community worker to be able to identify the principal groupings of people in the community, to secure representative leaders from these groups, to establish communication between groups, and the like. The five episodes in this section suggest different practices in respect to these matters, and it is left to the teacher and students to explore these sufficiently to identify useful principles. Again, however, it is emphasized that principles must be related to some basic philosophy and that some consideration should be given to the various approaches suggested in Chapter 1.

The main section of the book, Part Four, deals with more substantial documents in which community projects of several kinds are reported. Here, a whole community (either functional or geographic) is involved in, or affected by, the projected undertaking. Perhaps it is more important here than in the earlier sections to distinguish in each of these episodes the particular purpose that motivates the worker or workers and the methods employed. When this is done, there is adequate foundation for evaluating the project in light of its aims and for considering whether another approach would have been more or less appropriate.

It is not suggested in any of the records that what the worker or group or community did is "right" or "good" or "desirable." This is left for those analyzing the episodes to discuss and decide. I insist only that such evaluation be made solely on the basis of some explicit formulation of objectives, and methods consistent with these objectives. Further, what must be clearly realized is that there are numerous goals and consequently numerous approaches which are useful in community work. Only when we have decided what we are trying to accomplish can we decide which approach is the proper one and which methods are consistent with the end we have in mind. Such a decision is an essential prerequisite for evaluating any of the records in this book.

I am indebted to the Russell Sage Foundation for permission to use the records of "New Mexico" and "Parker Valley," and to the Anti-Defamation League of B'Nai B'Rith for permission to use the account of developments in "Centertown." I am also indebted to Harper & Brothers for clearance to use the records of "Mrs. Fisher" and "Bellville," which, while they came to me many years ago from other sources, appear in rather similar form in Clarence King's book on community organization. I am grateful also to students and friends from whom I secured other records which appear in this book.

I wish to express appreciation to the H. M. Cassidy Research Fund for assistance in this project and to Mrs. Florence Strakhovsky, the Research Secretary of the Fund who supervised the preparation of the manuscript and made many valuable suggestions as to its content and organization. I thank also Mrs. Betty Kitazaki who typed the manuscript.

MURRAY G. ROSS.

Toronto
January 1, 1958

Part One

The Theory of Community Organization

Conceptions of Community Organization

DISTINCTIONS IN COMMUNITY WORK

ONE WAY to define "community organization" is to say that it is "what community workers do." As will be evident from some of the records in this book, "what community workers do" in the community varies greatly, and it might lead only to further confusion to classify these different approaches under a common title. This is not to suggest that the achievements of one worker are better or more effective than those of a worker using a different approach. It is simply to suggest that that there are a variety of ways of working in the community, each with a somewhat different philosophy, method, and (usually) result. We might well avoid the confusion which ensues when these differences are blurred and attempt to see more clearly what distinct approaches exist at the present time. We shall later restrict the term "community organization" to just one of these.

In working with individuals, there are, of course, well-recognized differences of approach. When we hear terms such as "interviewing," "counseling," "casework," "psychotherapy" or "psychoanalysis," we immediately assume distinctions between each of the corresponding realities. True, each involves a face-to-face situation and, prob-ably, a "helping" relationship. But there are significant differences in the depth of diagnosis and analysis, in the degree of involvement of both parties in the relationship, in the subtlety of factors and feel-ings explored, in the complexity of methods used by the professional workers. However similar the situation, the general goal of helping, and the method may be, few would claim that the differences men-tioned are insignificant or that the approaches are anything but quite distinctive. Any confusion as to the difference in these ap-proaches creates practical difficulties. For example, the counselor who confuses what he is attempting to do in an interview at camp or school with what only a psychotherapist ought to try to do, may find himself in a situation which he has neither the training nor the skill to handle. The advantage of being at least aware of the nature and limits of each approach is obvious in working with individuals.

There are, similarly, marked differences in methods of working with communities. As a beginning, we distinguish five approaches, which might be placed on a scale as shown below. It is not suggested that there are only five, or that these identified approaches carry special value because of their position, or that they are discrete units spaced at equal intervals. These words simply name approaches or orientations to the community which represent different ways of working in the community; each has its own philosophy, values, and results.

Five Approaches to Working with Communities

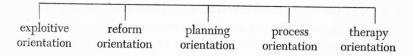

| exploitive orientation | reform orientation | planning orientation | process orientation | therapy orientation |

For the purpose of our discussion we will ignore the polar posi-tions, which imply at one end of the scale *sub rosa* and manipulative procedures to secure private goals, and at the other end of the scale something approaching depth analysis of community forces. The three midpositions identified, however, require some discussion, for it is in these areas that most of our current conceptions of community organization fall.

THE REFORM ORIENTATION

In this approach it is usual for a small group, or more rarely, one person, to seek action with respect to a specific reform or project it thinks is desirable and beneficial to the community. The reform may be something like getting the penal code changed, securing legislation to provide for certain adoption procedures, or increasing allowances to widowed mothers. Or there may be a project in mind, such as the establishment of a new recreation center, a new marriage guidance clinic, or a new program of well-baby clinics. No matter what the particular reform or project may be, the important thing to note is that *this* (the reform or project) is the primary objective of the group. The group is convinced of the merit of the reform or project it advocates, and the focus of its work is that kind of action which will secure the reform or project. The conviction is formulated, the answer is known, the goal is clear. The group, therefore, approaches the community with its mind already made up. If the interest of others is solicited at all, it is not with a view to exploring the need or modifying the plan; it is to secure support for predecided action of a particular kind.

What distinguishes this position is that a minority group (be it the Congregational Church, the American Legion, or the Welfare Council), seeks to secure an end it believes to be desirable *in* and *for* the community. The steps it takes to reach its goal vary greatly, but they often include the following methods.

Reform Approach: Purpose—to Secure a Specific Reform

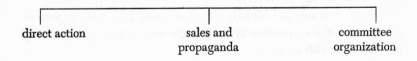

direct action   sales and   committee
                            propaganda   organization

In some situations, *direct action* by the group concerned is possible. It may be that the group need only call the attention of officials to a laxity in the enforcement of certain legislation, or to unmet needs which could be met under existing legislation. Or the group may have sufficient authority, status, or power to secure its ends either by pressure or by proceeding with the reform or project on its own (for example, it may itself raise the money and build a new home for unmarried mothers). Thus direct action may be an adequate method in some situations.

But the problem of securing its ends may be more complicated. It may be known that other individuals and groups in the community are either indifferent to the group's proposal or opposed to it. In such cases, sufficient support must be obtained in the community to assure successful action. Here, either of two methods may be used.

In the *sales method* the group seeks to "sell" the community and either win the indifferent to its side or win over the opposition by persuasion. The arguments for the proposal are put forth in speeches, in discussion groups, in newspaper columns, in film strips. Authorities supporting the proposal are quoted at length, the evils which the reform or proposal seeks to remedy are described in detail, and the soundness of the reforms proposed is emphasized. This educational campaign is often an essential aspect of the reform orientation.

The other method of securing action here, one not exclusive of the first method described, is the organization of a large *committee* or *conference group* to support the proposed reform. It is important to note here that the committee or conference is not called together to formulate just any proposal, but to provide support for the proposal previously formulated by the original group. There may, of course, be exploration of the need, or of a variety of reforms to meet the need, or of other aspects of the problem, but the committee or conference is not organized to develop another solution but to endorse and support a solution already decided upon. The real purpose of constituting the committee or calling the conference is to get help to implement *this* solution.

There are, of course, other variations here, but perhaps this description is sufficient to distinguish one specific approach to the community—that in which a minority group seeks to secure changes it considers desirable in the community. This approach represents common practice in American society. It is undoubtedly acceptable practice in a democracy such as ours, and provides a means by which any alert group of citizens may seek improvements in the life of the community. It is, perhaps, an especially important and appropriate approach for professional groups such as social workers and doctors or lawyers who have special knowledge with regard to certain aspects of community life, and special views as to what is needed. Many of the advances in social welfare were undoubtedly the result of such an approach by individual social workers or groups of social workers who had conviction about welfare needs in the community and took action with respect to these needs.

PLANNING ORIENTATION

In this approach, someone begins with what he feels is a difficulty, with a feeling of concern, with an awareness of a problem which he feels needs to be explored. This concern may be specific, such as concern with the financial difficulties facing families on relief, or quite general, such as a feeling that a better balance of welfare services in the community is needed. Usually this concern is communicated to an existing agency, such as a Welfare Council, or a new committee or council may be formed to deal with it.

But in any case the purpose in the initial stage is *exploration*. It is not, as in the reform approach, to move towards a *particular* solution. The orientation is rather that of planning—of exploring the nature of the difficulty and the means for its resolution. The initial orientation of the planning approach is, then, somewhat different from that of the reform approach. (It is obvious, however, that should the planning group develop conviction about a particular solution, it may then follow some phase of the pattern suggested in objective not only a solution to the problem (a plan) but also an the reform orientation, although, as will be shown, this is not the only method for securing action.)

There are, of course, various ways in which the planning may be undertaken; the method selected indicates, if not refinements of the primary objective, at least important sub-goals. The different ways of organizing committees to do the planning illustrate some of the differences in goal orientation. Again, however, these may be shown by other means, such as the differences in the orientation of the professional worker, differences in dealing with minority opinions in the community, and differences in the use of communication channels in the community.

Planning Orientation: Purpose—to Explore and Resolve a Felt Difficulty

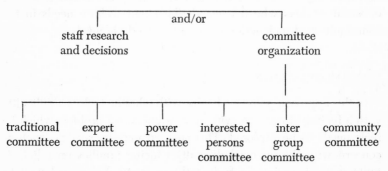

The planning task may be assigned to the staff groups or to a committee, although frequently it is a joint undertaking, with the staff doing the basic research. What kind of committee is formed may reveal how the sponsors view the purposes and nature of the planning task.

It may be a *traditional committee,* one organized simply because it is common practice to form committees to deal with such problems. Where the committee is formed simply because it is "the thing to do" or because "all such decisions are made by committees," it is often made up of "the old reliables," all of whom hold essentially the same point of view—a view which is probably not at all representative of the community.

Another way to go at the problem is to organize a *committee of experts,* through which persons with special knowledge or competence about the problem under discussion are brought together to plan. Or there may be organized a *power committee,* the members of which are prominent among the power hierarchy in the community, people who are probably able to secure implementation of any plan upon which they agree.

A different pattern is the *interested persons committee,* which seeks to bring together those individuals with a special interest in the problem under discussion. Thus a committee formed to consider juvenile delinquency might have an outstanding worker in a church, a juvenile court judge, a police officer noted for his work with youth, or a well-known public recreation worker. Seldom, however, do the advocates of this method go so far as to include some of the individuals most interested, such as parents of delinquents or even juvenile delinquents themselves.

Still another pattern is to bring together on the committee representatives of the major groups interested in the problem or likely to be affected by the decisions made, to provide what we call the *intergroup committee.* Here the groups most concerned are asked to send representatives to the committee. Thus such a committee on juvenile delinquency would ask the Y.M.C.A., the Juvenile Court, the Mental Health Clinic, the Public Recreation Department, etc., to send representatives to work through the problem and to formulate a plan, satisfactory to all, for its solution.

The *community committee* varies from the above in that it seeks to bring together not simply the persons or groups interested and concerned about the problem, but representatives of the most important groupings of people in the community, whether interested or not. It includes not just the traditional agencies, but ethnic or religious groups that have meaning for large groups of people in the community.

Obviously, a committee may be organized which combines some of these patterns, and in fact this is often the case. Nevertheless it may be useful to delineate the patterns of organizations in this way, for it suggests some of the differences in orientation that exist. These differences may be classified (if we leave out the traditional committee) as representing a desire:

1. to have a good (i.e., technically adequate) plan. Thus the use of experts is essential.

2. to have a plan that will be implemented. Thus power figures in the community are used.

3. to have a plan that is accepted and supported by individuals who have an interest in a particular problem area. This often represents both a desire to have a plan that will work (i.e., not be opposed by professional or other vested interests) and a desire to have such persons learn to work together on a common problem.

4. to have a plan developed and supported by the groups most concerned in the community. Here also the objectives may be twofold, namely, to have a plan that is acceptable and to secure collaboration among these groups.

5. to secure a "community" plan. This orientation may have as an objective not only a solution to the problem (a plan) but also an attempt to further community integration by involving most of the people in a community, through their organized groups, in a cooperative process of planning.

While a good deal more could be said, perhaps this brief list is sufficient to suggest that real differences in goals and methods do exist, even within what we roughly call the planning orientation.

PROCESS ORIENTATION

Here the purpose is to initiate a *process*. The process is one by which a community seeks to identify, and take action with respect to, its own problems. The purpose is not (as in the reform orientation) to take action to secure a specific reform, although this may at some point be involved; nor is it, as in the planning orientation, to plan in a particular problem area, although such planning may also be undertaken at some appropriate point. The purpose in the process orientation is to encourage the community itself to identify what it considers to be its problems and to work systematically on these problems; the underlying belief is that such an experience will increase the capacity of the community to deal with problems which will confront it in the future.

This orientation presumes that there is some way by which a community can collectively identify its problems. Such identification is relatively simple in the rural village or in the small town. But in the large complex city, there are many functional communities (discussed later in this chapter), many neighborhoods, and there is, of course, the city itself. Study of any of these should reveal subgroups whose leaders may represent very well the desires, problems, and attitudes of these groups. A council or committee of such leaders may in a significant sense represent the people of a particular community.

With such a group, it is assumed that it will become more deeply involved, more willing to work together, and will develop greater capacity for coöperative work if it deals with problems about which there is common concern and conviction. How these problems are to be identified may vary in the way shown below:

Process Orientation: Purpose—to Develop Community Capacity to Work on Common Problems

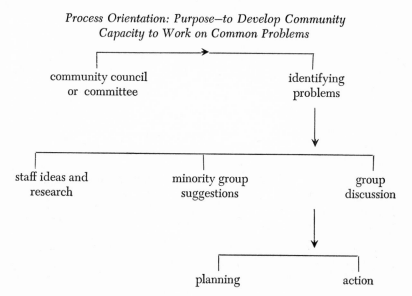

The identification of the problem for study may be made by the staff or research group, may come from some individual or group in the community, or may result from council discussion. It is recognized, however, that if the objective is to be attained, the leaders of community sub-groups in committee must themselves agree—with some feeling of conviction—on the prime importance of the problem. When the problem has thus been identified, the procedure calls for planning and action which might follow some of the methods indicated in the planning orientation and the reform orientation. Advocates of this approach, however, insist that to be consistent, a "community committee" is required to do the planning; they also say that when such a committee agrees on a plan, action inevitably follows, since it has the full support of the community.

It is evident that the three orientations discussed above are not necessarily found in all purity in any real operation. Each represents, conceptually, an approach separate and distinct from the others; yet, in practice, they may be merged in a single approach with planning and action representing stages or elements of the process orientation.

The advantage, however, of careful analysis of each orientation and of the differences within each orientation is that one can see that indiscriminate use of these approaches and methods may make for a program that is inherently inconsistent and self-defeating. It is easy, for example, to proclaim adherence to the goals of the process orientation yet to be so caught up in the desire for action that one organizes a power committee to get the job done, regardless of the feelings of the community's sub-groups. This, in fact, is undoubtedly what frequently happens.

If community organization is to have any meaning at all, it is preferable to use the term to refer to a process which is at least inherently consistent. If the major aim of a given group is to remedy the inadequacies of the welfare services of the local community, it may use a wide variety of methods, including political maneuvering, without offending its claim to consistency. If, however, the objective is to plan in such a way that the community's capacity for under-standing, planning, and coöperative action is increased, then we are limited to methods which will support, and not defeat, this purpose. Then, as in case work and group work, we are committed to definite methods. In this case, we are committed to working the problems through in the community, to using methods that require the com-munity to define, to understand, and to deal with, its own problems.

COMMUNITY ORGANIZATION AS A
SOCIAL WORK PROCESS

If community organization is to be part of a more general practice of social work, this fact sets further limits on what it may properly include. It has been commonly classed as a "social work process" and if we believe it to be so, then community organization must conform to certain fundamental principles in order to qualify. Unfortunately, while there have been frequent discussions of the "social case work process" or the "social group work process," there has been little systematic analysis of the generic "social work process." However, translating roughly some of the concepts often used in connection with case work and group work, one might demand that the process to be called "community organization" meet at least the following conditions:

1. It must deal with problems which the community recognizes as its problems.
2. It must provide for community self-determination.
3. It must engage the community in an active way in the solution of its problems.
4. It must move at a pace that is comfortable for the community.
5. It must encourage growth through problem-solving.
6. It must encourage community self-understanding and integra-tion.

If this necessarily rough and inadequate list of criteria is accept-able, it immediately limits what may properly be called community organization. The reform orientation *per se,* or many types of the planning orientation *per se,* may be useful and valuable in our society, but they cannot be the whole of community organization, if this latter is to be considered a social work process. On the other hand, the community committee (even when it is in the planning orientation) and the process orientation, which seeks to initiate a process by which the community is involved in identifying and solving its own problems to the end that it will develop increasing capacity to function coöperatively, could, it appears, meet these criteria.

Deep in the tradition of social work is the tendency to press for social change and the improvement of welfare services in the community. On this Lurie says: "The responsibilities of the practitioners of social work . . . include those aspects appropriate to all members of professional groups that render a public service *as well as the special qualities in a profession that has an obligation to foster the social changes necessary to attain social welfare objectives . . ."* [1] This obligation of the profession is still widely accepted, and community organization is often considered the means or the method by which we fulfill this objective. This point of view presumes that we (the profession) know what is required, and by a variety of devices, including involvement (since social psychology suggests this as a way of obtaining support), we secure action on that which we believe to be professionally sound. Without denying the obligation of the profession to work for welfare objectives in the community, a legitimate question is whether the means of achieving these ought to be through the use of a social work process. This latter seems to mean the use of insight and skill in helping individuals and groups work through to a satisfactory solution of their problems. We do not insist, much less prejudge, in case work that a client should or should not divorce her husband. We do not in group work insist that the group listen to good music or paint with oils. Why then should community organization be considered the means by which

[1] H. L. Lurie, "The Responsibilities of a Socially Oriented Profession," in Kasius (ed.), *New Directions in Social Work,* New York, Harper & Brothers, 1954, p. 31.

we get a group or council or board in the community to secure certain welfare objectives which we have predetermined to be "good"? Why should not community organization be a process by which we use our insight and skill to help communities, either geographical or functional, to work through their problems?

Ought the task of the professional worker in community organization be to secure certain welfare reforms and objectives in the community, or ought his task be that of helping the community increase its capacity and competence to deal with its problems? Or are these two aspects of the same process?

Since the various approaches described in the first part of this chapter are quite different, it might be better not to refer to all indiscriminately as "community organization." Moreover, if we define community organization as a social work process and if we accept the conditions that seem to be implied by that term, we are logically compelled to accept the process orientation, or some modification of it, as that which (by definition) we will call "community organization."

This does not invalidate other approaches to community work. Indeed, we have already suggested that other approaches have special uses and values. But we must recognize that just as the case worker may teach, interview, counsel, advise in various situations (i. e., she may use a method other than case work in working with individuals), we may use various methods of work in the community. In some situations we coerce, in others coax, in others coöperate. But community organization as a social work process has now a very special meaning and must not be confused with concepts and methods which are inconsistent with it, or incomplete aspects of it.

DIFFERENCES IN STRATEGY

Another way of exploring this problem is to analyze the ways in which different goals emerge even when workers begin with the same basic assumptions. This is illustrated in the diagram and dis-

cussion which follow.[2] We cannot here, of course, investigate all
the different types of social workers who hold or profess to hold the
same beliefs and values, but we will show the emergence of certain
differences in the character of work, and then concentrate on two
types of community work.

Diagram I

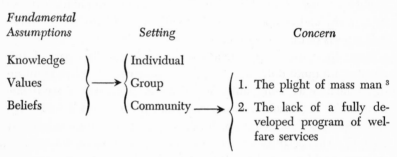

Fundamental Assumptions	*Setting*	*Concern*
Knowledge	Individual	
Values	Group	1. The plight of mass man [3]
Beliefs	Community	2. The lack of a fully developed program of welfare services

Social work rests upon a certain body of knowledge, a system of
values, and a set of beliefs regarding method. It is not necessary to
enter here into a prolonged discussion of these ideas since the reader
can readily find references to these in other sources.[4] Suffice it to say
that social workers accept the following propositions: that human
behavior is purposeful; that human beings have needs which are
met more or less adequately in given environments; and that persons
consistently seek methods of adjustment and adaptation, each in his
own environment. Further, social workers for the most part sub-
scribe to certain beliefs about the essential dignity of man, the
ultimate worth of the individual, the superiority of human over

[2] All the diagrams in this section could well be combined in one more nearly
complete diagram. Space does not permit an extensive diagram of this kind
but the reader should notice that the diagrams overlap and are meant to represent a continuous line of thought or development.

[3] "Mass man," as used herein, means modern man submerged in the mass of
humanity of the urban center.

[4] See, for example, Murray G. Ross, *Community Organization: Theory and
Principles,* New York, Harper & Brothers, 1955, Chaps. II and III.

mechanistic values, and so on. In terms of method they believe that the most effective way of furthering these aims, given what we know about human behavior, is to encourage individuals, groups, and communities to define and come to grips with their own problems as effectively as possible. This is the foundation upon which social work rests.

These views inform the worker's approach no matter what social unit he is dealing with. His task may involve work with individuals (case work), work with groups (group work), or work with communities (community organization). While each procedure calls for certain additional assumptions, each nevertheless builds from the same foundation. But even in dealing with one such unit, various special and distinct approaches develop, because other assumptions are added to the common base, because this base is defined differently by different workers or groups of workers (e.g., the functional and diagnostic schools of case work), or because the setting differs (e.g., the setting of the psychiatric social worker as opposed to the medical social worker, etc.).

Such differences are probably to be found among workers in the community as well. But the major distinction in the community arises because of the nature of the concern which focuses the attention of the worker. As suggested in the diagram above, one worker might be concerned about the plight of mass man—his lack of intimate social relations, his lack of control over any of the major forces which govern his life, the lack of purpose and meaning in his life. To this worker, this is the great and indisputable fact which dominates his outlook. A second worker with essentially the same background and philosophy might be concerned about a different problem, or a different aspect of the same problem in the community. He may even see the problem that is the concern of the first worker, but his conception of the problem might be somewhat different. He may see social and physical poverty and suffering, but believe that if welfare services (or adult education services, or recreational services, or health services) were adequately organized in the community, blocks to individual growth and development would be removed and the problems of mass man, in his view, thus resolved. What this second worker sees, then, is a very specific need for better welfare services (or for better adult education or health services). This becomes his focus of concern.[5]

Diagram II

Concern	Most General Goal	More Specific Goal
1. The plight of mass man	→ 1. To create a community life in which man has dignity	→ 1. To get the community to identify and mobilize itself to deal with its own problems
2. Lack of welfare services	→ 2. To secure a well-balanced program of welfare services	→ 2. To get a team to plan and organize welfare programs

The difference in concern leads naturally enough to the establishment of different goals by these two types of community workers even though they begin with assumptions which are similar in some respects. The first type of worker might think of his general goal somewhat as follows: to stimulate and help create a quality of community life in which man has significant contact with his fellow men, some control over his environment, and an awareness of meaning and becoming in his life. The fundamental assumptions from which he operates lead him to construct a specific goal: to get geographical or functional communities engaged in a process of identifying and understanding common problems, and to work in collaboration with these communities on those problems they feel to be important. The result, he feels, will lead to a sense of participation and responsibility on the part of all participating members of the community, which in turn will give them new meaning and movement in life.

[5] There are, of course, other focuses of concern and we select these two merely by way of illustration. It will be seen, however, that whatever the concern selected for primary attention, it influences the goals, sub-goals, methods, etc., of the worker.

The second type of worker, because of his concern with the lack of certain types of services or with the need for the coördination or extension of existing services, conceives his goal as that of providing a well-balanced program of welfare (or adult education or health) services which will meet the needs of people in the community and will facilitate individual growth and development. Thus, he may see the provision of an adequate floor of relief and insurance measures as essential for the protection of human dignity. The nature of this goal leads him to prefer certain specific objectives in the community, namely, the development of certain health and welfare services which he believes essential for individual and community development. His primary attention is devoted to these services without which, he believes, the values he accepts stand in danger of being lost.

Diagram III

Specific Goal	*Sub-Goal*	*First Steps*
1. To get community to identify and mobilize itself to deal with its own problems	→ 1. To get action on problems selected	→ 1. Explore what people conceive to be their problem
2. To develop a team to plan and organize welfare programs	→ 2. To help people understand and participate in change	→ 2. Study and list welfare needs of the community

As suggested in Diagram III, these primary goals have important sub-goals. The first worker has, in addition to the objective of getting all parts of the community involved and working on a common problem in such a way that it develops capacity for dealing with its own problems, the secondary goal of helping the community to cope successfully with those problems about which it is concerned. On the other hand, the second worker is primarily committed to finding ways and means of securing advancement in his area of interest, be it welfare, adult education, or transportation services. His secondary goal often involves the desire to secure community understanding and support for this program of services. It is suggested here that the major goal of the one approach may be a sub-goal of the other approach. The difference, although a matter of degree, is of sufficient importance to make for considerable variation in the way each worker functions in the community.

The first worker seeks in the beginning to find what community problems are of deep concern to the people of the community. He attempts to discover where the problem is located by the people of the community, and what they feel to be its nature, content, and importance. He then seeks to help people throughout the community become aware of, and concerned about, this problem to the extent that they are ready to begin to take action to alleviate the problem. The second worker, on the other hand, begins with a technical study of needs in the area in which he is most interested, and secures the opinion of informed laymen; but, before he moves into the stage of organization, he already has an idea (largely his own evaluation) of what the community requires in his area of specialization.

When the stage of organization is reached, differences are again obvious. The first worker is primarily concerned with involvement of all aspects of the community (either geographical or functional) in the process of resolving the problem. The structure he seeks to develop is one, therefore, which seeks representatives from all the major groups in the community. The second worker seeks to develop an organization which involves people who understand, who are interested in, who are able to help in a technical way, or are able to support because of personal wealth or power, the planning that will lead to more effective programs in the worker's area of interest. In the latter kind of organizing there is awareness of the power structure of the community, and an effort to secure the participation of those without whose interest and support effective action might not be possible. The difference here is quite sharp. The first worker wants an organization which represents the community.

The second worker wants a strong team that will be able to implement sound technical plans in his area of interest.

Diagram IV

Initial Steps	*Structure*	*Method*	*Strategy*
1. Explora- → tion with people	1. Com- → posed of indigenous leaders of major subgroups in community	1. Move → with interest and needs of community	1. Encourage community movement
2. Technical → study of welfare needs	2. Com- → posed of people with knowledge and power to plan and implement	2. Move on → prior welfare needs	2. Encourage balanced welfare programs

The methods of the two workers involve other differences. The first worker uses methods which bring out the concerns of people. The second worker uses methods which create concern for the problem, or gather support for the plan, in which he is interested. The first worker guides consistently in the direction of helping people to discover for themselves the problem and the process by which to resolve it. The second worker guides people in the direction of the area of concern defined by his profession, and of the steps he believes must be taken to deal with this concern. The major difference in method is that the first worker is more expert in process and less so (in some cases, not at all) in terms of the specific problem. The second worker's emphasis tends to be on the problem (welfare, adult education, etc.), and much less on process. The first worker in some ways may be compared with the therapist, the second worker with a teacher. The latter, however flexible he may be, must move in directions defined by the law and his professional interest; the therapist moves at a pace set by the patient, and with respect to problems largely defined by the patient.

The strategy of the two workers is, therefore, basically different. The one aims primarily at developing the capacity of all the people to work in collaboration on common problems and therefore seeks to involve the major groups in the community in meeting together through their representatives. The strategy calls for helping these representatives to understand and accept one another to the degree that they are able to work together. What must be developed are active lines of communication which bring to all parts of the community a common sense of belonging. What must emerge is an organization with increasing power to regulate some aspects of communal life along lines defined by members of the community. The second worker, primarily concerned with well-balanced services, seeks to build an organization with enough insight and power to develop this balance. His strategy requires that he find and mold a strong team with the sophistication and skill to plan and implement. He is not necessarily concerned that this team be representative of the community (though he may desire that it be as representative as possible) but only that it be wise and strong. He is concerned with communication primarily to the extent that it provides data for planning or is used to build support for his team's efforts.

The differences we have been attempting to make clear may be illustrated by reference to two recent statements on community organization. Both discuss, for example, how problems or needs are identified in working in the community. The following statement tends to be consistent with the approach of the first worker we have described.

. . . the representative leaders, in consultation with members of their groups, identify a problem or problems about which they wish something might be done. It is simply a process of becoming conscious of "things we don't like," "things we need here," "things we wish we could do," etc. Elementary as this may sound, it is of great importance in community organization, for it is from the feelings which surround these expressions of opinion that will come the motivation for action. Many workers in the

field take too much for granted that consciousness of these problems or needs on the part of people in the community already exists. Actually, many people live with their problems for such a long period that they adjust to them or learn to accept them to such a degree that their feelings about them lie deeply buried. In community organization, the problems, needs, concerns, and hopes of the community come to consciousness, feeling about them is expressed, emotion is discharged and harnessed.[6]

On the other hand, a position which describes the approach of the second worker has been well stated, in the following concept of community organization: "It derives its 'problems' by applying a broad conception of human welfare to practical situations; needs and intermediate goals are evaluated in the light of this broad conception of human welfare, and the course of the community organization process is directed toward goals rooted therein. Present-day community organization abounds with instances in which the professional worker deliberately and skillfully redirects the trend of a group's efforts toward specific goals by evaluating such goals in this broader perspective." [7]

It is apparent that quite different ways of formulating problems are identified here. In the first instance the attempt is made to have the problems or needs emerge from, or be "teased out" of, the representatives of the people in the community. In the second case, the worker or some small group applies a criterion of "good" to the community and identifies by this process the problems or needs which require attention. Not only does the worker or small group thus determine the needs, but they also accept responsibility for directing attention to these needs, even though the community may be concerned with quite different problems.

The above distinction is further clarified by the following two statements on the role of the worker:

At this point the worker can assist greatly in processing the expressions of desire or need. But he does not determine content. This latter is de-

[6] Ross, *op. cit.*, p. 44.

[7] Canadian Seminar on Community Organization, Report of Discussion Group No. II (mimeographed), 1955, University of Toronto School of Social Work, p. 1.

pendent upon the community. It is a need because they feel it is a need, not because it is reasonable, logical or scientific. The "feeling about" is a prime determinant of the importance of a problem for community action. Now every professional worker will have his own conception of the community's needs and problems. He will have inevitable biases. Some feel he should be completely objective (which is impossible) or that he should not reveal his own conception of the problem (which is hardly honest). Our own conviction here is that the professional worker has a right, if not a responsibility, to reveal his own appraisal of the community and its needs. This responsibility is not unlike that of the psychiatrist who does analysis and interpretation at appropriate times but does not claim infallibility and does not insist on acceptance of his ideas. Similarly, the community organization worker has the privilege of contributing his conception of needs. But rather than press for acceptance of his formulation, his emphasis is on having the people rank his objectives along with the many others which may be suggested.[8]

The second statement suggests a much more direct approach by the worker:

. . . this conception of community organization implies that the community organizer should not wait for "clients" to bring forward problems, but should take *initiative* in identifying problems and needs, as well as in taking steps to deal with these. This is in fact in accordance with actual present-day community organization practice.[9]

It can readily be seen that the second worker plays a far more aggressive role in deciding not only what problems will be given attention, but in initiating action on the problems. This distinction is made even sharper as the worker's role is discussed in detail.

The first statement indicates:

The professional worker is not averse to encouraging discussion, asking leading questions, focusing thought, etc., on problems he believes important. He does not operate completely in terms of impartial interest and objectivity, but he is controlled by his primary goals of helping the community itself to become aware of its own needs and to find the means of working co-operatively at these needs. His control over his disposition to establish direction and pace in the community is, of course, a matter of degree. At times he may unconsciously interfere, use undue influence, or

[8] Ross, *op. cit.,* p. 45.
[9] Canadian Seminar, *op. cit.,* p. 2.

take over the direction of a project. At other times he may deliberately take a "calculated risk" and intercede because he recognizes certain danger signs, or the need for emergency action, of which no one else in the community is aware. But his basic assumption in respect to his work forces him to recognize that in the degree to which he accepts responsibility for content, pace, or action in the community, in that degree he may be defeating his own purposes. Thus his work is always being regulated by awareness that at the point at which he takes responsibility away from the community, the possibility of learning and growth in the community is thereby reduced.[10]

The second statement frankly admits that manipulation is involved if the worker's goals are to be secured, suggests that this is inevitable, and calls for frank recognition of this fact:

The term "manipulation" is, for our present purposes, used without any value connotation. It is used to refer to the process of assessing the various component elements in a situation, and deliberately introducing new elements with a view to initiating and directing change towards a known objective.

In this sense "manipulation" will be "good" or "bad" (a) according to whether the objectives are "good" or "bad," and (b) according to whether the methods employed are or are not in conformance with whatever criteria are used to determine what is "good" or "bad."

The practical application of scientific knowledge is essentially manipulative in the sense just defined. It consists of the deliberate introduction and direction of processes of change which are designed to bring about a pre-determined goal.

The principal argument for recognizing the manipulative nature of social work in general, and of community organization in particular, lies in the following considerations:

(a) The tendency to confuse ideology with operational principles and to see social work as based upon the principle of self-determination, tends to restrict the scope of activity of the profession, and to produce rationalizations for not facing the task of clearly articulating professional goals.

(b) The use of manipulative methods without recognizing them as such not only is intellectually dishonest, but prevents the development

[10] Ross, *op. cit.*, p. 204.

of the proper professional discipline, controls, standards and dis-
cretion which are required for the protection of worker, client, and
society.[11]

These statements illustrate, as we have already implied, the two
different approaches we have attempted to identify in this section
of the book. Someone has suggested that the first approach represents "what social workers think they do" and the second, "what
social workers actually do." There is little question that the second
approach represents common practice not only in social work but in
other professional approaches in the community. This is undoubtedly
due to the fact that "things have had to be done" and initiative and
direction are required from professional groups. Professional workers are also conscious of problems about which communities either
are unaware or wish to avoid. Further, many situations require such
an approach; it is foolish to sit around discussing whether fire is a
hazard while men's houses are burning down. There can be no
question that achievements of great community value have been
reached by this second approach.

But we must ask to what extent community cohesion has been increased by all this effort. Are communities any more competent to
deal with their problems because of all the effort of the reformers?
Does "mass man" feel more a part of the community because of the
improvement of health and welfare services? Has modern man more
self-respect, dignity, spirit, as a result of the effort of these community workers? Has he more interest in, and feeling of responsibility for, the community because of the work of those whose concern is the reform of particular services? It may be suggested that if
the answer to these questions is in the affirmative, it is accidental
and not likely the direct result of the reformers. Their concern is not
primarily with these questions but with the quantity and quality of
certain services. On the other hand, these questions are of first importance to the process worker, for his objective is to increase the
community's capacity to work in collaboration on problems of common concern.

[11] Canadian Seminar, *op. cit.*, pp. 2–3.

It is obvious that one cannot say that one method is superior to or better than the other. They are simply different ways of working in the community. What approach is used depends upon the purpose the worker has in mind, the goal he seeks, the kind of problem which he confronts, the demands that are placed upon him, the situation he faces, etc. But it is important to note that the concerns, goals, methods, and strategies of the two workers described above represent two distinct orientations to community work.

THE CONCEPT OF "COMMUNITY"

Another area in which clarity in community organization is required is in the definition of "community." There are at least three relevant definitions of community which need to be considered. The first two of these are suggested by Lindeman in his classic essay on the community.[12]

1. The community in its "explicit elements" is defined as any consciously organized aggregation of individuals residing in a specified area or locality, endowed with limited political autonomy, supporting such primary institutions as schools and churches, and among whom certain degrees of interdependency are recognized. Such a definition includes the village, town, city, and may, without undue strain, include the suburb or city ward. In any case, this is the traditional sociological concept of community and the one, perhaps, most commonly accepted.

2. Lindeman suggests, however, another definition of community which, defined in its "implicit elements," is any process of social interaction which gives rise to more intensive or extensive attitudes and practices of interdependence, coöperation, collaboration, and unification. This definition refers not to a geographic area or a group of people, but to a process that operates in an area or in a group; it defines, in part at least, the nature and movement of relationships among the people in the given area or group. "Community" exists, or is coming into existence, when these relationships are character-

12 Eduard E. Lindeman, *Encyclopaedia of the Social Sciences,* Vol. IV, p. 103.

ized, or beginning to be characterized, by attitudes and practices of interdependence, coöperation, collaboration, and unification. Community in this sense is not a place; it is a process by and through which people are learning to relate to one another in such a way that capacity for coöperative and collaborative living is developing.

3. A third definition is that of the functional community, which would include those groups of people in any geographic area who share a common function or interest of sufficient importance in their lives to induce recognition among them of a common bond which draws them together in association and organization. Thus, the welfare agencies in a given geographic area may recognize their common function and interests and come together in a council of social agencies. Such a council is representative of a functional community. It does not include all the people in the geographic area; it includes only those groups of people who, recognizing a common bond in their work, come together in formal organization. The welfare council is representative of a broader functional community. It brings together, not all the people in the geographical area (although it sometimes claims, quite falsely, to represent all the people in the geographic community), but those individuals and groups interested in the coördination and development of welfare services in the community. The welfare council is thus a functional community and represents the "welfare community" in a specified geographical area.

These three conceptions of "community" are important, and it is necessary that they be seen as quite distinct concepts. What community organization, as we have defined the term, seeks to nourish is growth and development of the community process (2) in either a geographical community (1) or a functional community (3). This is consistent with the conception of community organization implied previously—that it is a process that makes for greater capacity to function coöperatively in respect to common problems in the community.

If this be accepted, there is still the possibility of confusion concerning the nature of the community in which this process is to operate. For example, is the welfare council a creature of the geo-graphic community dedicated to nourishing the development of the community process in the geographic community? Or is the welfare council a functional community seeking to develop the com-munity process in the welfare community but with quite a different relationship in, and obligation to, the geographic community? Many welfare councils at present tend to confuse their objectives and methods at this point. Ideologically, they often appear to be committed to one type of community; in practice, they work with a different community.

It seems reasonable to suppose that the welfare council has a responsibility to develop coöperative and collaborative attitudes in the welfare community. This is clearly one of its tasks. Another responsibility is that of planning and developing welfare services in the geographic community. These two tasks are easily reconciled and may be carried on in such a way that each supports the other. But this does not commit the welfare council to the development of the community process in the geographic community. The welfare community is a minority group in the geographic community, which, although it may wish to support the community process in the larger (geographic) community, may nevertheless seek to secure its welfare service goals in the same manner as other minority groups—by pressure, by appeal, by propaganda, by education, by conference, etc. This is what, in fact, frequently happens, and it is straining reality to expect welfare councils always to seek consensus in the whole of the geographic community. But within the welfare community (a functional community) the approach is one which should be that of community organization.

The neighborhood council is, or may be, quite a different matter. Here, the worker attempts to nourish the community process in the geographic community—the neighborhood. When the neighborhood council is made up of the most important sub-groups in the neighborhood, or when there is representation by streets or blocks, this frequently is the case, although there are situations in which, as we know, the neighborhood council is simply a welfare council at the neighborhood level, and represents not the geographic community but another functional community.

CONCLUSION

The approach for which we choose to reserve the title "community organization" has already been revealed. We do not believe, however, that this in any way disparages other methods or approaches in community work. Each has its particular values and brings its particular result, as we have constantly emphasized. The records of community work which follow show a variety of approaches. It is suggested that there is some value in the student's identifying the particular approach in each, appraising its consistency, evaluating its effectiveness, and speculating as to whether it is the most useful approach in the particular situation described.

Part Two

The Community Worker and the Individual

Mrs. Fisher

Mrs. FISHER, the founder of the Travelers Aid in Glenview, was the wife of a well-to-do physician. She was a person of great energy and executive ability. She had two children, both of whom were married and living in another city. Her husband was docile and easily managed. She spent most of her energy as program chairman of the women's club of her church which sponsored a Sunday-night forum. In seeking a speaker for this forum she learned that a field secretary of the National Travelers Aid Society would be available. Mrs. Fisher had no special interest in Travelers Aid but she wanted a good speaker. The field secretary proved to be an excellent speaker. She made a most stirring appeal and explained that Glenview as a railroad and truck center with a population of 150,000 should have a travelers' aid service. She painted a sad picture of the fate of some young woman who might find herself stranded at the Glenview station that night. Mrs. Fisher vibrated with interest. Still excited, she later drove the speaker down to the station and put her on the night train. Most of the night she lay awake making plans.

She was at the station early the next morning and "bulldozed" the station master into setting aside a corner of the station for her use. She borrowed an old desk from her husband's office. She got a friend of her husband, who owned a truck, to move the desk to the station,

33

and by 10:30 Monday morning the Glenview Travelers Aid was born! It was as simple as that. There was a little delay in getting a telephone but with Mrs. Fisher's energy all things were possible. She spent all of every day at the station. She was the Travelers Aid. When she got hold of a "case" she hung on to it; she didn't "refer" it. But even she had to leave the station for lunch or to do things for her clients. So she finally admitted another woman to the partner-ship, a coworker in her church club. For some time they financed their work with what money Mrs. Fisher could secure from her husband. But eventually more funds were needed. Mrs. Fisher went through the formality of organizing a society with a board. The president was a manufacturer who was a member of her church. She herself was vice-president. The board never met, but it did contribute money. About this time a Community Chest was formed in Glenview. The writer became the Executive of the Chest and Council of Social Agencies. All the other agencies complained of the lack of standards of the Travelers Aid and that Mrs. Fisher did not "coöperate" or "refer." She, in turn, alleged that the social workers in the various agencies were inhuman and hard-boiled. All the other agencies had salaried workers paid with money furnished by the Chest. Reluctantly Mrs. Fisher accepted a small salary. Finally the executive of the National Travelers Aid Association was called in. He insisted that Mrs. Fisher either resign as salaried worker or as vice-president. She remained as vice-president, and a trained social worker was employed.

A few weeks later Mrs. Fisher came in to consult the Council of Social Agencies about the need for an old people's home in Glen-view. I explained that there was an old men's home and two old women's homes. "But you see," said Mrs. Fisher, "there is no home for *old couples*." She was fairly patient with me while I explained that we would call a meeting of the case work division to discuss the matter with her. They asked her to bring in a list of the couples who needed this service and adjourned for a week. Mrs. Fisher brought in a list of 12 couples. Their names were run through the Social Service Exchange. Ten of them were already under care of social agencies in their own homes but two couples were not known to any agency. "Then you will help me build the old couples' home?" But the chairman of the committee explained that it would be better and less expensive for the two couples to find families who would board them. For a moment Mrs. Fisher was disheartened. "What a pity," she said, "for I already have an option on a wonderful piece of property in the West End, and you know Miss Green who has just been let out as superintendent of nurses at the hospital? She would make a wonderful matron."

Today there is an Old People's Home in Glenview on the plot in the West End and Miss Green is matron. When Mrs. Fisher's plan was disapproved by the Council of Social Agencies she went to the national headquarters of her church and proposed that the home be built as a national memorial to a famous hymn writer of that denomination and that old couples from all over the nation might be sent to the home through their local churches. A skilled money-raising firm in New York was engaged. A national campaign was put on, and the home was built.

Questions for Discussion

1. Do you think Mrs. Fisher should be encouraged or discouraged in her efforts? If the latter, what should be the nature of the discouragement? Should she be prohibited from starting a home for old couples in Glenview? If so, how?

2. What do you think of the way the worker and the Council dealt with Mrs. Fisher? What other ways might there be for dealing with her? Was she, for example, given any acceptance?

3. One commentator writes: "This is a typical social work case record. It reveals the bias of the writer, who I presume is a social worker, and his complete disapproval of Mrs. Fisher. I would ask why shouldn't Mrs. Fisher be admired? Isn't her initiative and enthusiasm that which makes our free enterprise system operate? And would there be a travelers' aid or an old couples' home in Glenview without Mrs. Fisher? And aren't they both good projects? Who is to say not? Only the social workers who must have things develop through established channels?" What do you think of this comment?

Steve Bishop

THE MORNING following a most successful welfare council board meeting, Jack Sorenson, the executive secretary of the council, had a telephone call from the chairman of the board, Mrs. Sawyer. "We have a little problem on our hands with Steve Bishop," she said. "Will you be free at eleven if I drop in?" The time was agreeable to Sorenson and she rang off without saying more.

Sorenson pondered the nature of the problem with Bishop. The latter was a well-known accountant in the city who had accepted the chairmanship of a committee to plan the annual meeting of the council. It was not a large task but it was an important one. When Bishop had accepted the position in the late spring, he had been full of ideas and enthusiasm. Sorenson, being a relative newcomer to the community, did not know Bishop well but he was a little suspicious of the latter's gaiety and optimism. It did not seem quite real, and the grandiose plans he recommended, while admirable in themselves, seemed to be considerably beyond the resources or needs of a council annual meeting. For all Sorenson knew, however, Bishop might be able to put these ideas across without, as Bishop stated over and over again, "its costing the council a cent." Sorenson did not interfere or attempt to steer Bishop towards more modest plans. His job, he felt, was to encourage others to act and to use their resources, and he did not want to be a "wet blanket" on plans that were more imaginative and daring than he himself could develop. He had, however, raised the question with Mrs. Sawyer in the spring, but she had said of Bishop, "If he can do it, more power to him. We need something like his plan to stir up the agencies in this city."

At the first board meeting in the fall, Bishop had been called upon to report. He seemed pale and listless and had indicated that he simply hadn't had time to move further with his plans. He apologized profusely for not getting his committee together during the summer but promised to do so immediately. Shortly after this meeting, Sorenson had phoned to see if he could be of any help. Contrary to earlier conversations, Bishop seemed confused, stuttered and stammered, and was far from coherent in what he said. The burden of his reply seemed to be that he could look after things all right.

The "next board meeting" had been the previous night. Bishop reported no further progress because of "many pressures." The members of the board made numerous but kindly suggestions for alternative plans and programs, and with all of these Bishop agreed with: "It's a dandy idea," "Very good," "We'll do that," "That's excellent." But still Sorenson could not but feel that Bishop was simply grasping indiscriminately at straws.

When Mrs. Sawyer came to Mr. Sorenson's office, she first showed him a note she had received in the morning mail from Bishop. It had been written and posted immediately after the meeting the previous night. It said simply, "I can't go on. I want to do it but I can't. Will you get another chairman to take my place?"

"What," asked Mrs. Sawyer, "are we to do?"

"Do you mean about getting another chairman or about Bishop?" asked Sorenson.

"Well, both. We have to have an annual meeting but we can't just cast Bishop aside. He'd lose any self-respect he has."

As they discussed the matter, Sorenson discovered that Bishop had always been "up or down" either saying too much or too little. He asked Mrs. Sawyer whether she thought Bishop was a sick man. This she had not considered. Sorenson explained that he was not an expert, but some of the symptoms of mental distress were there and that perhaps this was a problem beyond their ability.

"Well, let's go and see him anyway. Let's make him realize we understand and will help him in whatever way he thinks best."

They drove over to Bishop's office, choosing a direct approach rather than phoning for an appointment. Bishop received them at once. He was pale and quiet and apologized for "letting the board down." Mrs. Sawyer was sympathetic and said it wasn't important; they had just dropped in to see whether they could help a friend in need.

"Is there some part of the job that is more difficult than another, Steve?" Sorenson asked. It was the first time he had ever used Bishop's first name. Bishop rubbed his hands over his eyes. "No! No! No!" he exclaimed, "I can't do anything these days. I am afraid to phone. I can't write letters. I can't meet people. I am a mess."

"Have you been able to get any help with this?" Sorenson asked quietly.

"Yes, I've been going to Dr. Rideout [a well-known psychiatrist], and I think I've been getting hold of myself but it's really tough going. I think I see the way, and I think I'll make it, but last night really set me back. I hated to fail on that job."

"You haven't failed yet, Steve," Mrs. Sawyer said softly.

"What does Dr. Rideout say, Steve?" asked Sorenson. "Does he say you should keep away from committee work or does he think you should be kept active in things like the council?"

The air seemed to clear a little for Bishop. Some of the strain was gone and he seemed calmer and clearer in what he said. "No, he thinks I should try to keep going. Not on jobs that are too big or ambitious, but that I should take on little jobs that I could probably do well and easily. I thought the annual meeting committee was one of them. I feel terrible about that."

"Wouldn't you feel better if you took another try at this job?" Sorenson asked.

"Oh God! yes, but I can't do it. I am stumbling."

"Look, Steve," Mrs. Sawyer said firmly, "you can do this job, and

40

Jack and I will help you. We'll be a committee of thr work together. No one is going to know you haven't don job—and you will, but we'll help you. We'll get through it and in six months you'll feel better than if you gave up."

"I would, I certainly would," exclaimed Bishop, "but you don't know how I am. I can't even dictate a letter."

"Well, you'll do some," said Mrs. Sawyer positively, "and those you can't do, we'll do. What say, we get to work."

Their first meeting was held there and then. They outlined a plan for the annual meeting, and each took on some of the jobs to be done. Bishop was given relatively easy tasks but he had two difficult tasks (for him), namely, inviting two important guests from out of town.

They met three days later; all had completed their work except Bishop who had not invited the two guests. The other jobs he had done. Mrs. Sawyer did not press the issue and the group worked on other matters. Toward the end of the meeting she said, "I believe everything is in shape, Steve, except for inviting our two guests. Why don't you phone them now?"

"Well, yes, that's an idea," said Bishop and reached for the phone. "But you know Mrs. Richardson better than I do. Why don't you ask her and I'll ask Dr. Peters? I know him well enough."

"O. K.," said Mrs. Sawyer.

Within 20 minutes the phone calls were completed and successful.

At the next board meeting, Bishop reported the completion of details for the annual meeting with considerable pride. He gave credit to Mrs. Sawyer and Jack Sorenson for considerable help, but there was no doubt that he felt he had made his own significant contribution. At the annual meeting itself, he introduced both the guest speakers. This he did at first nervously but with growing confidence, and his second introduction was, all agreed, well done. Sorenson thought, "This is only half as good as he feels inside."

All this was a year ago. Bishop is not what might be termed a "healthy and well person," but he is not so much "up and down," not verbose at one meeting and silent the next. He has steadied considerably.

"I don't know about his psychiatrist," said Mrs. Sawyer the other day, "but I think we helped that man. We gave him a lift when he needed it. If you can do that in community work, you're doing a good job."

Sorenson nodded. But he was less sure that their personal work with Bishop was part of the job.

Questions for Discussion

1. Do you think the function of a community worker includes personal attention to the needs of a person like Bishop? Why?

2. Evaluate the role of Sorenson in this case. Do you think he performed well in this situation? Why?

3. In this situation, should the knowledge that Mrs. Sawyer and Sorenson gained of Bishop's personal problem be kept confidential? What should the other persons who were asked to serve on Bishop's committee be told?

Mrs. Fraser Ronson

WHEN WE first organized the Sheltered Work-shop Committee, we were very careful to secure a representative from the Jewish community. This was not only because there was in the Jewish community a good deal of interest in the question of sheltered workshops, but also because we were anxious to do what we could to close the gap between Jew and Gentile. I had been in Colton for only a year but I was soon conscious of what seemed to me to be widespread anti-Semitic attitudes in the Protestant and Roman Catholic groups. As secretary of the Health Department of the Council, I had reminded my committee members many times in private that we did not have one Jewish member on the committees in our division.

It was, therefore, an event for me when Mrs. Sidney Johnson, who had been appointed chairman of the Sheltered Workshop Committee, suggested that we get a Jewish committee member. It was agreed, and I was asked to consult with a few friends and to suggest a person. I talked the matter over carefully with Sam Lippman and Sora Rose, both prominent social workers in the Jewish community. We finally decided to suggest Mrs. Karl Saltzman. She had served on several committees in the Jewish community, was well informed about sheltered workshops, and could, we felt, make a contribution to the committee. She was not a very forceful person but was quiet, determined, and had considerable status and prestige in the Jewish community. It was agreed by our division to invite her, and Mrs. Sidney Johnson wrote her a personal note asking her to serve on the committee. Mrs. Saltzman agreed.

While there were 22 members on the committee, only 3 of these members concern us here. One of these is Mrs. Saltzman. She was the wife of a wealthy Jewish doctor and, as intimated, had considerable status in the Jewish community but was unknown to any of the other members of the committee. Mrs. Sidney Johnson, the chairman, had many years of service in various Council committees but this was her first term as a chairman. She was a kindly woman, thoroughly interested in Council work, and devoted to several other community projects including a large settlement house. She was not a wealthy woman nor a clever one. In fact, she had only limited ability and was inclined to get easily flustered, but her tireless interest and energy won her a recognized place in Council affairs. The third person in the triangle was Mrs. Fraser Ronson, a woman who had at one time served as chairman of the Council board and was enlisted on this committee to give it some status as well as a spokesman when time for action came. Mrs. Ronson was from an old wealthy family and stood as high in the social scale as anyone in the Council. She was a powerful, dogmatic, and in one sense, a sadistic woman with a sharp tongue and a "fighting way" of talking. Personally, I was secretly afraid of Mrs. Ronson. I had seen her turn on lesser lights with devastating results, and I feared the day she would turn her scorn on me.

We had not anticipated Mrs. Ronson's reaction to Mrs. Saltzman. Indeed, it was not immediately apparent. But by the end of the second meeting, the pattern was clear. Every time Mrs. Saltzman spoke, Mrs. Ronson followed with a comment. And her comment was always in a tone which deprecated what Mrs. Saltzman had said. Her dislike of Mrs. Saltzman was becoming more apparent. At the third meeting, Mrs. Saltzman had bravely referred to an experience in a Jewish sheltered workshop she knew about. Mrs. Ronson almost sneered at this, and said the experience of "foreign groups" was not an adequate basis for planning a community program in Colton. Everyone was embarrassed. Mrs. Saltzman flushed but remained quiet and the chairman became quite flustered.

After this meeting, Mrs. Johnson and I had a long talk. What could we do? If the truth were known, we were both terrified of Mrs. Ronson. We hesitated to raise the issue with her, yet we knew we must do something. The open hostility of Mrs. Ronson toward Mrs. Saltzman was ruining our plan to bring the Jewish community into the Council. Finally, we decided that before we did anything else, we should consult Professor Jacks at the University. He was a brilliant psychologist with wide experience in committee work.

He was most interested in the account of our problem. "I've always been interested in this problem, but short of psychotherapy, I must confess I don't know how to deal with this kind of person. I have only one suggestion to make and this I read in a book the other night. I don't know whether it will work but I'd love to see it tried. The assumption is that people like Mrs. Ronson are basically authoritarian people. They like to give orders, to boss others, although they also will accept orders and be bossed by others. But they will recognize authority only from someone 'higher up.' If this is true, I'd say try to get someone that Mrs. Ronson recognizes as higher in the social scale and ask the new person to support Mrs. Saltzman. If this theory works, Mrs. Ronson will accept the judgment of the new authority."

There was a good deal more said, but Mrs. Johnson and I were not impressed by the theory. It seemed most implausible. Nevertheless, we returned to it after we had considered every other possibility. It seemed the only idea we had worth trying. But to find the right person to do the job was another question. Mrs. Johnson and I spent three hours discussing names. It wasn't that there were so many names but it was difficult to decide who, if anyone, would help. Finally, it seemed clear that Mrs. Benson Hopkins was our woman. She was the wife of the publisher of the largest newspaper in the city, a former international president of the Junior League, a brilliant woman with charm, wealth, position, and influence. We were certain from several addresses she had made that she was not anti-Semitic. She had served as chairman of the board of the Art Gallery and her superior status (over Mrs. Ronson) was clear. She had never served on Council committees although she had been one of the honorary chairmen of the Chest campaign. As I look back on it now, I realize we were naïve and brazen to approach Mrs. Hopkins. We didn't realize it at the time, and this was fortunate for us.

Mrs. Hopkins, when she received us, was most charming. She captured us immediately, and I am frank to say that I am now a lifelong fan of hers. I had to do most of the talking because Mrs. Johnson was so impressed by the Hopkins' library where we were received that she could hardly speak. But gradually we got our story out without mentioning names, told her about the professor's theory, and our hope that she would save this experiment in Jewish-Gentile relations. She was, of course, busy but she agreed to try it if three meetings would be adequate. We thought it would, and it was so agreed. We then named names and agreed that no word of our discussion would ever go beyond the three of us.

There were a good many things that Mrs. Johnson and I had not considered. Did we have the authority to bring Mrs. Hopkins on the committee? Would Mrs. Saltzman ever come back to the committee? Should we be manipulating the situation like this? Why did we not encourage others on the committee to fight Mrs. Ronson? But the die was cast and we now had to follow through.

Before the next meeting, Mrs. Johnson sent a little note to every member saying that she had met Mrs. Hopkins and invited her to sit with us on this committee and expressing the hope that everyone would feel as happy as she that Mrs. Hopkins had accepted. I happened to meet Mrs. Saltzman and we were able to speak frankly about the difficulty with Mrs. Ronson. Without mentioning anything about our plan, I said that I hoped she would not allow herself to be silenced, that I thought most of the committee appreciated her contribution. She smiled and said she had planned to give it one more try.

I must confess I was excited at the next meeting. Mrs. Hopkins had a very gracious way of meeting people and everyone seemed to warm up to her. Mrs. Ronson immediately edged up to her, "taking her over," and sat next to her at the table, and even while the meeting was going on, explained in a loud whisper what it was all about. The meeting moved on to routine business. Then came some discussion about a possible location for a sheltered workshop. Mrs. Saltzman mentioned an old but vacant factory on Pearl Street, and Mrs. Ronson snorted audibly and said, "In *that* district?" Mrs. Hopkins came in immediately with "You know, I rather think that is a good idea. I was thinking of that factory myself. It's near both the subway and bus line and also has parking space around it. You and I think alike, Mrs. Saltzman."

I couldn't help peeping at Mrs. Ronson. One would think a blow had been struck but she recovered quickly and the next time she spoke it was in favor of the factory site. We had one more incident like this during the meeting when Mrs. Ronson slashed at Mrs. Saltzman. Again, Mrs. Hopkins came to the rescue in a most sensitive and understanding way, and again Mrs. Ronson "changed her line." At the next meeting, Mrs. Ronson did not once attack Mrs. Saltzman, and in fact followed Mrs. Hopkins in support of a suggestion put forward by Mrs. Saltzman. In the meetings that followed there were no further attacks, and Mrs. Ronson became very cordial to Mrs. Saltzman.

Did the professor's idea work? I'm not so sure it did. I feel Mrs. Hopkins made it work as she would make anything she tried work. But certainly this problem was solved nicely. Incidentally, Mrs. Hopkins became much interested in sheltered workshops, stayed on the committee until the job was finished, sat with Mrs. Johnson and Mrs. Ronson on a committee to meet with the executive of the Chest to request a grant for this purpose, and was, of course, the influential factor in our getting every cent we asked for. But when I tried to get her as chairman of our division the following year, she refused— with graciousness, of course, but still a refusal. She was occupied as a member of our country's delegation to the United Nations.

Questions for Discussion

1. How much validity do you think the professor's theory has? Is it an idea that could be tried in other situations? In what situations?

2. What do you think of the questions the worker and the chairman asked themselves (see Chapter I)? Do you think they were manipulative? Were they justified in what they did? Why?

3. Are there other ways of handling a situation like this? What are they? What is the particular value of each?

Mrs. Taylor

THE FIRST week I was in Brocton I attended a cocktail party where I met Mrs. Taylor. She was a striking woman, tall, with handsome features and a mind as sharp as a whip. We conversed briefly and I asked if she were active in welfare work (as were, I knew, many of those present). "Lord, no!" she exclaimed, "I have interests of my own but they don't include that kind of 'do-goodism.'"

In spite of the nature of our first contact, I felt the tremendous potential of Mrs. Taylor and was aware of the contribution she could make to welfare work in general and to the Welfare Council in particular if she could be induced to work with us. When I made a list of people I thought might be useful in the Council, Mrs. Taylor's name topped it. At the end of my first year in Brocton most of those on my list had assumed positions on various Welfare Council committees, but Mrs. Taylor remained aloof and apart. Certainly she was active in the community—in the Civil Liberties League, the Adult Education Association, the local branch of Consumers Union—but she refused invitations to serve on two different Welfare Council committees. It was clear in this and other ways that Mrs. Taylor wanted no part of us.

The Welfare Council in Brocton was not an organization to evoke the admiration of the objective observer, and no one knew this better than I. I felt a primary part of my job was to build a strong effective council, and to do this we needed people like Mrs. Taylor. So I didn't give up. I discovered that, among other things, she had taken graduate work in food chemistry, and while she didn't do much about it now, she had never lost interest in this field.

The next year we had a committee doing a study of the diet habits in one of the depressed areas of the city. We hoped through this study to show the need for nutritional education and probably the need for free milk being served in school. It suddenly struck me that this was a topic that would interest Mrs. Taylor. I called and said, "I am not calling to invite you to join a committee or to do a job, but there's a problem I have on which I need help. Could you spare me a half-hour today?"

"Certainly," she said. "Can you come to tea?"

Mrs. Taylor and I spent an hour going over details of the study. She was genuinely interested and her advice was extremely valuable. As I was leaving she said, "Look, Miss Rogers, this project interests me; if I can be of further help, let me know."

"Well, I know how busy you are, and I don't want to ask you when you're already fully occupied."

And so we left it at that. But when our questionnaires were ready and our sampling procedure set, I called Mrs. Taylor to see if she would go over them with me. "I'll be glad to," she replied. "I was just beginning to wonder if I'd hear anything more about this project."

Again she was most helpful, and when I left she asked if she could sit in on the meeting when the replies were tabulated. I said we'd be delighted to have her. She came and was of tremendous help to the committee in pointing out implications of the data we had.

Now thoroughly involved, Mrs. Taylor asked openly if she could continue to work with the committee. Everyone was most happy with this and she played a major role in the remainder of the work of the committee. She also came in contact with other aspects of our program, and toward the end of the year she said to me on one occasion, "This is a better outfit than I had imagined."

The next year we asked her to take the chair of a committee on housing that had been recommended by the diet study committee. This she agreed to do, and she did a brilliant job. The following year she became chairman of the Child and Family Division, and as such sat on our board of directors, where she did a good deal to improve the quality of our work. Two years later she became chairman of our board and she served in this capacity for three years with great effectiveness and skill. Our council became recognized not only in Brocton but in many other parts of the country for its strength, influence, and effective work. Much of the credit for this was owing to Mrs. Taylor.

She is now the president of a national organization in the welfare field and her contribution continues to be felt throughout the country. I have often felt that my own best contribution to social work was that of getting Mrs. Taylor interested in our work.

Questions for Discussion

1. "Here is a good example of a missionary. She gets a convert and she's happy. Is this what social work is? What about the idea of autonomy, self-determination, etc., that you throw around? This is pure unadulterated salesmanship—convincing people that they must think and act as you want them to think and act." What do you think of this comment?

2. Do you feel this worker was justified in pursuing Mrs. Taylor? Should she have cleared her approach with her board? With the committee involved?

3. Do you think this worker used good techniques in building "the welfare community"?

Carl Anderson

CARL ANDERSON was what is often called an "eager beaver." Having none of the advantages of education or a good home, his formula for success was enthusiasm and hard work. Already at the age of 39 he was general manager of a small industry, and it was obvious that he intended to go much further. He had served on several small Welfare Council committees and this year had been elected to the board of directors. Again, it seemed obvious that he considered this a stepping stone and that eventually he hoped to become president of the board. Or at least so it seemed to some who watched him closely.

At the first meeting of the board that Anderson attended, there was considerable discussion about how to get action on a public housing project long advocated by the Council. Anderson was soon in on the discussion but on a new vein: "Mr. Chairman," he said, "if I may make a suggestion, I happen to know the president of the Board of Trade very well. I'd be very happy to get his support on this project and if we can get the Board of Trade behind this I know it will go through." There was no doubt that the support of the Board of Trade would be highly desirable, and the chairman replied that if Anderson could do this, it would undoubtedly help.

The next meeting, a month later, gave Anderson a chance to report. He had seen, he said, the president of the Board of Trade, the president of the Rotary Club, and "several important business-men," all of whom were interested. If the president of the Welfare Council would have lunch with them at Anderson's club, he was sure the matter could be quickly settled. The chairman agreed, and after the meeting a date for the luncheon was set. On the appointed day, none of the men Anderson had mentioned turned up, but instead came the paid secretary of the Board of Trade and a junior public relations man from the firm used by Anderson's industry. Neither knew much about the project and when it was explained, the Board of Trade secretary said it was not the kind of thing his organization would undertake. The meeting, as far as Mr. Bufford, president of the Welfare Council, was concerned, was a waste of time and he was extremely annoyed by the whole incident.

A few weeks later, Florence Jefferies, the executive officer of the Council, had a call from Mr. Bufford. "We have to do something about that fellow Anderson," he said. "He has been around to see several top businessmen saying he represents the Council board and he irritates them all. Either you'll have to tell him to pull in his horns or we'll have to get rid of him."

Miss Jefferies was reluctant to take on this kind of job. She believed that part of the learning that comes as a result of committee work should be that of handling people like Anderson. She discussed this at some length with Mr. Bufford without convincing him, but they agreed to carry on.

At a later meeting a similar problem came up, and again Anderson offered to "contact some influential people." Meanwhile, many members of the board had become suspicious of Anderson because of his failure in the earlier project and they were ready when Mr. Bufford said, "It is good of you to offer but I am not sure we should be making hit-and-miss informal approaches to individuals in the community. Shouldn't we let the committee in charge work out the strategy for this?" Several other members spoke in favor, and it was agreed to follow the chairman's idea. Miss Jefferies felt sorry for Anderson, and when later in the meeting they were discussing preparation of the list of persons to whom invitations to the annual meeting were to be sent, she asked if Anderson and she might not do that job. It was agreed, and Anderson eagerly accepted.

He threw himself into the job with great vigor and, except for his desire to send out a group of special invitations over his own name (an idea which Mr. Bufford vetoed), he did a very thorough job. Miss Jefferies mentioned his good work in this respect at the next board meeting and Anderson beamed.

At this same meeting, the program of the annual meeting was being discussed. One part of the program was to be a brief buzz session and there was some discussion of a chairman for that rather difficult job. Anderson spoke up, "I'd be very glad to do that, if you wish, Mr. Chairman!" If they were surprised, few board members showed it, and Mrs. Jones said, "That's a job I hoped we'd have someone from the University do." And so it was agreed. One of the last jobs to be assigned was the securing and instructing of ushers. The chairman asked Anderson if he would be willing to help in this way. "Sure, I'd be glad to do it," said Anderson. And he did this and did it well.

Gradually, it seemed, the board came to understand Anderson. He didn't mind the little jobs although he wanted to get to the big ones. But the board refused to let him handle anything "big," anything that brought him too much before the public until they thought he was ready. His willingness to do anything brought him considerable acceptance, and he was treated with cordiality, if not always with respect, in the board.

But, Miss Jefferies reflected, both the board and Carl Anderson are learning how to work in a committee. Perhaps Mr. Bufford or I should have taken him aside and told him the facts of life, but I think both he and the committee have learned more this way.

Questions for Discussion

1. Evaluate Miss Jefferies' handling of this situation. Should she have provided help on a personal basis for Anderson? Why or why not?

2. Compare Miss Jefferies' handling of this situation with that of the

workers in other episodes in this section. Are the workers operating with different goals in mind? If so, what are these in each case? What are the specific differences in goal and method?

3. Would Miss Jefferies' method be equally satisfactory in all situations? Specify.

4. After reviewing your analysis of each of the episodes in this section, try to list some of the factors which define the role of the community worker in dealing with individuals in the community.

Part Three

The Community Worker and Community Groups

The Finnish Group in Dorchester

SHORTLY AFTER World War II began, I was asked to go to Dorchester to help the citizens there organize a War Bond Drive. When I arrived I found a committee already organized with Mr. Cooke, the owner of the largest radio station and newspaper, as chairman. The first night I was in Dorchester there was a meeting of the committee, and I had to admit they had their campaign in good shape. I was able to help on a few details, but on the whole it was plain to see that they knew what they had to do and how they were going to do it.

At one point I said, "The government is most anxious that the bond drive represent an effort of the whole community. I would guess by the size and nature of your committee that you have representatives from all sections of the community, but I'd like at least to raise the point." A number of members smiled, and Mr. Cooke said, "There are three major groups in this community: the service clubs, the Roman Catholic Church, and the labor unions. We have very good representation from all of these. Is that not so?" Everyone nodded in the affirmative and I said, "That's wonderful."

During the next few days I had a chance to look the city over and to study some statistics on the population. There were two major minority groups: French and Finnish. I was interested in this and inquired around. It seemed that almost all of the French group were members of the Roman Catholic Church and that this was the traditional institution through which they were represented. But the Finnish group was in a somewhat different category. They lived in a separate part of the community, had their own newspaper, church, clubs, etc. Those of this group to whom I talked felt that they were not represented in the three groups to which Cooke had referred. The Finnish editor said, "It is always this way; no matter what we do we're segregated, left on the outside. We've never been recognized as part of the community."

At the next meeting of the central committee, I raised the question of the Finnish group. The answer was that most of them were represented in the labor group. I was not satisfied with this answer and persisted, "If they would prefer to have their own group organized and related to this committee, would that be possible?" There was considerable reluctance to accept this idea but finally it was decided that Cooke and I should meet with them, and if they wanted to have a campaign among the Finnish people they could do so and also have representation on the central committee. Their quota would be $20,000.

I arranged a meeting with a group of Finnish leaders, and they were obviously proud to meet with Cooke and me. We discussed some details, such as how to avoid overlapping with the union campaign. As it turned out, few of them were members of local unions, most of them being engaged in shops, small industries, or independent one-man operations. They appointed two men to represent them on the central committee.

At the next meeting of the central committee I became conscious of the fact that, with the exception of Cooke and myself, the two Finnish leaders were unknown to most of the others who were present. When discussions of quotas took place one of the Finnish representatives said, "We have discussed our quota and feel that we can raise not $20,000 but $50,000." To this Cooke replied, "Wouldn't it be better to take the $20,000 quota and then if you get it, you will have more satisfaction than if you take a large quota and fail?" With this most of the members of the committee agreed. But the Finns were adamant. They had gone over their resources carefully and felt they could raise $50,000 and they wished to do their share.

The next few weeks were busy ones for me and I did not see much of the Finnish people except at meetings of the central committee. Here they fitted in well. They were quiet and modest but willing to help with any of the little extras that were required. They reported their own work progressing satisfactorily.

At the first report meeting, the Finnish group were the last to be called upon. Most teams had reported around 20 percent of their objective, the highest being 41 percent. None of us was prepared then for the captain of the Finnish team who reported 210 different purchasers for a total of $52,500 or 105 percent of their objective. The applause was terrific and the Finns were delighted. They had evidently planned this surprise to show what they could do, and they were more than pleased with its reception.

Three days later they reported another $3,200, and since they had just about completed their canvass they offered to cover any other cards or to make any other calls the committee wished them to make. Their offer was taken up and they worked conscientiously and effectively at these additional tasks. At the final "success dinner," Cooke signaled out the Finnish team for special praise, and again there was prolonged applause. There was no doubt that this ethnic group had established itself in Dorchester. Before I left, Cooke said to me, "You know they're a great people. I never quite realized there were so many of them here. Funny how you can overlook the obvious in your own community."

As I thought about this later I pondered on why the Finnish group came through so well. National pride was certainly a factor. But perhaps, also, this was the most important group association these people had, and they worked more effectively and enthusiastically in this group than they would if they were asked to serve separately in churches or labor unions. In any case, it seemed to me that there might be an idea here that would be of value in community organization. But I never had an opportunity to try it out again.

Questions for Discussion

1. Why do you think the Finnish group was successful in this campaign?

2. Do you think the community should be broken up into relatively small homogeneous groups for a campaign effort of this kind? Why?

3. What lessons are there in this episode for community organization?

The Watertown Rotary Club

CHARLES JEFFERY was president and Jim Peterson was executive secretary of the Watertown Welfare Council. They were consulting with the president of the local Rotary Club regarding representation from Rotary on two new committees which the Council was setting up. The Council considered it essential that the Rotary Club be involved in its planning, since this club represented the most powerful group of people in the community, and their support, or lack of it, often determined whether a project would succeed or fail.

The two new committees were (1) to study the needs of children with cerebral palsy in Watertown, and (2) to consider setting up an experimental group work program in the Swamp area, an area with the highest delinquency rates in Watertown.

After some discussion it appeared that the men whom the Rotary should place on these committees were John P. Wicket and Ralph R. Albright. Wicket was a man approaching 60, the head of a chain of restaurants, wealthy, affable, but with a strong antagonism toward "eggheads, radicals, and communists." If the truth were known, he was inclined to regard with suspicion any new idea not considered "practical." He was, however, a staunch Rotarian, an "inner member" so to speak, and two years after this writing was elected president of the Rotary Club. It was felt that he would be a good member for the cerebral palsy committee. It was agreed that the second representative should be Albright. He was a Y.M.C.A. secretary and secretary of the Rotary Club. This latter position usually was assigned to the Y.M.C.A. secretary, who was given free membership in the Rotary Club for his services. Albright was a capable, competent person, and although 46 and younger than most Rotarians, was well liked by them. He was not, however, an "inner circle" member like Wicket. It was difficult to analyze his position in the club—he was rated higher than the pianist certainly, yet he was not quite given the status of a "regular" member. Nevertheless, it was felt, that because of his group work knowledge, he would be of great assistance to the Swamp area project. Jeffery and Peterson had privately agreed that it was unlikely that Rotary would support anything as sophisticated as the area project—it would be sufficient if they were kept informed and did not oppose it. On the other hand, it was quite possible that they would rise to the appeal of the cerebral palsy clinic or whatever was needed to help these handicapped children. Indeed as they talked over the two ideas with the Rotary president, their views of how Rotary would rank the two projects were strongly confirmed.

The best of plans, however, sometimes go amiss, and certainly this one did. At the next meeting of Rotary, the president, by some accident of fate, announced that Albright was being asked to sit on the cerebral palsy committee and Wicket on the area project committee. This was, of course, the opposite of what had been planned. Later in the week Jeffery tried to straighten the matter out, but the shadow of things to come was Wicket's refusal to change. As he put it, "I want to see what these boys are up to." He was not going to be pushed around! In light of this, neither Jeffery nor the Rotary president felt like putting pressure on him, and it was left that this rather rough and outspoken man would serve on the area committee and Albright on the cerebral palsy committee.

This latter committee moved well, and Albright's skill and insight were of tremendous help. A survey was conducted which showed 35 cerebral palsy children in Watertown who could not go to the regular public school. Only 20 percent were able to go daily to the nearest school for cerebral palsy some 45 miles away. When it came to action, a very simple plan was developed. It was decided to set up a special school in Watertown. An old house was available, and Albright agreed to ask the Rotary for $5,000 to purchase the house. The parents of cerebral palsy children would fix it up with their own hands and provide materials needed. The government would care for the salary of teachers and therapists. Everyone was enthusiastic. Albright demonstrated his competence in a clear, concise, and touching appeal for the $5,000 to the executive of the Rotary Club. There were adequate funds in the treasury, yet there were half a dozen reasons given why such a grant could not be made. It was refused. The cerebral palsy school idea lingered on for over a year before funds were available and even then, a mortgage was required to purchase the old house.

Meanwhile, the area project committee proceeded with difficulty, and the source of much of the difficulty was John P. Wicket. Many of the members of this committee were professional workers, and Mr. Wicket was likely to explode at the least semblance of "jargon." "What in heck does 'integration of personality' mean?" he yelled one night, when this phrase was used by a professional social worker. When the worker tried to explain in a way which can only be said to have made the concept more confusing, Wicket blurted out "Eyewash!" Nevertheless, Wicket attended every meeting. He seemed to become fond of Peterson, the Council secretary, and would often stay after the meetings to chide him. "An awful lot of rubbish you fellows talk, eh?" he would say, or "I am never going to be integrated," or "How's your self-determination tonight?" Peterson entered into the spirit of this ribbing, and although their conversation never went much beyond this level, a kind of friendship developed between them.

In spite of the fact that the committee had to stop to define every difficult word for Wicket, they moved slowly toward a plan. This was to employ a skilled worker to spend all his time working with the three or four natural gangs in the area. The worker was not to try to reform the groups or to start athletic leagues, or to get them to church. He was simply to associate with them, allowing hostilities to come out—in short to begin something like a therapy program. It was a project much favored by social workers at this time and one that seemed to amuse Mr. Wicket very much. He was asked at one point to report to the Rotary Club on this committee. His report was simply: "I tell you men, that group talks the greatest amount of rubbish you ever heard. I don't understand what it's all about, but they're kind of nice fellows and for all I know they may come down to earth yet."

When the area plan was finally in shape it was evident that $10,000 would be required to get the project underway the first year. Wicket was asked if he thought the Rotary Club would be interested in putting up the money for this purpose, and he said gruffly but with a twinkle in his eye, "They're not used to throwing their money away on things like this, but I'll see."

At the executive meeting of the Rotary Club, Wicket interpreted the request approximately as follows: "What we want to try to do is to get those kids in the waterfront area on their feet. We all know the trouble they've caused—robbery, arson, rape, even murder. The problem is, what do you do with kids like that? Put them in jail, of course, but first you have to catch them. Even when you do, once they're out they are as bad as before. We've tried all the things, Sunday School, camps, sport programs, a settlement house, and none of them works. Now we want to try sending a trained worker to go in there and live with them. He's going to try to provide what you and I got in our home—the understanding and guidance of a parent. We think these kids, if they have this, will snap out of it. They've never had a chance and we want to give them one. Now the advantage of this is that it works. At least it has in some other cities. No results are guaranteed, of course, but we think it will work."

There was some discussion of this project and its costs. Finally one member asked, "What do you think, John? Is it worth $10,000?"

"Yes," said Wicket soberly.

"That is good enough for me," the member replied. "I move we provide the $10,000 grant."

And thus it was done!

The committees worked out rather differently from what Jeffery and Peterson had expected. Nevertheless, they were pleased. "It almost makes you think," said Peterson, "that a committee should not move too smoothly. That Wicket was a constant thorn in the side of the area project, yet when I look back on these committees, it was the area committee that was really dynamic and interesting."

"What surprises me," said Jeffery, "is the difference in understanding which the Rotary Club has of these two projects. Albright did a far better interpretive job than Wicket. Yet not only do they buy the area project idea but they seem to understand it, and they haven't any idea what cerebral palsy is all about. It's as if they couldn't hear what Albright said, but anything old Wicket says is just what they'd say if they were in his place."

Questions for Discussion

1. Which of the two committee experiences was more productive? Why?

2. What do you think of Peterson and Jeffery's summary of the experience? Are both valid?

3. What principles for community organization emerge from this experience? Would they be valid in all situations? If not, in which situations?

4. What suggestion would you have for a chairman of the committee of which Wicket is a member?

Civil Liberties in Melville

W HEN WE first organized the Civil Liberties Association in Melville, we were a small group of young people, all under 40 years of age and sometimes referred to as "eggheads." We were mostly business, professional, or labor people who had a strong common conviction that we were needed to protest infringements against the freedoms men were guaranteed by law in our kind of democracy. After a year of operation we found ourselves involved in a number of legal suits which we had initiated to fight for the rights of certain minority groups we felt to be illegally discriminated against. This required a good deal more money than the small foundation grant we received, and we were forced to consider ways of securing support from the public.

We felt at first that this would not be too difficult, and we apportioned a number of organizations and individuals among us for canvassing. Our first disappointment was the labor union. One of our members, a junior officer in one of the larger unions, sought its financial support. Its executive voted us a $25 grant but we had wanted $200 from them. Other disappointments followed. Of 12 businessmen we were to see, we could get in to see only five, and in each case were told that prior commitments prevented them from giving.

After long deliberation we decided that the only way to meet our problem was to build up an organization that would include senior business and labor people and to ask them to help us, not only in raising money but in carrying forward our program. We went first to see the publisher of the major local newspaper to ask him to serve as our president. He was a man of considerable status, trusted by business, yet known for his broad liberal views. He asked us many searching questions about our organization and then suddenly said, "I'll serve as an officer, though not necessarily as president unless it seems best that way, if you get Charles Malcolm, John Simpson, and Ralph Stern to serve as officers also."

We agreed, but we knew it was a tall order. Malcolm was the vice-president of perhaps the largest business empire in the country, Simpson was president of the largest labor union in the country, and Stern was a wealthy Jewish brewer. But we started out to see what we could do. We now believe Dawson, the publisher, paved the way for us with phone calls to each of these men, for each saw us and gave us courteous interviews. The result was that each agreed to serve if Dawson would act as president.

To have these men in our organization made a great difference in our work. We had status and respectability and usually won what we fought for. But we were not only respectable; we were, I felt, much more conservative. Ideas for which we would have fought previously were considered "poor strategy," and we were constantly being told that "to win a war you have to lose a few battles." Personally, I wouldn't have minded losing some of the battles; what I objected to was not fighting at all on some of the issues.

However, the purpose of this paper is primarily to recount our experience in raising money. When our budget came up for discussion, Dawson said: "Do you think you could get us $1,000 from the labor unions, John?" and "Charles, could you raise $5,000 from your companies?" and "Ralph, could you get us $2,500?" All agreed, and Dawson said, "Let's plan then on a budget of $10,000 and I'll make up what the others don't get." Within two months the checks began to pour in and we had our budget secured for the year. Interestingly, with the checks, came some nice notes, especially from businessmen congratulating Malcolm, Stern, or Dawson on getting something like the Civil Liberties Association going—"We need this kind of organization," said one with a check for $300. It all seemed too easy compared with the hours we had formerly spent writing letters, pounding the pavement, making phone calls with so little to show for it.

One other aspect of our new set-up was interesting. It happened that one of the professors at the local university made a speech in which he accused businessmen of "profiteering at the expense of the country" and in which he used words like "sabotage," "black and white Christians," etc. This was not the first time he had delivered a speech of this kind, but a considerable furor arose on this occasion, and we learned that there was a definite move to have him fired from the university. His case was discussed in our association. Since he was a distinguished professor of classics, most of us felt he should not be fired. Dawson and Malcolm, I think, privately believed that anyone so stupid should be fired, but that this might do more harm than good. In any case our association decided to support the professor. A short note was sent to the president of the university urging that the professor be retained. But the real work was done by Malcolm, who held a little dinner at his club for a few businessmen, including several key figures on the board of governors of the university. The matter was discussed at this dinner and policy decided upon—informally, of course. The professor was retained with only a word of warning from the president.

Questions for Discussion

1. What does this case tell us about lines of communication in the community? What principles of community organization does it suggest?

2. Does involvement of "outside persons," such as Dawson and Malcolm, in such an organization entail modification of purposes and policies? What are the gains and costs of involving such leaders in the organization?

River Street in Spadina

In ORGANIZING the Spadina area council we asked residents in each block in the area to vote for three members to represent them on the council. This worked fairly well except on River Street, which was perhaps the worst street in the area—dirty, dilapidated, and congested. The ballots from River Street were not filled in on this particular item. Some residents put in a question mark, others wrote "don't know," but most simply left a blank.

During the first year of operation we got along without representatives from River Street but we recognized this as a gap in our organization. The second year we made a determined effort to organize River Street but we found what we had suspected, that the people did not know one another, and in any case, most of them did not wish to be bothered. We compromised by selecting three people from River Street who agreed to come on the council. They were good people and were an asset to our organization, but it was clear before the end of the year that they had little influence on the people in River Street.

One of the area projects was a clean-up week during which every street was to clean and paint up as best it could, and prizes were to be offered for the two best streets. The three people from River Street worked hard, visiting personally every family on the street seeking to secure coöperation in the project. But few were interested and only one family bothered to help in any way. At the end of clean-up week, River Street did not look much better than it had before. We thought the people there might be shamed by the changed appearance of other streets around them but apparently they were not.

During the third year of the council, the Executive Committee spent almost a whole evening discussing River Street. We realized that this street was so heterogeneous and disorganized that it was impossible to get representatives from it. What we had to do was pretend River Street was an area and could be organized like an area, with representatives from each block—only in this case each house would represent a block.

We began with interviews with each family: How did they like living here? Was it a good place to raise children? What kinds of problems were there? Would they be willing to help tackle some of these problems? Who in this house would be the best one to meet with people from other houses? It was hard, hard work. We were met with suspicion, indifference, a sense of hopelessness. We had to be tactful, encouraging, confident that something could be done.

At the end of the week we had our list of problems and people. We went to see each of the 26 appointed as representatives, and almost forced them to promise to come to the first meeting in the basement of an old church just around the corner. Twenty-four of them came, and we started with the problems they had provided: rats, leaks in plumbing, crowding, dirty neighbors, children running wild in the streets. There was much feeling about these being the problems, but no confidence that anything could be done. One of our members told what his street had done about rats. A flicker of hope in the River Street group quickly dimmed; it could be done only if everyone would help. "Sure it's hard," we told them, "but are you content to live in filth all your lives?" It was a shocking thing to say but it turned the tide. The River Street Council began.

There is no need for details here but the Council has made real progress, beginning with the rats. It was too busy with its own affairs to join the Spadina Council, although it coöperated in clean-up day. But this year, three years after the River Street Council began, it sent three representatives to sit on our area council. They are among our most effective members, and seldom does the River Street Council refuse to give help when asked.

Questions for Discussion

1. What values are there in having representatives from a group or area that is lacking in cohesion or awareness of "commonality"?

2. Do you think our way of handling this problem of representation from River Street is effective? Why or why not?

The Birth Control League in Crofton

T HE ADULT Education Association of Crofton is fundamentally a coördinating and planning body. It does not operate programs of its own except on rare occasions when it initiates an experimental program. Rather, it seeks to bring together representatives of all organizations interested in adult education so that they may plan together on ways of supplementing each other's work and developing new programs in light of new trends and needs.

In 1952, the secretary of the Adult Education Association received an application for membership from the local Birth Control League. He referred this to a small standing committee established for the purpose of screening such applications, and in due course this committee brought to the board a recommendation that the Birth Control League be admitted to full membership. It was immediately apparent that there were profound differences in the board respecting this application. Father James McQuire from the Catholic Coöperative was openly opposed, and some other Catholic members, although less firm on the matter, followed his lead. On the other hand, there was considerable support for the recommendation from other members of the board. Sensing this to be an important issue, the chairman attempted in many ways to secure a compromise or to change the nature of the issue in one form or another. He was unsuccessful and finally, because the hour was late and he was tired, he called for a vote. The result was that the Birth Control League was to be admitted by a majority of two votes.

Following the vote, Father McQuire said he accepted the decision of the board but that he must be frank and say that all Catholic clubs and organizations might, as a result, be forced to withdraw from the Adult Education Association. In view of this, the chairman asked that the board's vote be held in abeyance and that the matter be further explored by a small committee consisting of Father Mc-Quire, the chairman, the secretary, and Dr. Robinson from the university.

This committee met twice and explored the matter carefully. Dr. Robinson argued that the objectives of the Adult Education Association had nothing to do with birth control, that the groups came together because they had something in common, and that this in no way affected their differences. There were Catholic, Protestant, and Jewish groups in the association and this did not eradicate certain differences among them; they came together because they shared a limited common purpose. His argument was: If we all want better education in the community, why can't we join together for this purpose regardless of whether we're white or black, Protestant or Catholic, conservative or radical? Father McQuire, who was a reasonable man, was almost persuaded, although he pointed out that birth control was something on which his church took a firm position and coöperation with such a group would appear like a compromise in the Church's position at the present time. At the second meeting he said he had discussed the matter with the archbishop, who was adamant in his statement that if the Birth Control League were admitted, all Roman Catholic organizations must withdraw. He was sorry, said Father McQuire, but no other course of action was now possible for him.

In light of this, the committee recommended to the board that the Birth Control League not be admitted. The chairman had discussed the matter privately with a number of board members, and the recommendation was accepted with 17 voting in the affirmative, five abstentions, and two opposed.

Questions for Discussion

1. Must one accept the fact that certain groups in the community cannot be brought together in the same organization? Why or why not?

2. Do you think the Adult Education Association should have submitted to the pressure, posed by the threat of withdrawal, by the Catholic groups? Why or why not?

3. What other ideas might be introduced to secure a compromise or even integration in this matter?

4. Review all the episodes in this section and list good practices for community workers in dealing with groups in the community.

Part Four

The Community Worker and the Community

The West End

WHILE I was employed by the Family Services Association near the end of World War II, a wave of juvenile delinquency swept across the country, hitting particularly the large urban communities. Our district office of Family Services Association was deluged with requests for help by parents who were having difficulty in coping with teen-age children who were members of antisocial gangs in the neighborhood. Such gangs as the notorious Toppers Gang were committing offenses ranging from vandalism to armed robbery. (The parents of the Toppers Gang leader were clients of our agency at the time.) Our district office was situated in the southwest part of the city—a low-income, poorly housed, industrialized, boarding-house section of the city. An emergency housing center was included in the district. This housing center, operated by the city, had an extremely bad reputation for inadequate plumbing, filth, and overcrowding. Hundreds of families who had been evicted and could not find new housing at moderate rentals were herded together. Those families that did not have social problems when they entered this center, soon developed them after moving into this area.

In a staff meeting at our district office, we discussed our heavy case loads and the unusually high intake figures for the month. We were having limited success in our work with these disturbed parents and their teen-age children. It was generally agreed that here was a problem that needed to be tackled on a community level as well as a case work level. Perhaps better services were needed, services such as recreation, housing, vocational counseling, etc. It seemed that the roots of the problem lay in social factors as well as in individual family problems. Such postwar problems as absence or death of fathers, working mothers, upheaval of families by frequent moves from one community to another were contributing factors, it seemed to us, to this kind of social disorganization.

A decision was reached in the staff meeting to bring this problem to the community. While it seemed reasonable to me as a young inexperienced worker, I was later to find that this was unusual procedure for a case work agency, or for that matter, for a church, or service club, or recreational agency—the practice being apparently "to do one's own job well." In any case, we decided to lay the problem of delinquency before other groups in the community in the hope that by combining efforts we could work more effectively than by each group working separately.

We selected a wide group of people including ministers, teachers, public health nurses, visiting nurses, social workers from the Children's Aid, Protestant Children's Home, Catholic Children's Home, from the Y.M.C.A., the Y.W.C.A., church organizations, service clubs, from the Public Welfare Department and the Public Recreation Department. In all, 100 invitations were sent out to a luncheon meeting planned for April 25th, and we were pleased to have favorable replies from 81 of those invited.

The director of our agency acted as chairman and proceeded with the brief agenda we had planned. She explained the purpose of the meeting as being "an effort to find a way to cope with the rising problem of delinquency in this area of the city." She illustrated the problem by reading extracts from case histories from our agency's records. Then she introduced the speaker of the day, a professor from the local School of Social Work who discussed (in a rather theoretical way, I thought) some of the causes of juvenile delinquency. This was followed by animated discussion with many complaints about housing and other conditions in the area and with many illustrations of delinquency or predelinquency to confirm some of the speaker's points.

Our staff plan had been to make this a preliminary meeting, to have the group meet again, organize, and begin a program to reform the area. However, quite spontaneously there came a suggestion that a committee be organized to study the problem and to suggest a program of action. Our director raised the question of whether we should not keep the larger group together so that they could remain close to the problem. It was agreed that as soon as the committee was ready to report, another large meeting should be held. It was not specified who should call this meeting.

A committee of ten, which included our director, was appointed with Reverend John McCreary as chairman. McCreary was a young, very vigorous, and highly intelligent person. At the first meeting of the committee he suggested that the terms of reference of the committee be (1) to set forth the causes of delinquency and (2) to suggest a program of community action. The committee decided to tackle this job by organizing several study groups composed of parents and teen-agers. They would also try to work through student organizations in the high school.

The committee met weekly to develop these plans. After four meetings, however, the chairman accepted a call to a church in another city and was unable to take the initiative in planning another committee meeting. No one else felt responsible, and the committee never met again. Since there was no committee report, there was no reason to call the larger group together, and no meeting of that group was held.

We discussed all of this in a staff meeting. Some of us felt that we had an obligation to get Reverend McCreary's committee together again, others that we should call another community meeting; most of the group, however, felt we had done our share and if no one else felt any responsibility, we should not push ourselves forward. Fundamentally, however, I think the reason we never did anything else about this matter was (1) we were very busy with our own cases, (2) we really didn't believe in the plan of the McCreary committee nor did we agree with many of the suggestions which came from other groups at the community meeting, and (3) we felt a bit overwhelmed by the size and importance of the group at the community meeting. In any case, no further meetings were held and there was no follow-up of the problem on a community basis.

I have often wondered about this project and I have often felt guilty that we didn't do something better or something more. But what we should have done, I am not sure. One thing that impressed me was that while everyone at the community meeting seemed enthusiastic and deeply convinced about the need for a community approach, neither I, nor any of my colleagues, heard even one person ask why there had been no follow-up in the year following.

Questions for Discussion

1. List the reasons for the failure of this project. Which do you think were of crucial importance? How could the reasons for failure be overcome?

2. Do you consider it unusual that no one at the enthusiastic community meeting bothered to ask why another meeting was not called? Why or why not? List some of the reasons that might create this situation?

3. Should a case work agency, such as the one in this episode, take the initiative in encouraging community organization? If so, what conditions must be present if they are to do it successfully?

St. Peters

St. PETERS has a population of about 38,000 and is the only city in St. Peters County, which has a population of some 60,000. It is a small industrial city, surrounded by farms and a fairly large number of summer homes. Much of the shopping of both farmers and summer residents is done in the city of St. Peters.

When Joe Sommers came to St. Peters in 1950 as Executive Director of the Children's Aid Society, he found that his agency provided services to the whole county. He discovered also that his predecessor had been corresponding with the provincial Department of Health regarding the lack of mental health services in the county. Apparently the Children's Aid Society, when it had a disturbed child to help, had to take that child to Ronto, some 200 miles distant, for psychiatric treatment. As Sommer's staff soon pointed out, continued psychiatric service was not possible under such circumstances, and many who needed help simply had to do without it. Several specific and touching examples of disturbed children and adults in the community who were unable to secure help were described to Sommers by the staff.

At the second meeting of his board, Sommers raised this matter of deficiency of mental health services, and fortified by several case histories, made a strong case for the need of a psychiatrist in the community and especially as a consultant to the Children's Aid

Society. With this there was unanimous agreement, and a small committee was organized to approach the provincial government both for a grant for this purpose and the name of a psychiatrist who would be suitable and available. This committee met in two weeks' time and with the help of Sommers began preparation of a brief to be submitted to the provincial government. Some six weeks later the brief was ready; at the next board meeting it was approved and later sent with a personal letter from the president of the board to the Deputy Minister of Health in the provincial government. Several weeks later an indifferent letter was received from one of the assistants in the department indicating that while funds were allocated to assist local communities in securing adequate mental health services, these funds had already been spent for the current year. However, the letter went on to intimate that the supply of psychiatrists was so meager that even if money were available, it would be impossible to secure one at the salary level the province could provide. This letter came just seven months after Sommers had first introduced the matter to his board!

During this period, Sommers had been active in the organization of a council composed of those who worked in the health and welfare agencies in the city. Included were the Department of Health, Department of Welfare, Victorian Order of Nurses, Y.M.C.A., Y.W.C.A., Institute for the Blind, Family Court, and the Children's Aid Society. Sommers hoped this group would support the effort for more adequate mental health services. This matter, among many others, was discussed and there was considerable interest in the project, but it was decided, in light of the action taken by Mr. Sommers' board, that the other agencies merely be kept informed about developments. When, however, Sommers reported the discouraging letter from the government, interest and concern were sparked anew and the council formally decided to ask the Children's Aid Society board to take the initiative in organizing a representative committee of citizens to pursue this matter further.

It was now June of 1951 and since the Children's Aid Society board did not meet during the summer, the matter was not considered until September of that year. Some of the earlier interest and concern had been lost during the ensuing months but the council recommendation was briefly discussed although action on it was delayed. One member almost carried the day when he said, "If the social workers are so interested in the problem, perhaps they should pursue the matter." The matter was not considered again until the November meeting, when it was decided to organize a community committee to consider further the need for mental health services. The chairman of the previous committee, E. J. Ferguson, and Sommers were asked to organize and call such a group together.

Ferguson was out of town a good deal in November and it was not until January, 1952, that he and Sommers met to draft a list of those to be invited to serve. Sommers had already consulted his colleagues in the council and had a ready list, most of whom Ferguson approved and to which he even added names of his own choosing. The committee, when finally organized in February, included prominent persons who served on the boards of major agencies, persons from the Departments of Health and Public Welfare, in addition to several prominent businessmen from service clubs, the heads of two leading women's groups, and the school superintendent. In all, 26 persons attended the first meeting of the committee in mid-February, 1952. It had been decided by Ferguson and Sommers that at this meeting Sommers would describe the problem, illustrating it with several case histories; that Ferguson would next describe the action of the Children's Aid Society board; and that the committee would then be asked to discuss further possibilities for action with the hope that all would agree to prepare and sign a petition on behalf of their respective agencies or organizations. While the first part of the meeting went as planned, the group had other ideas about what to do. There was agreement that psychiatric service was required, but it was felt that the petition would have limited value. Rather, the group decided to explore the matter with the local member of the provincial government and with people in Hamlinton, a city the same size as St. Peters, where they had a mental health clinic. Two small sub-committees were appointed to arrange for these consultations. It was April before a meeting was arranged with the provincial member. He was interested, but asked for time to investigate the matter fully. Some expected immediate action as a result of what they thought would be his intervention in the matter, but no word came from him until June, when he wrote that his efforts had been in vain: there was simply no psychiatrist available at the salary the province was able legally to provide. It was also June before the other sub-committees were able to arrange a visit to Hamlinton and since no committees meet in the summer in St. Peters, it was late September, 1952, before the committee met to hear the report about Hamlinton.

The three people who had visited Hamlinton were enthusiastic and optimistic. Hamlinton had had some of the same difficulties; they had found they had to organize a branch of the national mental health association to interpret consistently to the public the need for mental health services and to keep pressure on the city and the province to provide such services. The job was much larger than merely securing a psychiatrist, important and essential as that was. Some of the enthusiasm of those reporting spread through the committee, and it was agreed to ask the national mental health association to send a representative to meet with them at the first possible moment. It was November, however, before such a meeting could be arranged.

Dr. Parkinson from the national office of the mental health association was more than helpful. Not only did he outline the problem of mental health in all its ramifications, he was able to suggest practical steps for action, especially with respect to the establishment of a mental health clinic. The latter could be set up as a private community operation which could raise money of its own, secure grants from both provincial and municipal governments, and hire and pay a psychiatrist whatever it wished. On the spot, the group organized themselves into a mental health association with their principal project the establishment in St. Peters of a mental health clinic. At an early date it was decided to hold a public meeting both to secure new members and to build support for a program of mental health, and especially for the clinic.

But while the group met several times during the winter of 1953, there always seemed to be some reason why a public meeting could not be held. The winter was not entirely wasted, however, as far as Sommers was concerned. He and other members of the council supported a small membership drive for the local mental health association, and before spring had come, over 100 citizens had paid the five dollar membership fee. Literature from the head office began to be circulated in the city, the editor of the local paper was enlisted as a member and became interested enough to write several editorials on the problem, and there was more talk and more acceptance of the need for mental health programs than Sommers had expected.

Finally, at a meeting of all members in September, 1953, it was decided to hold the public meeting. In order to make adequate preparations, the date was set for December 3. The Council of Social Workers gave its full support and vigorously promoted attendance. Many of the branch members asked for the first time to do something besides pay a fee, and also did an effective job in promoting attendance at the meeting. Meanwhile, a small committee worked out a tentative constitution, program, and budget for a mental health clinic in St. Peters. Dr. Parkinson and Dr. Soward, the provincial minister of health, and Mayor Jones of St. Peters, were asked to be the main speakers. Soward was unable to attend but it was later learned that he had sent a junior member of his department as an observer.

The meeting was a most enthusiastic one. The attendance was 427, a number which was far beyond the expectations of the group. Parkinson again did an excellent interpretive job, the Mayor promised support, and several people in the audience among them a wealthy industrialist, indicated that they personally, or some group they represented, would support any effort to provide adequate mental health services in St. Peters. When the draft constitution, program, budget, and list of suggested board members were presented, they were unanimously endorsed.

The members of the new board of the mental health clinic, all of whom had previously agreed to serve, ten of whom had been members of the original community committee on mental health, met briefly after the public meeting. Since the budget was the crucial item in the future, individuals were assigned to negotiate with the three sources of income: the province, the city, and private corporations. It was agreed to meet in January, at which time a report on the possibilities would be heard.

At the January, 1954, meeting, there was evidence of substantial support from both local industry and the municipal government, but the explorations with the provincial government were inconclusive. It was decided that a small committee should seek an interview with the provincial minister of health, but that in the meantime investigation should be undertaken to secure a competent psychiatrist to direct the local clinic. After much waiting, the interview with the minister was arranged, and although he hedged on many matters, he finally agreed to contribute $8,000 during the next year for the psychiatrist's salary. With this financial foundation and with Dr. Parkinson's help, a young psychiatrist was secured at a salary of $12,000 per year. The new clinic was opened in September, 1954.

Meanwhile the local mental health association was busy on several new projects. Several meetings with home and school associations were held, films and literature were made available, and an investigation launched into the care of mentally retarded children.

A month after the new psychiatrist arrived, he met with his board, and in his first report he spoke about the understanding of, and support for, his work which he found in St. Peters. "I have worked in only two other communities," he said, "but I find here far more recognition of mental illness as an illness rather than a plague, and far more desire for prevention and treatment than in these other communities."

Joe Sommers, a member of the board, smiled at this. It had been four years of hard, and at times exasperating, work to get the psychiatrist here. "But perhaps," he mused, "the four years were necessary for us to be ready for him."

Questions for Discussion

1. What was Sommers' objective in this situation? Could it have been secured with less difficulty and in a shorter period of time? If so, how? Would anything be lost by another kind of approach?

2. Evaluate the steps taken in this project. Were all useful and valuable? Why?

3. Appraise Sommers' work in this project. Do you think he pushed his idea too much, or is it necessary for someone to push an idea like this? Do you think persons other than the social workers in the community were deeply conscious of the need? If so, how did they become conscious of it?

Bellville

WHEN JOHN JONES was elected by the voters
as Commissioner of Public Welfare in Bellville in 1929 there were
only 20 cases under care outside the poor farm. Jones was a loyal
though undistinguished member of the Republican party, a real
estate agent of modest success, and when his health failed, he was
given the post of commissioner by the party leaders as a reward for
his work in the party and as a means of supplementing his meager
income. It was understood that the commissioner's post was an easy
part-time job, and the salary of $1,500 per year was considered both
by Jones and party leaders to be quite generous. Jones had no particular qualifications for the job, having only a high school education
and experience as a reporter on the local paper and later as a real
estate agent.

When, however, the depression struck Bellville in the early 1930's,
the problem of relief became a major issue. Bellville was a town of
36,000 with a per capita wealth exceeded by few communities on
the continent. Throughout the city there were large estates each of
which employed many domestic personnel such as maids, gardeners,
and chauffeurs. With the depression, many of these people were discharged, and for this and other reasons, the number of persons
applying for relief increased at an alarming rate. The position of
welfare commissioner became a serious and difficult full-time task

which swamped Jones with his inadequate budget and his staff of one stenographer.

Little help on the problem of mass relief was available from private agencies. This was not their particular concern. The only possible agency that might help was the Bellville Family Welfare Society, but its funds were very limited and it had but one trained social worker on its staff. This agency therefore specialized on family personality conflicts and problems, and carried a limited case load. It apparently saw no reason to change its policy in light of the new situation. The other welfare organizations at this time included a boys' club, a Y.M.C.A., a Y.W.C.A., a day nursery, Boy Scouts and Girl Scouts, a Red Cross chapter, a municipal recreation department, and a juvenile court.

Before the year 1931 had ended, the problem of relief was a community problem. No one was satisfied. Those on relief were unhappy with the administration; those not on relief were unhappy with the huge relief budget—even though it was quite inadequate. Democrats were charging that Republicans could get relief while Democrats could not. Republicans were concerned with rapidly mounting costs and the need to keep the tax rates down. For some time the dissatisfaction was whispered and muffled but gradually it became more overtly expressed, especially by leading Democrats in speeches throughout the community.

The Board of Estimates and Taxation, which confronted this problem most sharply, considered the possibility of appointing a bipartisan committee to supervise the work of the public welfare department. It was felt by this group of Republicans that there was no solution to the problem of relief at that time, and if the Democrats could be involved and were to fail at the task, the Republican party would emerge in a much less dangerous position at the next election. Jones himself greatly feared and opposed the idea of a committee, but his feelings were sacrificed to the interests of the party.

Accordingly, therefore, the Board of Estimates and Taxation appointed such a committee with the following seven members:

Colonel Henry, as chairman (a military man, chairman of the

Republican Committee, and drawing a salary as business manager of the school system; influential in the national guard; cautious, crafty, and a clever manipulator of political forces).

Mr. Brown, as secretary (manager of a large moving and storage company; young, vigorous, popular, impetuous, and headstrong; likely to act before thinking; a hometown boy; member of the Rotary Club; president of the Chamber of Commerce and the Y.M.C.A.; a partisan Democrat).

Mrs. Bellwood (wife of a young mutimillionaire; active in Republican circles; president of the Children's Home. She was emotional but vigorous and enthusiastic, and devoted nearly all of every day to working in Commissioner Jones' office, organizing a campaign for the collection of old clothes, undertaking to find new quarters for the department in a large vacant mansion, etc.).

"Doc." O'Grady (a druggist and landlord, owning several tenements in West Bellville; an active partisan Democratic politician; very influential in this separate village area. There was bitter antagonism between Commissioner Jones and Doc. The Commissioner believed, probably with some truth, that Doc O'Grady was using his position on the committee to get deserving Democrats on work relief. Doc believed, probably with some truth, that Colonel Henry influenced the commissioner to give preference to deserving Republicans).

Reverend Mr. Leonard (Congregational minister; young, vigorous, eloquent, announced Socialist in a wealthy church supported by conservative Republicans; social-minded and keenly conscious of his opportunity to steer the committee toward constructive results. He held the balance of power between the two factions).

Father Murray (Catholic priest and Democrat appointed on the committee as a matter of courtesy to balance Reverend Mr. Leonard. He was conscious of this and seldom attended. He was soon to be transferred from Bellville, probably because he had not succeeded in establishing leadership among the large Italian population. He did not approve of Doc O'Grady and was unwilling to act as his political and religious ally. He desired to offend no one and was therefore inactive).

Mrs. Westcott (president of the Family Welfare Society, appointed in her absence from the city because of her position. She was a Republican, somewhat social-minded, and influential).

The committee was immediately faced with difficulties. There were basic differences in loyalties and outlook. There was the open Republican vs. Democrat feud. There were those who wanted to increase the relief budget vs. those who wanted to keep the budget at its present level. There were those who trusted Jones and those who didn't. The first few meetings were distinguished by the appearance of these differences in conflicts of various kinds over a variety of matters. For example, at one of the early meetings, Commissioner Jones reported that there were 1,200 active cases—people applying for various amounts of relief. Several members disputed this vigorously, Doc O'Grady going so far as to say "deliberate padding." Mrs. Bellwood, in a characteristic manner, made her own private count from the commissioner's files and reported bluntly and untactfully at the next meeting that she could find only 900 cases. This started a heated discussion with the meeting breaking up in disorderly fashion. It seemed doubtful if the committee would meet again.

Mr. Leonard was convinced that the committee must do its job. He personally was committed to a position which would increase the relief budget, but he decided he would submerge this conviction to play the role of conciliator in, and facilitator for, the committee. It seemed to him that the only hope for continuing was a new attack with the help of an expert who would be unbiased and who would have the confidence of all members. During the three days following the meeting he privately visited each member of the committee and Commissioner Jones. Each one of the members felt the committee had been a failure, and none was anxious to continue. Mr. Leonard's argument with all of them was about the same. "What will happen if we quit?" he would ask. "Who will do the job, if we don't?" and "What kind of people are we if we can't do a job like this in a time of crisis?" He let each stumble over these questions before putting forth his proposal to bring in an expert to provide some facts and direction for their work. All agreed to try again. Commissioner Jones felt threatened by the idea of "an expert" but Leonard helped him to see that such an expert might point a direction which Jones could follow with the full support of the committee, and indeed of the whole community.

Mr. White, the expert, a staff member of a national organization interested in promoting better standards in social work, arrived and worked inconspicuously in Bellville. He spent a week going over the records and in discussions with Commissioner Jones. His relations with the latter improved daily, as it became clear to Jones that White came not to criticize or condemn but to help where he could. At the end of the week, there began a series of daily meetings with the committee. The major item of business was the preparation of a budget for the following year. This, of course, had considerable political, not to mention social and ethical, implications. The determination of the budget was crucial. Mr. White was able to clarify many issues for the committee, among them the number of active cases in the department. Mr. White's case count proved that both Mr. Jones and Mrs. Bellwood were approximately correct, Mr. Jones reporting total registration, which on October 31 was 1,246, whereas the number currently active in October was fluctuating between 700 and 800 with the possibility that the number of currently active cases might reach 1,000 with the approach of cold weather. On the basis of numbers of cases in the past and forecasts of the future, Mr. White was able to project three probabilities of what the committee might expect in the way of a case load in the year ahead. For each of these probabilities there could be three budgets depending upon the kinds and quality of relief the committee thought appropriate. Thus, there were nine possible choices the committee could make. This was the extent of Mr. White's help, but it was considerable. Certainly, after his visit, there was no question in the mind of any committee member of maintaining the present inadequate budget. The question was by how much it should be increased. On the whole, the Republicans tended to favor the lowest of the nine possibilities, whereas the Democrats leaned toward the top of the scale.

An additional issue was Jones—Doc O'Grady was intent on getting rid of Jones. At the first meeting following White's departure, the underlying tensions in the committee again came into focus. Doc O'Grady stalked out in anger shouting that he was resigning, and again the meeting broke up with seemingly no hope of agreement of what budget would be recommended. Again, Mr. Leonard undertook to visit each member of the committee. He was able to persuade Doc O'Grady that it was unwise and futile to persecute Jones, who was a sickly man who had only two years to run in his office. "If we can keep the ship afloat for two years," he said, "then we can get another commissioner if things aren't right." O'Grady agreed to come back and to accept whichever budget the committee agreed upon. The other committee members were all a bit regretful about what had happened but in almost every case referred to some member of the committee (a different person in each case) who seemed to block the work of the committee. In each instance, Leonard encouraged a discussion of this person to secure some of the reasons why he was considered difficult. He then moved on to suggest that it would be impossible to get rid of any committee members—"It will be the whole committee including you and me who will fail"—and to suggest that perhaps they could help "the difficult person" or at least compromise with him or her. Thus when the next meeting was held, each member of the committee came with some determination to try to help the person who bothered him most, or at least to compromise if need be. Mr. Leonard was able to secure one other change for this meeting. He persuaded Colonel Henry to invite the committee to his home for the meeting which could be held there without the help or burden of papers, staff, agenda, etc.

The committee met in the living room of Colonel Henry's beautiful home, and whether or not it was this setting, Mr. Leonard's interviews, or a general change in the attitude of the committee, or some other factor, the atmosphere was entirely different. Colonel Henry explained that there was no need for an agenda, that he thought only the question of the budget required decision at the moment, and that he had called the meeting here so that the matter could be discussed informally and without the need for a decision, although the committee must be conscious of their responsibilities to the community. Doc O'Grady plunged in with a mumbled apology regarding his hasty departure from the last meeting and with the statement that he had thought over the possibilities, and while "you all know which budget I'd like, still I am agreeable to any budget recommended by this committee and I'll support it for all I am worth in Bellville." With this gesture of good will as a beginning, the meeting progressed almost too well, Mr. Leonard thought. He smiled to himself at the constant indications of mutual good will and willingness to accept the judgment of others as to what the budget should be. The mood was almost spoiled by Mrs. Bellwood, who suggested that "since it is so difficult to agree on the exact amount, why don't we let Colonel Henry set the budget and we'll support it, whatever it is." Good will and mutual trust had not developed this far, and Mr. Leonard hastened to step in and say that while he had faith in Colonel Henry's judgment, he would like to see the committee face its responsibility and make its own decision. Most heads nodded approval. He went on to say that the issue was between "what was needed to do an adequate job" and "what the taxpayers would stand"; but if the committee asked for a small budget and then were required to overspend, was it being fair to either the taxpayers or to itself as a committee? Personally, he was in favor of the second highest budget, both because it was almost surely going to be needed and because it would be an honest estimate for the taxpayers. There was considerable discussion of this proposal with the committee finally agreeing on the third highest projected budget. Colonel Henry asked again for a show of hands of those who approved and who would fully support such a budget in the community. The vote was unanimous.

This budget proposed a possible rise in case load to 1,200 currently active cases and an average of 800 per month throughout the year, an adequate staff for Commissioner Jones, and a total relief budget of $410,200 and an administration budget of $33,730. Since the previous year's budget was only $90,000, the increase requested was almost five times that of the former budget.

The next step was to secure the approval of the Board of Estimates and Taxation. In order fully to explain their budget, it was agreed to invite the Board to meet informally with the committee. Accordingly, Mr. Brown was asked to arrange a tea for the following Sunday at the Y.M.C.A., of which he was president. This meeting went well, with rather skillful and sharp questions coming from the Board members about various aspects of the proposed budget, and drawing out the basis for the committee's desire both for an "honest budget" and a budget that provided for adequate personnel "to see that the money is spent wisely and well." The meeting broke up in a united and cordial spirit.

The following day the committee met to put its report and budget in final shape. It was noticeable that spirits were high, that a new *esprit de corps* had developed, and that there was a considerable feeling of confidence and achievement. Gradually the members whipped their report into shape. After reviewing the situation and the anticipated case load, the report read:

The full significance of these statistics will be appreciated when it is understood that they indicate that approximately one-sixth of the children of Bellville must depend for their existence this winter upon the relief funds you are appropriating. Unless these funds are not only ample, but also wisely administered, our children will be undernourished and the physical, mental, and moral stamina of our people will be seriously impaired for years to come.

We recommend that the commissioner be provided with a staff of investigators large enough to permit each a maximum load of 100 cases. We are convinced that a capable investigator will more than save the cost of her salary in the more careful expenditure of the relief appropriation which will result from her work if she is not overburdened with too many cases. The commissioner has asked us to act with him in selecting additional staff. The compensation for such investigators should average $150 per month. The commissioner, we believe, should have a chief assistant, or case supervisor, capable of relieving him of the detailed supervision of the investigators. The sum of $3,000 will probably be necessary to secure such a person. The commissioner himself is now giving full time to his work and in view of the heavy burden he is bearing, should receive at least $3,600.

A few days later, the committee attended the public hearing before the Board of Estimates and Taxation. The previous unofficial discussion of the department's budget in the informal setting of a Sunday afternoon tea at the Y.M.C.A. helped to lay a successful basis for the formal hearing. Mr. Brown made an eloquent plea for the acceptance of the committee's recommendations. The Board of Estimates and Taxation ultimately approved the administrative appropriations exactly as requested by the committee ($33,730) and allowed $330,030 for relief. While this was less than the "ideal" budget suggested by the committee, it was four times the original sum for which the commissioner had dared to ask.

Under the Bellville charter the total town budget as proposed by the Board of Estimates and Taxation must be approved by a town meeting at which all qualified voters of the town might attend and vote. The town meeting might reduce but could not increase the appropriations recommended by the Board. For the previous year the total town budget was $2,976,000, raised by a tax rate of .016 on a grand list of taxable property of a little over $185,000,000. The grand list which would be used for the impending tax had shrunk to a little over $180,000,000. Nevertheless, in order to finance an increased public welfare budget, the Board recommended a total town budget of $3,057,000, and in order to keep the total at this figure they reduced the allowance for every other function of town government below that granted for the previous year (except payments on the town debt which were contractual and could not be reduced). The net result was a proposed tax rate of .017 per dollar of assessed value, or another point rise in the tax rate.

Mr. Brown was selected as the spokesman of the committee to "sell" the proposed increase in the welfare budget to the voters of the town. He was a fluent speaker, an active worker in the "opposition party," and a popular member of many clubs and organizations. He addressed the Taxpayers Association, the Chamber of Commerce, the Rotary Club, the American Legion, and many other civic groups, explaining the recommendations of the committee and the need for a larger budget. His remarks were published in the daily paper together with the entire report of the committee.

Reverend Mr. Leonard also made several speeches and influenced key members of his congregation. Mrs. Bellwood was no less effective among her large circle of influential friends. She made no formal speeches but used that very effective technique which has been called "organized conversation." At the bridge table, at the dinner table, and on the golf course, she and many others energized by her "sold" the new budget enthusiastically.

Colonel Henry, aided by Commissioner Jones, swung the Republican Committee into line and thus set in motion that far-reaching word-of-mouth publicity at which they were adept as professional politicians. Doc O'Grady worked tirelessly among ward-heelers and "lower-class" Democrats. His open support of the report did more than anything else, perhaps, to stifle opposition from the small taxpayers.

When the town meeting was held, there was no serious opposition to the welfare budget. Two hours were spent wrangling over an item in another department's budget. At 11:30 p. m., after one minor criticism of Commissioner Jones' administration, the public welfare budget was passed as recommended.

Questions for Discussion

1. What would you consider to be critical steps in this process? Why were they critical?

2. Evaluate the role played by Reverend Mr. Leonard in this situation. What was his special contribution? What was his philosophy and strategy?

3. How can one explain the change in attitude in the committee? Does this often happen in committees?

The South Side Center

I_N 1948 a well-known community organization specialist was imported by the Welfare Council of Summerville to make recommendations regarding its existing youth recreation services. The action of the Welfare Council was primarily initiated by the Executive of the Summerville Neighborhood House who was about to retire and who wished to turn over the future fate of the House to the community. The board of the House concurred in her thinking, applied to the Welfare Council, and the Welfare Council happily acceded to the request. The survey conducted by the specialist revealed that the public recreation services, which were operated through the community board of education, were on the whole excellent but that the programs could stand some enrichment and some professionalization. The Y.M.C.A. and Y.W.C.A. were doing an adequate job. However, two of the existing agencies required some drastic revision.

First was the Summerville Neighborhood House which had had a 25-year history of serving as a settlement house in a neighborhood not far from the university. The population was primarily Negro, Italian, and Jewish, as well as "poor white." The latter category included people of Irish and Scandinavian descent, and people who had moved in from the Southern states. The House was operated chiefly by the director and her sister who were two sweet, Southern

ladies of relatively independent means. They had had no professional training, their moral attitudes were strict, and they definitely
considered themselves to be in a totally different class from the
people they served. In fact, it was difficult to distinguish their home
visits from snooping expeditions. They advised new workers never
to take their hats and coats off when they entered a home, always to
wear gloves, and never to sit on a stuffed chair because of the danger
of vermin infection.

In the 25 years that had passed, the community had changed considerably. The Italians and Jews who had arrived as immigrants
were giving way to a second generation of Italians who had been
born in America. The Negroes had almost completely replaced the
Jews in the neighborhood. It was obvious that the sewing and cook-
ing classes, the weaving and piano lessons, which had been major
programs, were no longer meeting the needs of the neighborhood.

The second agency was the West Side Center which had grown
out of the community's wartime experiment with a Youth Mayor's
Council. The latter some years past had created this center, which
had a very active dramatic group, held dances, and operated an
active after-school bowling league. The teen-agers who met at the
center were primarily of middle-class American and Jewish stock.
Women in the neighborhood volunteered their services for the well-
baby clinic. The program, though excellent, was limited in scope,
there was an exclusive air about the activities, and the staff was
untrained.

The survey recommended that the two agencies be amalgamated
under a single director and overall executive, but that they continue
maintaining separate boards for the present. A further recommendation was made that this new agency take the initiative in developing
recreation facilities on the South Side.

The South Side was a genuinely deprived area. There was not a
church, or a school, or a playground in the area. Although geographically small, the population was relatively dense. The South
Side had originally been a trailer camp which had somehow become
permanent. People who had come to Summerville during the war

had frequently decided to stay on, purchased a small lot and built themselves small homes. In every block there were a number of homes which merely consisted of a cellar and roof, the family having postponed completing the house until they had found additional income. Some homes were really two or three trailers stuck together. The population was mixed and consisted of some old-time Summerville residents, Negroes from the south, former white sharecroppers, and some of the less acceptable second generation Italians. The police had the area tagged as a real trouble spot. Most of the rape and carnal knowledge cases were reported from this area. Most of the fights, wife beatings, and fires also occurred there.

The survey recommendations were accepted by the community, and the director for the newly named Summerville Neighborhood Centers was hired. Mr. Clinton was an experienced group worker who had done considerable student supervision at the University of Pittsburgh. He understood his job well and proceeded to do it. He first concentrated on the two existing centers and got them underway. He gradually came in contact with members of the community, such as professors at the university, the chairman of the board of education, the director of the public recreation program, the prosecuting attorney, and the police sergeant in charge of the juvenile squad. All of them liked Mr. Clinton who was a rugged former athlete. He fitted in very well with the direct friendliness of the small Midwestern community. He had no "highfalutin" ideas and promised everyone that he would not make any changes in his first year until he really got to know the community. He insisted that people who had lived in the city knew it best and that he would have to lean on them for guidance. His philosophy was "go slow," "learn to crawl before you walk," and "Rome wasn't built in a day." He insisted that group work was a special skill, but that everyone was more or less a group worker.

Nothing much happened in connection with the South Side until about February of the first year. During that month Summerville was rocked by a real South Side scandal. It appeared that two Negro men, one of whom was married, had had carnal knowledge of a 14-

year-old white girl living in the South Side. They had been discovered by police in a parked truck, and all three had been arrested.
Private conversations with the sergeant of the juvenile squad indicated that this girl had a few months previously entertained a group
of eight or nine South Side youths. The later situation might not
have aroused so much comment had the men been younger and
white, but now the community was galvanized into action.

The prosecuting attorney, the only elected Democrat in a
predominantly Republican community, immediately called a conference of educators and social workers and advised them of the problem. He made several speeches to service clubs during which he
stated that such situations were due to the neglect of the Republican
administration. In addition, the conference suggested that the
absence of recreation facilities in the South Side accounted for the
high ratio of adult and juvenile crime in the community. Mr. Clinton, who had attended the meeting, suggested that a group of interested citizens form a South Side community center board which
would promote the creation of social and recreational services on
the South Side. In this he had the support of the Welfare Council.
Mr. Clinton stressed that the board should make every effort to
include among its members citizens living in the South Side. This
was also accepted enthusiastically. Mr. Clinton was then given the
job of organizing such a board.

One of the first people contacted by Mr. Clinton was Mr. John
Dicks. Mr. Dicks was a stationary engineer at one of the small
industrial plants in the city who had lived in the South Side for
about 15 years. Mr. Dicks' picture had appeared in the local paper
when he had completed his own home single-handed. He was also
a frequent contributor to the "Letters to the Editor" column and
had expressed himself on diverse topics such as fluorine, the building codes, the commercialization of Christmas, and the lack of a
playground in the South Side. Mr. Dicks was happy to serve. Mr.
Clinton, the prosecuting attorney, and Mr. Dicks met to draw up a
list of possible people to serve on their board. Included in their
list were the milkman, the mailman from the South Side, the former

bootlegger to the university faculty who had made a fortune in the fuel oil business, and many others. All in all, the board was a very good one, consisting of many actual residents of the South Side ore people whose daily business brought them into close contact with the population there. Two or three wealthy citizens and members of the university faculty were also included. Early in March a general meeting was called. Meeting notices were distributed by the mailman in every South Side home. A notice was placed in the newspaper inviting all citizens to attend.

About 60 turned up for the meeting. A check of their addresses indicated that one-third were South Side residents. At the meeting, Mr. Dicks, Mr. Clinton, and the prosecutor explained the purpose of the meeting and expressed their hopes for the growth of recreation services in the South Side. The executive was elected with Mr. Dicks as president and the prosecuting attorney as secretary. The head of the local School of Social Work became vice-president and the treasury was taken by the police sergeant. The milkman also was in an executive capacity. No Negroes appeared at the meeting and none was elected.

The board had one meeting in April which was primarily social in nature, as it had been planned to give people an opportunity to get to know one another. They also discussed possibilities of developing a South Side Center. Mr. Peters, the head of the local School of Social Work, said that there were a number of large prefabricated buildings which had been used as movie theatres for the army not far from Summerville. These, he suggested, might be dismantled and reërected on a suitable site. The prosecuting attorney agreed to follow up channels to see if these buildings could be made available. Mr. Dicks volunteered to get a crew of South Side citizens to erect the building, and the remainder of the board decided to visit the South Side to find a suitable lot. Mr. Clinton was pleased with the meeting and felt it had gone very well. One of his major concerns, namely, finding a structure which would serve as a center, had miraculously taken shape as a realizable project. If all went well, there would be practically no expense involved, since the prosecutor claimed there were some federal regulations which would permit the free transfer of army surplus buildings for community purposes. The prosecutor again emphasized the beneficence of the Democratic regime. Mr. Clinton came out of the meeting chuckling and insisting that Mr. Dicks was "the salt of the earth." He also felt very warmly about the prosecutor, because Mr. Clinton had had active Democratic connections in the East.

In May something new developed. In past years the city recreation department had participated in a garden plot project. Close to the South Side there was a large open field which was especially fertile because it was drained swampland. The recreation department had subdivided this lot into small garden plots and invited local citizens to grow their own vegetables. The recreation department now wished to hand over this project to the South Side community center board. Mr. Clinton gladly accepted the offer and put his staff to work publicizing the garden project among South Side residents. Letters were also sent to all those who had registered for plots in past years. Again a meeting was called inviting everyone to attend. Many people did, but again South-Siders were in the minority and most of those who came were among those who had gardened in previous years. A committee was established to lay out the plots and a system of priorities was created. The meeting voted to give precedence to those who had gardened previously. No one suggested that South-Siders be given any kind of priority, and owing to the small turnout from that area Mr. Clinton hesitated to raise the question. During the course of the month the committee stretched string and made neat equally sized 30' x 30' plots. Mr. Clinton himself selected a plot right in the middle of the field and went out every evening in his shirt sleeves with his packages of seeds. He was personally thrilled at this opportunity to do some gardening. However, since he knew nothing of gardening he took advantage of his ignorance to ask others about type of seed, when and where to plant, etc. This gave him an opportunity to meet informally with an interesting cross section of community members. Almost all classes of people were attracted to these plots. The wealthier ones arrived with small power-driven plows, the poorer with rusty spades and rakes. At six o'clock in the evening the lot was the scene of great activity. Cars drew up and discharged husbands, wives, and children. Everyone was friendly and in a good mood. However, most people restricted their social contact to their own families, and each labored on his own plot.

The question of fertilization arose. Several members of the committee suggested that it would be cheaper and easier for all the plot users to buy a load of manure jointly immediately after the plowing. Again a meeting was called of plot users to discuss this question but only a half dozen people arrived. Now that everyone had his plot, each person evidently felt that he was attending to his onions and was not concerned with the project as having any overall community meaning.

Mr. Clinton planted radishes, carrots, cucumbers, lettuce, beets, and a few rows of corn. His crop thrived and he was thrilled with his contact with the soil. As the summer progressed he frequently brought samples of his vegetables to board meetings and categorically announced, "This is real fresh stuff, not like you get in the store." At one time he almost lost his sense of perspective when his corn was trampled one night by what he suspected were some South Side teen-agers. His sense of proprietorship was hurt and for about a week he was totally unforgiving.

In June, the program at the Neighborhood House began to slacken as the recreation department offered excellent services in the park across the road from the settlement. This left Mr. Clinton free to use his boys' worker and girls' worker more intensively in relation to the South Side project. Mr. Clinton at a staff meeting suggested that they go out and make a house-to-house canvass of the South Side to discover the community's needs. The girls' worker looked forward to the experience but was hindered to some extent by the disinterest of the boys' worker in the project. Exactly what was bothering the boys' worker in this situation may be difficult to analyze, but one of the factors was that he would be leaving the community at the end of the summer. He also felt that the burden of programming at

Neighborhood House had fallen on his shoulders, and he had been looking forward to the summer as a more relaxed time during which the job demands would be lessened. Nevertheless, the two workers began their house-to-house canvass of the community. Faced with the actual situation of pushing door bells, entering living rooms, and interviewing people, the girls' worker suddenly realized that she was rather fearful of actual social contact with the residents. As a result, the two workers visited each home together and most of the interviews were carried by the boys' worker. On occasion the girls' worker preferred to remain in the car when the house looked particularly "rough."

The two interviewers found that the community had no clear-cut ideas regarding its own needs. First of all, there was very little sense of community. Some of the residents preferred to dissociate themselves from the others and made references to the "poorer class of people." The two Italian prostitutes somewhat apologetically asked whether Negroes would be permitted to attend the new center and if so, would their attendance be scheduled at different times. Some of the Negroes were overpolite and their manner suggested that they didn't quite believe in the reality of an interracial center. Others were militant but were concerned about the "poorer types" of their own race.

In the meantime all progress on the building of the center suddenly halted. The prosecuting attorney was defeated for reëlection and Mr. Clinton was greatly disturbed. However, the Republican who was elected in his place (and who had held the office previously) began to display great interest in the project. Within two weeks of his election he had maneuvered the city manager into sending out a public works crew to dig the foundation and lay the cement for the centers. The city architect had been prevailed upon to draw up the plans and the new prosecuting attorney, Mr. Douglas, was making speeches to service groups regarding the deep interest of the Republican party in the South Side project. Word also came that the buildings were being dismantled and would shortly be shipped to Summerville.

During the course of the change-over, Mr. Clinton became concerned about offering to the South Side residents some visible evidence of the agency's concern. Since his staff had brought him no definite picture of community needs, he announced that he had hired a bus which would make two trips weekly through the South Side to transport for a nickel fare all children under 14 to one of the city's beaches. The two workers were to accompany the children and to supervise the swimming activity. Leaflets were to be distributed announcing this activity throughout the South Side. Further, the girls' worker was to assist the recreation department playground staff with its junior program three mornings a week. Not only had Mr. Clinton made arrangements with the recreation department regarding this, but he had also prevailed on the department to utilize the site of the forthcoming center as a playground.

The bus cruised slowly through the dust and the summer heat twice a week. As children saw the bus approach they ran out of their yards and began to climb aboard. Up and down the streets the bus went, and over 50 children were taken to the beach that first week. The following week there were 20 and the following week 15. By the fourth week the project was given up. Mr. Clinton was not too unhappy about this, because by then he had heard that the building was on its way. The playground was suspended as the works department brought out its steam shovels and dug the foundation. Mr. Clinton was initially disturbed at the speed with which Mr. Douglas and the city manager had moved. Mr. Dicks had been on the verge of organizing his committee of South Side citizens to help with the preparation of the foundation. When the city became involved Mr. Dicks abandoned his plan for the committee. Mr. Clinton tried to explain to him how important it was to get participation from the community so that all could feel that the center was truly theirs. Mr. Dicks conceded the point but countered with: "If you can get the city to do something decent for a change, don't discourage them."

The summer passed and two large Quonset huts stood on the South Side lot. The building had arrived and the community was interested and tripped through eagerly when they were invited to attend an open house. All of Summerville's dignitaries were present, and Mr. Douglas made an excellent speech in which he stated that through the initiative and coöperation of thousands of local groups of this sort America had grown strong. Nowhere did he strike a negative note or suggest that the center was a response to the community's concern about the South Side citizens.

After this, the observer left town and doesn't know much of what happened except that the South Side Center is in operation.

Questions for Discussion

1. Evaluate Mr. Clinton's work in the South Side area. What do you consider the strengths and weaknesses of his work?

2. Do you consider the South Side has "more capacity to deal with its own problems" than before Mr. Clinton began work here? What other things should Mr. Clinton have done?

3. Do you think the new South Side Center will be successful? If you were to become the new director of this Center at this time, what would you do?

New Mexico*

I. THE PROBLEM

FOR GENERATIONS Spanish American farmers in the Rio Grande Valley of New Mexico have grown corn as an important crop. As compared with midwestern United States farmers their yields are very low, and the quality of the corn is poor by any ordinary standards. In one community recently, a county extension agent of the United States Department of Agriculture succeeded in introducing hybrid corn which gave about three times the yield of that grown traditionally. Once the results of the new seed were seen, a majority of the growers adopted the hybrid variety. Four years after the first introduction, however, nearly all the farmers had ceased to plant the hybrid and were again using the old corn. Why did a seemingly successful introduction not ensure the establishment of an improved seed? What factors had the county agent failed to take into consideration?

II. THE COURSE OF EVENTS

In 1946 the county extension agent in ————— County, New

* Anacleto Apodaca, "Corn and Custom: The Introduction of Hybrid Corn to Spanish American Farmers in New Mexico," in Edward H. Spicer (ed.), *Human Problems in Technological Change*, New York, Russell Sage Foundation, 1952, pp. 35–39. Reprinted with permission of the publisher.

Mexico, decided to try hybrid seed corn as a way of improving the corn yield of farmers in his jurisdiction. He persuaded leaders in one village to allow him to present information concerning a hybrid variety. Discussions with the farmers proved more successful than he had hoped. Forty of the 84 growers in the village planted small amounts of the hybrid and doubled the production per acre of the preceding year. The following year 60 growers planted hybrid corn, and the county agent felt that the introduction had been successful. In 1948, however, although the high yield had continued, only 30 farmers planted hybrid. The other 30 who had planted it the year before went back to the traditional variety. In 1949 the decline in number of farmers planting the hybrid was even greater. Only three in the village planted it. They were farmers whom the county agent had long regarded as progressive. All the rest were growing the old corn, and the planting of hybrid had not spread to any other village.

III. RELEVANT FACTORS

Originally borrowed from the Indians, corn has long been a staple crop among Spanish American farmers of ——— County. They grow it for their own consumption, selling none of it outside the villages. Formerly, like the Indian women of the region, the Spanish American women ground the corn on stone slabs. Now it is made into meal at local mills. From the meal thin, round cakes, called tortillas, are prepared which serve as a major item in the diet. Also when crops are relatively abundant, corn is fed to the stock, and the stalks are used as roughage for the animals.

The corn grown prior to 1946 is a variety developed locally, which the farmers call "Indian corn." It attains medium height, producing a minimum of roughage. Its average yield is 25 bushels to the acre and the farmers save their own seed from year to year, mostly without benefit of selection. The corn is planted in small irrigated fields, for which there is usually a plentiful supply of water.

The county agent's relations with the farmers were good. He spoke Spanish in the same manner, was familiar with their background and agricultural practices, and had served as agent for several years immediately preceding this venture. The seed corn, he felt, had degenerated and he suspected that this was an important factor in keeping production low. He decided to introduce a hybrid seed that was known for high yield and proceeded carefully, consulting with the college agronomist, who selected a variety—Hybrid U.S.$_{30}$—that had been tested in the immediate area. It was considered disease-resistant and capable of producing a good growth, averaging 100 bushels to the acre.

Then the agent discussed the problem of low corn yields with the leaders of the village, having chosen this particular community as a likely place for a good response. The men readily recognized the need for better production and were willing to think that, perhaps, their seed strain was weakening after long continuous propagation.

The soils of the fields used by this village were tested and found to be of good fertility, since here, as elsewhere in the area, it had been customary to use some manure yearly. After discussion with the leaders of the various problems involved, a meeting was called in order to present the county agent's plan.

Everyone in the village was invited to the meeting. The agent showed movies of the hybrid corn and cartoons to enliven the demonstration. Then the leaders took over the meeting and explained in their own words the plan for introducing hybrid corn. All those present seemed to agree that the new seed was the answer to many of their problems and that they would be well able to afford the price of the seed, once it was available locally.

By special arrangement with a grower of seed, the new hybrid was furnished in exchange for the old seed. A demonstration plot which clearly showed a tripled crop was set up near the village, with the result that 40 farmers planted hybrid and each doubled his production the first year.

The whole procedure seemed to have been soundly based and to have got unusually rapid results. There was confirmation of this, when, in the following year, the county agent was able to report that 60 farmers, about three-fourths of all the growers in the village, had accepted the new seed. The seed was producing admirably; it was within their means and seemed a very profitable innovation.

IV. THE OUTCOME

Inquiry during 1949, after nearly all the farmers had gone back to planting "Indian corn," revealed the reasons for their rejecting the hybrid. The feeling of need for better yields was still stongly present. No one complained of lack of market for surpluses, which the extension agent had feared might be a factor. There had not, in fact, been any real surplus over the requirements of people and livestock. No one had had any particular difficulty in producing the new crop. All those who had grown it were still much impressed with the large yields, and some said it confirmed their belief that their own seed had become weakened through generations of inbreeding. Owing to increased production, there had been no difficulty in obtaining seed.

Gradually the agent secured responses to direct questions as to why those who had tried hybrid had not continued to plant it. The answer was simple. As one farmer said, "My wife doesn't like that hybrid, that's all." He and others explained that the new corn had not been popular from the first harvest. All the wives had complained. Some did not like its texture; it did not hang together well for tortillas; the tortillas were not the color of nixtamal (the corn flour dough to which they were accustomed). Few had cared for the flavor, but the farmers who persisted in planting it after the first year had hoped that they would get used to it. It made abundant food for the stock and they were reluctant to drop it for that reason. However, after three years they had not become accustomed to the flavor or texture, and their wives were up in arms.

V. ANALYSIS

This is an instance of careful procedure, up to a point, in the best tradition of agricultural extension in the United States. The agent moved slowly and carefully, and then only after a considerable period of observation and analysis of the specific local situation. He examined all the technical aspects of soil, growing conditions, and existing practices. A real need was felt for the new crop and he was able to induce farmers to formulate that need among themselves. He utilized local leadership and made no start until the people thoroughly understood what was to be done. He demonstrated procedure and results. It cannot be said that he ignored any of the well-tried, and often reiterated, rules of extension procedure.

Nevertheless, the agent's exploration of the context of the change sought did not go quite far enough. He had paid attention to the relations between the agricultural technology and the environmental conditions, and to those between farming practices and the social organization of the community. He failed, however, to inquire into the food habits and their influence on the selection of crops. By experiment, as it were, he found that food habits could not be ignored. He learned that the interests and wishes of the village women had to be taken into account as an important factor in the agricultural economy. Finally, he found that in the system of values of the community, corn quality was more important than corn quantity.

The agent had proceeded on the belief that increased farm production was the only important factor involved. He had not gone into the uses of the crop, nor had he tested it as a food prepared by the farmers in the usual manner.

He failed also to make allowance for the customary courtesy of the people, who were not used to correcting "experts" or to expressing themselves freely in the presence of the latter. On reflection the agent realized that some of the farmers had had doubts about the introduction, but had not felt that they should discourage his efforts.

It is probable that a successful procedure would have included the following steps:

Trial of several varieties of hybrid corn and the selection of one. More thorough testing of the corn to see how it fitted into the culture patterns. Continued demonstration of the advantages of the new seed. Close contact with the growers to detect any difficulties and to make modifications in the plan as needed.

By these means the taste problem might have been detected earlier and met through the use of a more suitable type of hybrid.

Questions for Discussion

1. Do you agree with the analysis of this project? What other possibilities were there? For example, are there other approaches to the community that might be useful in this situation?

2. Are there principles or lessons demonstrated in this project that are of general value? If so, identify them specifically.

3. How can the worker handle a situation in which the people are not "used to correcting 'experts' or to expressing themselves freely in the presence of the latter"?

Parker Valley*

I. THE PROBLEM

IN THE Colorado River Relocation Center, a settlement of involuntary wartime evacuees which had been recently formed in Arizona, people refused, when given the opportunity, to go outside the Center to pick cotton at current piecework rates. The income derivable far exceeded what they were receiving in token wages from the government. Was the failure to accept the opportunity due to lack of individual incentive, resulting from a plan for pooling the earnings in a common trust fund, to antagonism to the United States war effort on the part of these people of Japanese ancestry, to some other factors, or to a combination of these?

II. THE COURSE OF EVENTS

In October, 1942, farmers in the Parker Valley, Arizona, where the Colorado River Relocation Center was situated, sent urgent word to the administrators of the Center that the usual migratory labor on whom they counted to pick their cotton had not appeared.

* E. H. Spicer, "Reluctant Cotton-Pickers: Incentive to work in a Japanese Relocation Center," *Human Problems in Technological Change,* New York, Russell Sage Foundation, 1952, pp. 41–54. Reprinted with permission of the publisher.

They said they were faced with loss of almost their entire crop unless evacuees would pick it. From among the 17,000 persons in the newly established Center there should be enough labor to do the job.

The administrators talked the request over in staff meeting and decided that the evacuees should be given the opportunity to pick the cotton. They believed it would be to the evacuees' advantage in several ways. Not only would it bring more money into the Center, it would also improve the public relations of the evacuees with the local farmers and with the United States public at large. It would be a demonstration of the readiness of the Japanese Americans to participate in the United States war effort and thereby help to reduce the suspicion that had been aroused concerning them as a result of the evacuation.

The administrators also decided that indiscriminate recruiting by Parker farmers might disrupt the operation of the Center and that opportunities to make large sums by individuals would upset the framework of Center life, which was based on almost equal income for evacuees. Therefore, they proposed to present the request to evacuee leaders and urge a plan for turning what was earned by individuals into a Community Trust Fund, which would be used for community improvement.

Evacuee leaders and administrators came together in an especially called meeting. The evacuees concurred with the administrators in their view of the benefits and accepted, after some discussion, the proposal for a Community Trust Fund. They, too, believed that it would disrupt the pattern of life developing in the community if some individuals were permitted to make large earnings, while others continued to subsist on only the $12 to $19 a month paid to evacuee workers by the government.

The evacuee leaders presented and discussed the whole matter in block meetings in the Center. It was announced and advertised in various ways, until leaders were convinced that the plan was widely known.

Dates were set for the start of cotton-picking and members of the evacuee Community Council and the Issei Advisory Board and Block Managers (the three important over-all community organizations) themselves turned out to pick. However, only a very few evacuees, other than these officials, responded. Administrative staff and evacuee leaders were deeply discouraged.

What were the causes of the almost complete lack of response? With Parker Valley farmers ready to interpret it as disloyalty to the United States, what could be done to get a reasonable number of evacuees out to pick cotton?

III. RELEVANT FACTORS

At the beginning of World War II all persons of Japanese ancestry living on the West Coast of the United States were evacuated by the War Department and placed in "Relocation Centers" in inland wilderness areas. The Poston Relocation Center, situated in the Parker Valley on the Colorado River Indian Reservation in western Arizona, had a population of some 17,000 Japanese Americans.

The evacuation and incarceration of Japanese was an emergency war measure, described by officials responsible for it as required by military necessity. However, the relocation centers were placed in charge of an especially created government agency, the War Relocation Authority, which operated on the policy that the evacuees were in great majority not proved disloyal to the United States and that they might therefore be resettled outside the West Coast military zone. Temporary, and some permanent, resettlement of evacuees from the relocation centers had begun at the time of the cotton-picking issue in Poston.

Japanese Americans, in general, deeply resented the evacuation from their homes and businesses in California, Oregon, and Washington, which they had developed over a forty-year period. Different segments of the Japanese population reacted in different ways. A few believed that they might be better off in relocation centers for the duration of the war, thereby safe from any outbursts of anti-Japanese feeling on the West Coast as the war developed.

Many older people, who had never been allowed by law to become United States citizens and were still Japanese nationals, regarded this enforced neutral position as perhaps safest. However, most of the older people were concerned chiefly about economic losses caused by evacuation. They resented these and also strongly resented the refusal of the government to treat their children as other United States citizens were treated. Older people also tended to regard the evacuation as foolish policy and scoffed at the idea that they could in any way interfere with the United States war effort if left in their homes on the West Coast.

The great majority of younger men and women, born in the United States and regarding themselves as Americans, felt up against a blank wall in the relocation centers. Frustrated in their plans, resentful of treatment not accorded to any other citizens, many spoke of having lost faith in the United States. Some, however, persisted in seeking positive ways to "demonstrate their loyalty," writing to the War Department to open Selective Service to them and favoring such projects as the introduction of camouflage net factories into the relocation centers, in which they could work on the production of war materials. A smaller number, often young men who had received some of their education in Japan (the Kibei), objected strongly to doing anything that would help the United States war effort and expressed loyalty to Japanese cultural traditions and national aims.

People of all sorts of backgrounds composed the population of the Poston Relocation Center. A majority had owned, managed, or worked on farms, but nearly as many had been shopkeepers, small businessmen, or members of the professions in Los Angeles and other southern California cities. Those with agricultural background had grown truck crops, such as celery, melons, lettuce, or strawberries. A relatively small number, chiefly elderly bachelors, were harvest laborers, fruit and vegetable pickers, and of these only a very few had ever picked cotton. However, there were no strongly crystallized attitudes toward cotton-picking, despite some tendency to look down on it as the occupation of "Okies" (derogatory name for migrant workers from Oklahoma or Texas).

At the time the Parker Valley farmers asked for cotton-pickers, Poston had been in existence for about five months. People had settled with no overt resistance into a very dusty, barren, and extremely hot Army camp in the bottomlands of the Colorado River. Families had taken up residence in the wooden, tar-paper-covered barracks, usually one family to an unpartitioned room 20 by 20 feet. The barracks were arranged in blocks, with populations of some 300 each. Every block contained a common mess-hall at which all families ate their meals, a common laundry room, and common latrines. The pattern of communal life thus established by the War Relocation Authority was not accepted cheerfully by the evacuees. They continually objected to the overcrowding and they denounced the mess-halls as threats to wholesome family life. Resentment against the government for these conditions was strong at the time of the cotton-picking episode.

The Center was organized under regulations set up by the War Department and the War Relocation Authority. There were three geographically separate sections, of which we shall describe Unit I, having a population of about 9,000. The 36 blocks of this unit were patrolled at their border by military police in Army uniforms. In the area a civil service government employee, called project director, was the ultimate local authority, within the framework of the Authority as set up in Washington. He was assisted by a staff of civil service employees, who had charge of the distribution of food to the mess-halls, the organization of agricultural work in the Center, the medical services, and other aspects of Center life. Below the level of the civil service employees, evacuees were hired as assistants at the monthly wage of $12, $14, or $19.

During June and July the War Relocation Authority announced plans for "self-government" within the Center. A community Council consisting of elected individuals was set up as advisory to the project director and his staff. By War Relocation Authority regulation this Council was limited to young men and women, the Nisei, who, through birth in the United States, were citizens. In addition, an Advisory Board composed of Issei (men and women born in Japan

and by United States law ineligible for citizenship) was in operation. Members of the Board, which functioned in an advisory
capacity to the Community Council, were also elected. The basis
of representation was the block, each block thus having both an
Issei and a Nisei representative in the over-all organization.

The political structure that had developed by October also included Councils in each block, in which no distinction was made
between Issei and Nisei. Members of the Block Councils were elected
at large from the block. Weekly meetings were held, at which all
kinds of local and community affairs were discussed. There were
two topics that came up most frequently in the early months of the
Center. One of these was the mess-hall and its management, and the
other was block gardens and block beautification programs.

As the poltical structure had grown, there had at the same time
developed other types of organization. Church groups had formed
immediately on arrival of the evacuees in the Center. The various
Buddhist sects had been assigned barracks in which to hold their
services and meetings, and within each there was at least one recognized minister who had taken charge of affairs. Subgroups within
the Buddhist organization had also taken form, such as women's
groups (*Fujinkai*) and young people's groups (*Seinendan*). Similar
developments had taken place in the four Christian sects represented in the population, and there was a proliferation of small
social and athletic clubs.

Within this setting Community Council, Issei Advisory Board, and
Block Councils had begun to be the scene of discussion, either directly or indirectly, of a number of basic issues. These issues were
formulated in terms of the experience of the Japanese Americans as
a minority group in the United States during the past forty years
and had particular meaning and emotional content growing out of
the evacuation from their homes. One of the subjects that the
Japanese tended to keep more or less hidden from the administrators, lest their positions on it be misunderstood, was their relation
to the United States war effort. The people of Poston were split in a
number of ways on this question. One influential viewpoint main-

tained by many of the older men was that the evacuees must be careful to maintain a neutral position and must not allow themselves to be brought into any activities that directly furthered the United States war effort against Japan. They maintained that their status should be officially that of prisoners of war. In line with this position they opposed the introduction of camouflage net factories into the Center. Many other older men held that the neutrality position was probably the safest for Issei citizens of Japan, but that Nisei as citizens of the United States should have the opportunity to engage in the manufacture of camouflage nets and in other war production. The Nisei position on the issue ranged from a willingness to do anything their fathers said in order to maintain the last social unit left to them—their families—to vigorous denunciation of the neutrality position and aggressive espousal of opportunities for positive demonstration of loyalty to the United States.

Another question, which was for many not wholly separate from the neutrality problems, consisted in the over-all plan for life in the Center. Here again, as would be expected from the heterogeneity of the evacuees, there were many positions and shades of conviction and feeling. The essential issue involved may probably be stated as follows: Shall we as evacuees settle down in the Center to a peaceful, cooperative life for the duration of the war, unified in the aim of creating an ideal community? Such an objective fitted the views of most Issei regardless of their beliefs about relations to Japan and the United States as nations at war. It involved the concept of waiting quietly until the war was over and a basis existed for thinking about the future.

For many Nisei, however, it was not acceptable because it ignored the most important question on their minds: What will our future in the United States be? For them, the Center had to be tied into the life of the United States and there was no waiting for the future; the future was being decided momentarily. Some Nisei, however, accepted their parents' view that "we are all Japanese together" as a result of the evacuation. For them, waiting and meanwhile living peacefully with one's family in the blocks, seemed the only course open.

These issues of neutrality and the cooperative ideal community were the matrix of much discussion in all formal and informal groups in the Center. Such matters as exclusive Nisei representation on the Community Council and the crops to be raised in block gardens were frequently considered within the sentiment systems which grew up around these matters.

The Poston administrators at the time of the request for cotton-pickers were hardly aware of this state of affairs. The complexity of the Issei position in relation to the war was not understood, and aspects of it that came to their attention were usually interpreted in rather black and white terms of loyalty and disloyalty in an ordinary American community. Administrative understanding of the issues concerning the nature of the Center as a framework for life was much better. In fact, differences of opinion on this matter among administrators often paralleled those among the evacuees.

On the matter of cotton-picking the administrators took the position from the start that it would be beneficial to the evacuees in a number of ways: (1) If the evacuees saved the crop of the Parker Valley farmers, good will toward them would be stimulated locally and, consequently, public relations in the Parker area would be improved. (2) Participation in the salvage of a crop of some wartime importance would demonstrate to the people of the United States generally that the Japanese Americans were not all saboteurs. (3) The influx of cash into the Center would supplement the small amounts paid to the evacuees as wages and thereby help to ease some of the tension resulting from the frustration of confinement. It was on this basis that they presented the matter to the evacuee community leaders.

There was, however, one aspect of the problem which the administrators regarded as difficult. The Center had been set up by government regulation on the basis of approximate equality of income for evacuees. The income derivable from cotton-picking would vary greatly among individuals and many families would probably, for diverse reasons, be unable to send any member out to pick. Furthermore, if large numbers rushed out immediately to the work, as the administrators thought was possible, the routine operation of the Center might be seriously disrupted for weeks. With these matters in mind, the administrators conceived the idea of a Community Trust Fund, into which all wages would go for later disbursement as evacuee community leaders might determine.

The administrators, in short, believed that uncontrolled recruiting of cotton-pickers by the Parker Valley farmers would be disruptive and, hence, they decided that the whole matter would have to be presented to the community leaders who could, in turn, present it to the people of the Center. This plan was followed, and a special meeting of the community leaders was called for discussion of the farmers' proposal and the administration's plan for a Community Trust Fund. The importance of the cotton-picking as a community affair affecting evacuee public relations and as an opportunity for bettering the general welfare by increased funds was stressed in the administrators' presentation.

The evacuee leadership reacted in a variety of ways. Some councilmen and some Issei Advisory Board members wanted to have nothing to do with it—probably thinking of that segment of local public opinion which opposed any participation in United States war effort. Some were immediately enthusiastic, among both Issei and Nisei, and accepted the whole view of the administrators. Some professed to be surprised at what they called the administration's "socialistic proposal" for handling the wages as a trust fund. Discussion, however, resulted in a general acceptance of the administration's position by the evacuee leaders. Issei Board members in particular strongly espoused the idea of a Community Trust Fund, holding that all had been leveled in the process of evacuation and that the injection of individual differences in wage receipts would threaten the basis of solidarity in the Center.

Community councilmen and Issei Board members presented the matter to meetings in their respective blocks and it became a widespread subject of discussion for several days. In almost all blocks the community leaders stressed the opportunity for added income and better relations with Parker Valley farmers but did not mention the third reason emphasized by the administration. Demonstration of loyalty to the United States by means of picking cotton while confined in relocation centers was not regarded by those leaders who were closest to their constituents as a point that would have weight; on the contrary, they seemed to feel that mention of it would be likely to rouse opposition.

Community leaders, both Nisei and Issei, turned out to pick cotton on the days set for beginning the work, but a bare handful of other evacuees joined them. The general reaction seemed to be apathetic. The evacuee leaders, as well as the administrative staff, were surprised and dismayed. Among both groups there was a tendency to interpret the failure to respond as a result of anti-government feeling and some began to believe that it was a definite demonstration of disloyal attitude toward the United States. On the other hand, some among both groups were convinced that the basic reason for lack of response was the absence of individual incentive in the form of wages paid directly to the cotton-pickers. Within a few days, however, a change was made in the arrangements and large numbers of evacuees began to go out to pick cotton. What sort of change would bring about such results?

IV. THE OUTCOME

Here and there over the community, as councilmen presented the trust fund idea in block meetings, residents proposed a different approach. A few insisted that only individual wage receipts would result in bringing any number of persons out to pick cotton. In one block it was proposed that the money earned go, not into an over-all community fund, but into a block trust fund which would be used for improvements in the mess-hall, for block parties, and for other purposes of a strictly local character. Similar proposals came up in other blocks.

It was also proposed in block meetings that members of various church groups or social clubs put their wages into trust funds for the use of their organizations.

Gradually these proposals were taken up throughout the Center. Leaders saw many possible uses for block funds and they obtained approval from the administration for the establishment of such funds. They also developed methods for bringing the pressure of block public opinion to bear on individuals. Bulletin boards began to blossom with lists of individuals who would go or had gone out to pick cotton. People in the blocks began to talk about those who went out and those who did not go. Over a period of a few days the numbers picking cotton quadrupled.

It appeared that all who were going out, did so in response to the block, social club, or church fund arrangement. Steadily the belief that most evacuees were opposed to the United States war effort disappeared among the community leaders and the War Relocation Authority staff. A few blocks were turning out a majority of their able-bodied man and woman power. Young people became enthusiastic for cotton-picking as a relief from the dullness of Center routine. Statements praising evacuees as workers and loyal Americans began to be made at farmers' meetings in the Parker Valley. Totals in the various block funds began to be known throughout the Center. Some competitive spirit in working for one's block developed.

The Community Trust Fund idea was discarded by the Board and interest in cotton-picking steadily increased until the War Department prohibited movement of evacuees out of the Center.

V. ANALYSIS

This case illustrates the strength of local group or neighborhood as a social unit focusing the interests and activities of its members. It demonstrates the greater strength of the local group over that collection of local groups which constituted a community. It demonstrates that in a newly forming community of heterogeneous population the neighborhood tends to emerge first as the effective social unit. Its solidarity may appear in so short a time as four or five months. On the other hand, solidarity for the community as a whole (even when stresses are great for promoting the latter and when there is vigorous leadership for overall community interests) may lag very far behind neighborhood, or face-to-face group, solidarity.

The opportunity for cotton-picking was recognized by some staff members and most evacuee leaders as raising delicate issues, given the circumstances of existence in the Center. The staff, nevertheless, believed the matter worth pushing because of the great improvement in public relations for evacuees if the cotton were picked. They stressed, correctly, this aspect of the work along with that of its being an aid to the United States war effort. They did not believe the latter alone sufficient motivation in view of governmental action up to that point against the evacuees. The staff also wisely placed the matter in the hands of evacuee leaders for presentation rather than attempting individual recruiting on their own initiative. In doing so they were acting in accordance with their policy of building the conglomeration of uprooted people into a community and as nearly as possible in accordance with general public opinion existing at that time in the Center.

The presentation by the evacuee community leaders was in line with their own positions and with the policy of promoting community cooperation which they were formulating at the time. In advancing the trust fund proposal they were giving leadership consistent with the defined conditions of Center life. They showed that they recognized fundamental needs which the people felt, namely, the opportunity for variation in Center routine and for some participation in the life outside, as well as the need for supplementation of income. The community leaders also showed some understanding of the developing organization of the Center by carrying their proposal back for presentation in block meetings. Further, they demonstrated, as well as expressed verbally, their point of view by going out themselves to pick cotton. In addition, they showed recognition of the prevailing ambivalent attitudes toward the government and the United States war effort, by stressing Center community welfare in their appeals to the block rather than assistance to the war effort which the administrators tended to emphasize.

All this, good as it was, was not enough. The staff and community leaders obviously overestimated the solidarity at this point of the 9,000 people of Unit I. Thinking in terms of their own organization, the Community Council, they attempted to motivate the people with reference to the whole unit. The result was a general lack of interest. Besides themselves, only a handful of men and women, chiefly a few who were in contact with the administration and who were long since convinced of the importance of "demonstrating loyalty to the U.S.," responded by picking cotton. It is clear in view of what happened later that for the vast majority of persons in the Center, the "community as a whole" had little meaning.

What were the community interests? For what would money in a general trust fund be spent? Who would control its use: the administrators? councilmen from distant blocks whom one did not know? To give one's wages into a Community Trust Fund was like casting them away on a wind at sea.

Fortunately, at this point, the community leaders were no more rigid in their views than the structure of which they were a part. Out of the blocks to which they had taken their idea came proposals that had clear-cut meaning for the people. If the money could be spent for improving the kitchen and dining hall, for making the barren blocks more habitable, for parties to relieve the monotony, for equipment in an athletic club, or for a church, if it would be spent by men with whom one sat down to dinner and whom one saw and could make suggestions to every day, then the trust fund idea had real meaning.

To be sure, there were men and women in the blocks who held that any improvement in the kitchens ought to be paid for by the government which had evacuated them and placed them in these unpleasant circumstances, but even such people could not expect the government to pay for block parties. They realized they would have to do that themselves and here was a means for achieving such pleasures. Thus, despite differences of opinion in the blocks, arising from the complications of the Center situation, there could be some common ground on which people might accept the idea of a block or a church trust fund. The idea of a fund for a small local group grew rapidly as an expression of the kind of social organization which had developed up to that point in the centers. The community began to function in response to the outside stimulus, not as a single unified organization of 9,000 people but as a number of neighborhoods with similar interests and aims. The neighborhood leadership and neighborhood gossip began to push people out to pick cotton in response to the needs that almost everyone felt and saw about them in the drab and dusty blocks of barracks.

Questions for Discussion

1. Do you agree with the above analysis of the problem? What points do you believe to be valid? Are there additional factors to be considered?

2. What principles or lessons does this case reveal for (1) urban area organization, (2) welfare councils, (3) community chests, (4) Public Health programs?

3. If the administration, in the case above, had a new project to introduce, how should they go about gaining support for it in the relocation center?

The Parrmount Area

THE PARRMOUNT Civic Improvement Association was organized in 1945 by Miss Sybil Johnson, the headworker in the Murdock Neighborhood House. Miss Johnson felt that the work of her agency had a limited focus and that improvement in her constituency was dependent in part, at least, on improvement in the neighborhood as a whole. In addition, many of the problems which concerned her were of concern to other professional workers in the neighborhood—high delinquency rate, vandalism, dirty streets, poor health habits of residents, etc., were well known by all who worked in Parrmount as well as to most residents of Hampton, of which Parrmount was a notorious area.

Miss Johnson called an exploratory meeting in September. Attending this meeting were two Protestant clergymen, a Russian Orthodox priest, a Y.M.C.A. secretary who worked part time in the area, three case workers from family service agencies, a group worker from the Settlement House and Miss Johnson. In the discussion, it was clear that Miss Johnson's hunch was valid. There was a deeply shared conviction that some "coördinated and organized attack" must be made on the problems of the neighborhood. It was decided to organize. But on Miss Johnson's suggestion, it was agreed to include a wider group in the organization—some of the people who worked or lived in Parrmount: Dr. Somonski, a dentist; Mr. Potsom, the owner of a furniture store; Mrs. Bernstein, a member of Miss Johnson's Board; Mrs. Sokolsky, the manager of a large chain store; Miss Jaboski, a high school teacher, etc. In all, 20 names were listed which included several other priests, ministers, and social workers.

Within two weeks this group was called together and the Parrmount Civic Improvement Association was organized with Miss Johnson as president.

The purpose of the association was stated to be "to coördinate efforts to improve and develop the human and social resources of Parrmount." While members of the association did not formally represent agencies, organizations, or churches, it could be said that members came from 11 different churches, three schools, and six social agencies. In the beginning there was an obvious difference of opinion as to how the purpose could best be carried out. This was primarily a difference between "professionals" (social workers and clergy) and "laymen" (businessmen, doctors, housewives, etc.). The former were mainly concerned with coördinating and enlarging social services, the laymen with civic improvements such as street-widening, traffic lights, or a new bridge on one of the main thoroughfares. Gradually this difference was worked out and the association, in its first year, developed a list of "targets" which included (1) a permanent playground, (2) a wading pool, (3) a shelter house, (4) a public swimming pool, (5) closing the concession booth at the recreation center, (6) more drinking fountains, (7) more band concerts, (8) keeping playgrounds open longer, (9) better playground supervision.

Over the next three years the association struggled along with modest success in achieving these objectives. While there were 35 members of the association board, attendance at meetings seldom exceeded 15, and of these almost all were professionals. The interest of laymen seemed to lag, and while most of them attended at least one meeting a year, very few attended more frequently. Conditions in the neighborhood did not improve. To the contrary some of the things which first concerned Miss Johnson seemed now more acute than ever. Vandalism was particularly obvious. The new playground obtained through the efforts of the association was equipped with much fine play material including swings, backstops, sand boxes, and the like. Within two weeks all this equipment was damaged to the extent that it could not be used safely.

In the spring of 1948, Miss Johnson accepted an offer to work in another city, and at the final meeting of the association which she attended, she recommended that the association request the Welfare Council of the metropolitan area to make a study of the Parrmount area and recommend a course of action for the Civic Improvement Association. There was considerable discussion of this recommendation but it was finally agreed upon, and representations were made to the Hampton Welfare Council. These representations were well received, for widespread publicity was being given to teen-age gang wars in the Parrmount area. After several months of discussion and study, the Welfare Council recommended that a special Chest grant of $10,000 be made to do a thorough study of the "social and welfare needs of the Parrmount area and to recommend a program of reconstruction of this area." Two experienced research workers were employed, and in the fall of 1949 the study was launched.

The researchers spent six months in the area gathering data. Their method was unique in the sense that in addition to collecting the usual statistical material from the census and local welfare agencies, they devoted a good deal of time to extensive interviews with a carefully developed sample of both adults and young people in the Parrmount area. In addition, they developed little groups of local leaders for consultation, and by the end of the study period these leaders were familiar with the study, its methods, and its findings.

Briefly, the study identified ten problems in the area:

1. *Poverty.* The average weekly income and the average monthly rental were lower by a substantial margin than for any comparable area in the city of Hampton or the county in which Hampton was located. The researchers were impressed with the dire poverty in

many situations and the fact that relief was inadequately administered by the Hampton Department of Public Welfare.

2. *Housing and congestion.* Population density was almost twice that of Hampton as a whole. Later study proved it to be one of the most densely populated areas in the United States. Large families were crowded into a few rooms with the consequences which usually attend such congestion.

3. *Parental-child conflicts.* Almost two-thirds of the adult population were foreign-born, largely of eastern European origin, and the usual conflicts of parent and child were accentuated by the mores and customs of "the old country," to which parents subscribed, and those of the United States, to which the children were exposed in school and play. This difference turned up in almost every interview and was documented in the study report in most dramatic fashion.

4. *Nationality conflicts.* Thirty different nationality groups were identified as living in the area. Polish, Ukrainian, Slovak and Russian predominated. This was a typical mosaic society with the 30 groups separated by custom or religion from each other and jealous of one another's progress. Many of these groups were organized into churches, and the area was dotted with a multitude of small churches. In Parrmount there were five churches for every 1,000 families compared with an average of two churches for every 1,000 families in Hampton as a whole. Far from coöperation between these churches, there was competition and even antagonism.

5. *Health.* The researchers encouraged a health study of school children which indicated that 12 percent were pretubercular, that only one child in 93 was considered in perfect health, but that most defects were classed as remediable. A far higher proportion of hospital admissions in Hampton was from the Parrmount area compared with other areas in the city.

6. *Inadequate and uncoördinated welfare services.* In spite of Miss Johnson's efforts, the research team found the welfare services in Parrmount inadequate. Some families were served by several agencies; others in need received no help. Relief and health services were unevenly administered. No agency was concerned exclusively

with delinquency, gangs, or the preneurotic tendencies of many youth. Agency workers were largely unacquainted with the work of other agencies.

7. *Inadequate school curriculum.* The school curriculum was entirely focused on academic work as preparation for a university education, yet few children in this area would go to college. There were no vocational or domestic arts, nor any manual training classes. Children dropped out of school as soon as possible.

8. *Inadequate police protection and prestige.* The area was not patrolled regularly by the police, and when needed, such protection never seemed to be available. When officers of the law appeared in the area, they were objects of scorn and abuse. A constant battle to outwit the police was carried on by the 65 gangs of boys identified in the study.

9. *Inadequate recreational facilities.* The area was found to have fewer playgrounds, gymnasiums, swimming facilities, etc., than any other area in Hampton. Further, there was less play equipment and leadership than in other areas. In addition, there were few music, art, education and library facilities.

10. *Lack of citizenship programs.* In this area populated with such a large proportion of ethnic groups, no effort was made to provide English-speaking classes, citizenship classes, or other adult educational activities.

These briefly were the critical points emphasized by the research team. It was a picture of a highly disorganized area, poverty-stricken, congested, with the highest crime and delinquency rate in the city, "a center for the production of disease—physical, psychological, social." There followed in the report of the research team not a long series of recommendations but a discussion of philosophy for dealing with such an area: e.g., "Social work previously has always 'given to' individuals and communities, and tended to lift responsibility away from the local community. In this project we should shift back to the area some of the responsibilities for control of its own problems and for doing more toward solving them. If this attempted shift takes place, we will have made a real stride in community reorganization." It was conceded, however, that outside resources were required, and the Welfare Council of Hampton was urged to take the lead in channeling such resources into Parrmount.

The report was received with deep interest by the Welfare Council board and discussed at length. A committee was appointed to study and report on its implications for the Council. This committee recommended that (1) the Council establish a committee of 100 outstanding citizens to study the report and to take action to improve the services available to Parrmount, and (2) the Council provide an area worker to encourage the people of Parrmount to organize and deal with some of their own problems. This report was approved and action on it was taken immediately.

The committee of 100 Hampton citizens was organized and met early in June, 1950, under the chairmanship of Gerald W. Rope, a leading businessman in Hampton, widely respected, and well known for his whole-hearted support of various educational and welfare enterprises. The committee was made up of "a cross section of the community" and included, in addition to various well-known business and professional men, representatives from the divisions of the Welfare Council, the police chief, the fire chief, the director of public welfare, the school superintendent, the director of public health, the director of public recreation, the Y.M.C.A. secretary for the city, the head Y.W.C.A. worker, the commissioners of Boy Scouts and of Girl Guides, representatives from the Junior League, from the Public Library board, from the various service clubs, workers from the agencies in the Parrmount area, and 20 residents in Parrmount, all business or professional men.

The committee began its work by reviewing the whole report and then going carefully over each of the problems identified by the research team. Each of these problems was discussed and suggestions were made for action. When action was agreed upon, some one person or a small group was assigned to initiate the action. The committee worked throughout the summer and most of the next year. By that time, action had been secured on most items and a small executive committee was left with the task of following through on several projects, the most important of which was keeping pressure on the Housing Authority to implement a housing plan jointly agreed upon by the authority and the committee.

The variations of action taken were many. They can be summarized, in part, in the following manner:

1. The causes of poverty were attributed to a lack of a knowledge of English on the part of many breadwinners, lack of technical skills, and lack of knowledge of job opportunities. To meet these deficiencies the superintendent of schools agreed to open evening classes to teach English and several trades. The employment commission agreed to open an office in the Parrmount area, and several businessmen on the committee offered to employ people from the Parrmount area if they had been screened by the employment office. In addition, the director of public welfare undertook to make a complete survey of the area and to provide relief and supplementary assistance where necessary.

2. It was agreed that a public housing unit was required in Parrmount and negotiations with the Housing Authority were opened immediately. It required some four years to secure two large apartment buildings and these, even when opened, proved inadequate. However, congestion was eased somewhat by these housing units.

3. The conflicts between parents and children, and between various nationality groups proved to be elusive and difficult to attack directly. Interpretation, and effort to ease tension at these points, were promised by every agency worker. All agencies agreed to hold "parents' nights," to encourage children from various nationality groups to participate together, and to support community projects. The school superintendent agreed to help organize Parent-Teachers Associations. It was recognized that the area worker might have more success here than the committee.

4. In terms of health, substantial achievement was made. Two well-baby clinics were opened, a public health nurse was assigned to the schools, and two public health nurses were assigned to visit homes. These latter were resented by some parents but they were

able to secure the coöperation and good will of many others. Regular dental and medical examinations in the schools were also initiated. The Rotary Club established a free dental clinic two days a week in the Parrmount area.

5. The lack of coördination of welfare agencies was another difficult problem. The Community Chest, on recommendation of the "Committee of One Hundred," purchased a large building where all agencies had their headquarters. Thus brought close together, the workers began to meet one another and to share information and knowledge about their work and the community. But whether this compulsory joint housing in itself did much to improve coördination is an open question.

6. The superintendent of schools readily agreed with the criticism of the school curriculum and took immediate steps to introduce some vocational training classes in the high schools. But the need for a technical high school, obvious as it was, was not dealt with and remains a problem in the area.

7. The police chief was perhaps the one member of the committee most stimulated by the research report. During the discussion of delinquency rates and later of the attitude of Parrmount residents to the police, he had said over and over again, "Just leave this to me." Various suggestions were made by members of the committee but the police chief murmured, "I'll handle this." And who is to say he didn't?

After the meeting, the chief secured from one of the research team, the names and addresses of the leaders of the 65 gangs in Parrmount. Immediately, he went to headquarters and sent out five squad cars to round up and bring in all 65 leaders. It was then close to midnight and many of the gang leaders were routed out of bed and taken to the station. There is no record of the chief's conversation with these gang leaders but it is understood that there were some choice phrases used. In any case, and unbelievable as it sounds, the gang leaders left the chief, agreed that there would be no crime in Parrmount for a month and that they would work together to "get the community in shape." In fact, there was not a single crime reported in Parrmount during the next month. This was the point at which crime and delinquency rates reversed their upward trend in Parrmount, and since that time they have never approached the rates given in the research report.

The second part of the police chief's plan was to put five of his good young athletic officers in Parrmount with instruction to "make friends, start clubs, encourage athletics." Helped by the gang leaders, the young officers were most successful in getting several PAL clubs and Scout troops going. Again, seven of the gang leaders took special courses and became Scout leaders. So whatever the psychology employed, the tactics of the police chief had a sudden, profound, and lasting effect on Parrmount.

8. The lack of citizenship and recreation facilities and services was quickly dealt with. English conversation classes were started in the school, new funds were channeled into the Parrmount branch library to provide for a "beginners' adult" section and for a children's library. The librarian began a club for adults whose English was limited, and 42 members came regularly to read books together. Two new playgrounds were opened, one new recreational leader was assigned to Parrmount, and the new attitude of the police together with other factors, seemed to combine to prevent the destruction of new playground equipment.

This indicates in summary fashion the essence of the contribution of the "Committee of One Hundred." They acted vigorously and in some cases dramatically. The result was a coöperative effort of the major agencies and services to provide resources to meet the needs of people in the Parrmount area, as revealed by the study. The consistent support of the Welfare Council staff and the status of Mr. Gerald W. Rope were undoubtedly important factors in the effectiveness of the committee, yet many felt there was something about the idea of the committee, the kind of people who were on the committee, and the obvious needs of the area which combined to make the tasks undertaken challenging yet feasible.

The other major project of the Welfare Council was to encourage the people of Parrmount to organize in order to deal with their own problems. An area worker, Tom Banting, was appointed and paid by the Welfare Council with terms of reference which required him to live in the area and help the people develop their own leadership in combatting local problems.

The research report gave Banting a good start. He had a list of every church in the area and the minister or priest of the church; he had the list of all the gangs and their leaders; he could refer to the study's list of clubs—some 70 in number from the Polish National Singers Club to the Ukrainian Dancing Club; and, perhaps most important, he had the researchers' private appraisal of key persons in the area—persons respected and regarded as leaders by the people in the area.

For several weeks, Banting strolled through Parrmount and visited residents. He called upon every one of the 230 people on his list. The discussion always turned eventually to the study—what they thought about it, what they felt might be done. Banting had in mind an area council and usually put forward this idea. While there was no enthusiasm about the council, there was deep interest in the study, and, on the part of most, a shy and hesitant desire to "try something."

On the basis of these interviews, Banting called a meeting of the 230 persons. The "drawing card" was one of the researchers who was to be at the meeting to review the findings of the study. One hundred and ninety-one turned up for the meeting. The researcher carefully went over the study, emphasizing that in his view only the people in the area could make it a decent community by reducing tension in the home, and between groups and gangs; by creating an atmosphere where crime and delinquency are considered "wrong"; by building a place where children could grow up decently; and by making a real American community and not a European suburb. At points, he spoke forcibly and with ideas that were "fighting talk." But it went well and discussion was animated and vigorous. Banting suggested that a committee of 25 be appointed to explore what could be done and to report back to the group in two weeks. This was agreed and the 25 were appointed. This committee quickly decided there should be a Parrmount Community Council made up of two representatives of every club, church, agency or organization in the area; there should be an executive board of 20; the Council should help each member organization to do effective work and it should itself concentrate on carrying out community-wide activities in which every group would join and in which all would work together. Four projects were recommended immediately: (1) an Honor Roll in memory of those from Parrmount who died in the Second World War; (2) a Health Fair similar to that observed by one of the members in another community, which exhibited and demonstrated various health practices; (3) a Folk Festival where different national groups could perform native dances; and (4) a giant Halloween parade and party for the children.

These recommendations were adopted by the community meeting when it met, and an executive and four other committeemen were elected to carry out the projects. Banting had some reservations about them. He had not opposed any of them but privately the Halloween party was the only one he supported, for it seemed to be directed at delinquency, a problem about which he was greatly concerned. As he worked with committees on these four projects, however, he was forced to change his mind. The Honor Roll, for example, he felt a very poor project inconsistent with anything recommended in the research report. Yet the Honor Roll proved to be a project which everyone in the area approved: the names of young men from every national group in the area appeared side by side, and at the dedication service parents of all these boys stood together in a deep emotional experience. Banting had later to confess that the Honor Roll did more than anything else to bring the Parrmount area together. It broke down barriers, and besides being a significant project in itself, it made work on other community projects possible.

The Halloween party was a great success. Over 1200 children in costume were in the parade, and later movies and treats made a satisfying evening during which not one act of vandalism was reported. The Health Fair was not as successful as anticipated, the committee responsible having had difficulty in overcoming some of their differences. Nevertheless, it was held with the coöperation of school and health department authorities, and over 500 persons were tested for tuberculosis during the three days of the Fair. The Folk Festival was the *pièce de résistance*. It took over a year to organize, but when it took place it involved representatives of every national group in native costume. It was held in the largest playground, and over 4000 attended. There was hearty applause for every "act" or demonstration; mutual appreciation and respect appeared to be the mood of the day.

In all of these projects, Banfield had been surprised and pleased with the competence of the people in organizing their work. He came to trust their judgment about what should be done, who should do it, when it was appropriate to ask for something, and how one should ask. He had not thought of Parrmount as a community with a culture of its own, but as 10 or 20 small communities each with its own culture. Parrmount, however, had a culture and it "took some knowing." The committees knew the "ways of Parrmount" and steered their projects through difficult waters, the exact tide or movement of which Banting never quite understood. He often felt he was of most help simply by being pleasant, encouraging, and willing to chip in and work when the burden of detail became heavy on various committee members. He was a kind of focus which helped keep the group together. At the end of the first year, Banting encouraged the executive committee to take stock and develop new projects for the year ahead. All but the Folk Festival were now completed, and the committee was happy with its progress. As one of the members said, "We're a community for the first time." Banting pressed them, however, to consider the "things which bothered people most," "real problems," "things that Parrmount should or shouldn't have." With this encouragement, the group began to list problems like "the lack of traffic lights at Main and 7th," "poor housing," "rats," etc. Some 24 problems were listed. It was decided that at the next meeting of the Council, everyone should be asked to check the five most important problems to be acted upon by the

Council. This was done, and the new executive was asked to work on (1) housing, (2) rat control, (3) community parties, (4) folk festival, and (5) control of taverns, especially in the sale of liquor to minors. This provided terms of reference and objectives for the Council in the year ahead. And this became the pattern for operation of the Council: each year the selection of certain important problems for concentrated work in the year ahead. At the date of this writing, it has had four years of operation; each year new projects were taken on, and all of them, with the exception of housing, were completed to the satisfaction of the Council.

The total project involved research, the use of external resources provided by the "Committee of One Hundred," and the development of internal resources through the medium of the Parrmount Community Council. Those close to the project who have watched it over a four-year period feel it has been a very considerable success. On almost every point identified by the research team, progress has been made. Delinquency and crime rates are now below the average of the city as a whole, tuberculosis rates have been reduced, health practices have been improved, housing is somewhat better, the standard of living is higher, there seems to be less tension and conflict in the area, and, on the whole, reconstruction has begun, though substantial movement is not obvious. Some critics feel less optimistic. They feel no progress has been made on the basic problems of poverty and congestion, that Parrmount is being held together by "do-gooders" who are giving a service to this area that they cannot afford to continue, that the people are being "spoon-fed," and when these services are withdrawn the people of Parrmount will be less able than before to cope with the problems of slum life in an American city.

In the Welfare Council itself there is considerable satisfaction with the Parrmount project. Statistics alone provide proof of the success of the operation. And the movement that is evidenced in the work of the Parrmount Community Council suggests that this area may soon be able to handle its own affairs. But there are now two other areas in Hampton almost as bad as Parrmount was. The problem that holds the attention of the Welfare Council officers is the probability of repeating the Parrmount project. Can they afford the money for research? Can they afford the staff time required to launch the project when there are so many other pressing demands? Can the Committee of One Hundred be organized again? If so, will people be as enthusiastic? Will, for example, the police chief rise to the occasion again, and if so, what will happen to his PAL program in Parrmount? Can all agencies give extra service as in Parrmount? Who will pay for area workers in the new problem areas? In other words, the Council officers are considering whether Parrmount is a kind of "one shot" project and whether a different plan must be developed for other problem areas. If so, what kind of plan is feasible?

Questions for Discussion

1. Evaluate Miss Johnson's Civic Improvement Association. Is it a useful model for disorganized areas? Why?

2. Evaluate the work of the Committee of One Hundred. Do you think it was successful? Why or why not? Does it provide a model for reconstructing depressed areas in urban centers?

3. Evaluate the work of the Parrmount Community Council. Did it deal with the major problems of the area? Was its work successful? In what ways? What were its major achievements?

4. What were the strengths and weaknesses of this whole project? If you were a staff member of a welfare council and asked to recommend a course of action in a highly disorganized slum area, what would you suggest?

Henshaw

HENSHAW IS one of those pleasant progressive cities in which some of us more fortunate social workers are privileged to work. It is a city with a population of about 32,000, situated in a prosperous farm belt within a 100 miles of a metropolitan city, yet sufficiently isolated to feel a sense of independence and autonomy. The last census figures indicate that 74 percent of the people are associated with various Protestant denominations, 22 percent are Roman Catholics, and 3 percent are of the Jewish faith. Several large industries, including a paint factory, a farm machinery plant, and an automobile parts plant, provide the bulk of employment opportunities. The stores on the main street, which serve not only Henshaw residents but farmers in the surrounding area, have more than the usual number of managers and clerks. The city itself is well laid out with fine parks and play areas. There are the usual residential areas—both good and bad—but it cannot be said that Henshaw has a slum area; actually the poorest homes are well kept, almost all having a little lawn or garden.

Henshaw is a progressive city. I say this because I have not known any problem, which, once brought to the attention of the people here, has not been dealt with promptly and vigorously. There is an excellent school system in which the teachers are paid salaries comparable to, and in some cases a good deal higher than, those in the metropolitan city. In the last five years, two beautiful new high schools have been erected, each with a gymnasium and a swimming pool. There is a fine public recreation program with a well-trained staff. The library is one of the best for cities of comparable size in the country, and one librarian has a reputation throughout the nation for her pioneering work, especially with children. Similarly, the two hospitals are well regarded, and the Department of Public Health has a long record of outstanding work.

The social agencies are few in number: the Family Service Agency, the Children's Aid Society, the Crippled Children's Association, the Institute for the Blind, the Red Cross, the Y.M.C.A., the Y.W.C.A., the Salvation Army, and, of course, the Henshaw Department of Public Welfare. I have not known any of these agencies to have serious financial difficulty, and while I could wish that some of them would improve the quality of their work, they do provide useful service and work well together in the Welfare Council. Henshaw is a labor city and the workers in all the major industries are well organized. There was, of course, trouble when the unions first began to organize but that has long since passed. The unions are now accepted and carry a responsible role in community affairs.

I have worked in Henshaw for three years as Secretary of the Welfare Council and love it. Prior to this, I served as a division secretary in the nearby metropolitan Welfare Council. Here in Henshaw, matters are not only less complicated but the spirit of the people, if I may use such a phrase, is entirely different. There is a degree of mutual trust and acceptance that is new to me. Shortly after I came to Henshaw, for example, I mentioned to the president of the Council that Jewish people did not seem to have any place in Council committees, or for that matter in the community. "I hadn't noticed that," he replied in obvious surprise. Within the next 18 months several Jews were made members of Council committees, one came on our Council board, one was invited to become a member of Rotary, one was elected to the school board, and several became members of the golf club. I am sure there was no serious prejudice; it was simply that Henshaw folks had not noticed that they had excluded the Jews or that the Jews had excluded themselves. A few words and this situation was changed. If this seems naïve, let me say that while there is undoubtedly prejudice in Henshaw, I believe that, on the whole, Jewish people have acceptance as first-class citizens in Henshaw.

All this, I know, sounds a bit idealistic. But I merely report these facts both to suggest that Henshaw is unique in my experience and to warn you of my bias in this respect. There is more "sense of community" here than in any other city in which I have worked. This is reflected in the operation of the Welfare Council. It is made up of two representatives from each of the agencies together with six members from the Community Chest and six from the community at large. The Council meets four times a year, and an executive committee of eight meets monthly. There are four divisions: Children, Family, Recreation, and Special Projects. I am the only full-time worker, although we occasionally have additional help for special projects.

At a meeting of the Council in February, 1953, Mrs. Redford, a member-at-large, who had the previous month attended a province-wide conference of women, raised the question of elderly persons in Henshaw. Referring to her conference experience, Mrs. Redford said, "There seems to be an increasing number of elderly people in our society and no comparable increase in services for them. I wonder if this generalization applies to our community?" The chairman, Mr. Sidney Harrold, vice-president of the automobile parts plant, expressed the reaction of many when he replied, "I have no doubt that the number of older people is increasing, but there is no indication that this creates a problem in Henshaw. I assume that most older people here live at home and are well cared for there." However, Mrs. Redford persisted, and in the discussion that followed it was pointed out that quite a few older people were to be seen "hanging out" around the parks in spring and summer, and the representatives from the Family Service agency reported that from their experience it was clear that quite a few older people did not live with their families and were becoming a problem of increasing importance. I was, of course, asked what I felt about the matter and I indicated that many other cities were working on this problem but that in Henshaw we really didn't have the facts to tell us whether this was a serious problem or not. Finally the matter was referred to the executive committee, who at their March meeting asked Mrs. Redford and me to act as a committee of two to investigate the matter.

Mrs. Redford and I decided that we would report back to the executive committee in April, which meant that we could not really do a very throrough investigation in that short time. However, I was to get the statistical material and consult with case workers regarding their experience in homes and Mrs. Redford was to work through the churches. This took longer than we had expected, and we had to assemble our material hastily the day before the April executive meeting. At this meeting, Mrs. Redford reported that there were 1,967 people over 65 now living in Henshaw. This fact in itself stirred up controversy, but we were able to document it to the satisfaction of all. Still, as Mr. Harrold said, "who would have believed it?" Mrs. Redford went on to tell of some of the experiences of case and church workers. Apparently, many of these older folks lived alone in rented rooms, some were unable to get out at all, many had financial problems, and Mrs. Redford concluded, "While our data are quite sketchy, none the less the picture we have is of a number of older people living in Henshaw, many of them lonely and neglected."

The discussion again showed the surprise of many present that this situation could develop in Henshaw without the Council's knowing about it, and I felt that there may have been some feeling that I should have brought the matter to the attention of the executive committee long before this. It was not that I was unmindful of the situation but I felt there had been more important things for the Council to be concerned about last year. In any case, it was strongly urged that the Council appoint a committee not only to investigate further but to bring in recommendations for action. Mrs. Redford and I had anticipated this and we had a list of 14 names of possible members of the committee. Included in this list were two persons over 65, one a retired banker and one a retired public school teacher, both alert and active in the community. Also included were the personnel manager from the farm implements factory, a young Roman Catholic priest, a case worker in the Family Service Agency, the assistant public recreation director, a semiretired physician, an alderman, the administrator of the Old People's Home, the owner of a small nursing home for the aged, a Baptist minister, a lawyer from the Kiwanis Club, and the secretary-treasurer of the local trade union. This list was discussed at some length and to it were added Mrs. Redford as chairman, myself as secretary, and an official of the public welfare department. There were 16 in all—a heterogeneous lot, but one which represented fairly well the community's interest in this particular problem.

It was agreed that Mr. Harrold would write to these people on behalf of the Welfare Council, inviting them to accept responsibility on this committee. All but one accepted the appointment but we were able to get another lawyer from the Kiwanis Club in place of the one who was unable to serve.

The first meeting of this committee was held on Thursday, April 30th, 1953. All things considered, it was reasonable progress. Mrs. Redford had introduced the possibility of work on the problem of the aged in February and within two months we were underway. For this first meeting Mrs. Redford and I had set up as our objectives: (1) creating awareness of the problem and the desire to do something about it, (2) initiating a process of fact-finding and planning, and (3) encouraging good working relations in the group. In preparation, we had gathered some additional facts on the number of persons over 65 living in the Old People's Home, the number in hospitals, the number who were widows or widowers, etc.

Mrs. Redford, whose capacity I was to come to appreciate increasingly as this project developed, handled the meeting skillfully. She began by describing briefly her concern, the facts uncovered so far, the decision of the Welfare Council, which was not to supplement any of the existing services but to help them where possible to meet needs not now being met. She then introduced each member of the committee, saying a personal word about why the Council was so pleased that each had agreed to help. She suggested then that we talk informally for a bit about the problem: Were the data we had accurate? Could others add to them? Did anyone have any personal experience? Did anyone know any old people and how they were getting along?

On this personal basis the meeting moved in animated fashion. Almost all could recount a story or two, some of them most touching, and in about 40 minutes we were all convinced that here was a problem of the greatest importance. Mrs. Redford then moved us into a consideration of whether we were ready to act or whether we should investigate the matter further. Very quickly it was decided that we should have more facts and that we should try to discover something about the problems of old people in respect to (1) living arrangements, (2) medical and health services, (3) financial income, (4) recreation, and (5) employment. It was agreed that each member of the committee would try to explore these matters with at least one elderly person but that Mrs. Redford, the case worker from the Family Service agency, and I should try to do a more systematic study on the same questions with the help of the Social Workers Association of Henshaw. It was recognized that this would not be a "scientific survey," but it was felt that it would give the committee a somewhat more reliable guide. Further, it was decided to attempt to list all the organizations that were or might be interested in the problem, and to identify work now being done for the elderly.

The social workers group who had been looking for a project took on the interviewing task with enthusiasm. A rough one-in-40 sample was worked out and 50 interviews were scheduled. Of these, 41 were completed within a month and four more in the ten days that followed. When the committee met on May 30, a fairly interesting report was avaliable.

The May 30 meeting was a clear indication of the value of our strategy. Almost all members of the committee had done their "homework" and it was obvious that there was great interest in the project.

Mrs. Stevenson of the Family Service Agency reported for the social workers, and as she reported on their findings, she was frequently interrupted with exclamations of "That's exactly what I found," "That's precisely what old Mrs. MacCormick said," and so on.

Mrs. Stevenon's report, briefly summarized, indicated that about half of her interviewees lived alone, either boarding or renting a room and getting their own meals; only two were working, although many more would like to work part time; at least two-thirds had been ill for more than a week during the past year, and 15 percent complained of "never feeling well"; the only recreation for most was visiting or going to church, and most were lonely and felt unwanted; about half lived entirely on old age pensions, and Mrs. Stevenson guessed that many of these did not have proper meals.

The Social Workers Association was sent a hearty vote of thanks for its prompt and effective help, and I was forced to say that in a nearby city, the social workers group had fallen down very badly on a similar job and that we were especially fortunate in having a group like ours in Henshaw. With this all agreed.

The list of interested organizations was surprising, even to me. It was prepared by four of our committee people and included not just regular agencies and service clubs, but church clubs, women's associations, and lodges. More was being done with the elderly than we had thought, but a full report of all the activities could not be secured. This led to an important suggestion by Alderman Richards: "If this is a problem in Henshaw, why not put it before the people? In other words, why not call a meeting to which we would invite representatives from all these groups to hear our report and discuss with them what might be done?" This suggestion was discussed at some length and agreed upon. We were going, as my textbook said, "to spread the area of shared concern." The date for this meeting was sheduled for June 17, and Mrs. Redford was to send invitations on Council stationery to the organizations on the list presented to the meeting. Meanwhile, the committee would meet on June 7 to reconsider its findings and to plan the agenda for the larger meeting.

In preparation for our next committee meeting, Mrs. Redford and

I spent a good part of an afternoon working on various ways of summarizing our progress to date. Finally we decided on a face sheet summarizing Mrs. Stevenson's report,[3] followed by a listing in each of the areas of concern with "what we have," "what we need" and "outside sources of help" columns. Roughly the report appeared as follows:

Number of People in Henshaw over 65 Years of Age—1,967

Where do they live?
  50% live alone in a boarding or rooming house
How healthy are they?
  15% may be chronically ill, at least half have frequent illnesses
How do they manage financially?
  etc.

Our report then went on:

INCOME

We Have	We Need	Outside Resources
Old Age Security (federal), $40 per month to everyone over 70 years of age.	Supplementary assistance based on individual need administered by staff skilled in helping older people.	Statutes already cited.
Old Age Assistance (provincial), $40 per month on a means-test basis to people 65 to 69 years of age.		
Old Age Emergency Rent Assistance (sharable by municipality and province), up to $10 per month.		

[3] At the meeting, Mrs. Redford felt a little guilty about the blandness of some of our figures and told the group about the sample which made the report consist more of "reliable guesses" than "absolutely accurate figures."

We did this for each item—Employment, Living Arrangements, Recreation, Medical and Health Services. The whole showed in a fairly comprehensive way the situation at that time, what we needed in Henshaw, and what outside assistance was available, if any. (In this latter respect we found quite substantial grants available from the provincial government for hospitals and homes for the aged.)

While satisfied with our work, Mrs. Redford and I were hesitant about presenting this report to the committee. It seemed as if we were doing their work, putting the final report before them. We eventually decided that this was, perhaps, merely a minor extension of their thinking at the previous meeting, and that since it could be altered, it was proper to present it.

Actually, our report seemed appropriate. My impression was that the committee which met on June 7, felt this was merely a summary of what they had said, and although there was considerable discussion and some amendments, the report was agreed upon as a program for action.

When it came to planning for the community meeting, however, there was serious disagreement. Some wished to present what was now the committee's report, while others felt that to do this would be to provide the answers before the group was really aware of the question. Finally, it was agreed that Mrs. Stevenson should give her report on the survey as she had to our committee; there should then be discussion of the report; after which Mrs. Redford should ask each group to report what it was doing for the elderly or if it would be interested in helping. The report of the committee should be modified in light of this discussion and presented to the community group at a later meeting. I had myself some reservation about this procedure and raised the question of whether this was quite honest, and whether it wouldn't be better to show our report, but the meeting decided otherwise.

The community meeting was well attended—23 groups were represented by 41 persons, and, with our own committee some 54 persons were present in all. Our committee was in for a surprise, for we were not prepared for the interest and activity of the groups represented. Mrs. Stevenson's report was received with interest but without astonishment. When it came to reports from the groups, however, almost everyone was doing something, however small, for elderly persons. One church group arranged for cars every Sunday so that 11 elderly persons could get to church; one women's club visited a number of older people regularly, providing them with food and comforts; one church opened its basement for older people every afternoon and the minister provided checkers and other games for them; another church group took food baskets and reading material regularly to the elderly persons in need in their congregation; one man reported that he went next door three nights a week to read to an older man whose eyesight was failing. Perhaps the most dramatic moment came when a woman who visited several elderly persons told of one of her experiences. She had been visiting an old lady of 84 for several months, and on a recent visit they had a long conversation, after which she tidied the old lady's room, made her some tea, and fixed her pillows. As she was preparing to leave, she said to the old lady: "Now, is there anything else I can do for you?" The old lady hesitated a long time and then said, "Would you kiss me?"

"I just went over and put my arms around her and gave her a big hug and kiss," the visitor reported to the meeting. "But then I almost wept when the old lady said, 'That's the first time in 11 years that anyone kissed me!'"

By this time the meeting had been in session for more than two hours, and Mrs. Redford very skillfully brought it to a close. "What impressed me," she said to the group, "is how good the people in this city are. The milk of human kindness runs fully here. And thank goodness for that. But one of the things I think everyone here this evening recognizes is that none of us has any assurance that all of the elderly people are recipients of this kindness. There are 1,967 old people in Henshaw. The reports tonight would not cover services to more than 400 at the most. What about the other 1,500? Where are they? What is happening to them? Even the 400 contacted by us have problems that visits and food hampers will not meet adequately. How are those problems to be cared for? Now, the Welfare Council has a committee trying to develop a plan for meeting the needs of all elderly persons. After tonight's meeting, from which we learned so much, I think, we can work out a tentative draft which we'd like to present to this group. Would you be willing to meet a week from tonight to go over this plan?"

All agreed. On the basis of a little note from Mrs. Redford, I rounded up our committee for a 20-minute "post-meeting" meeting. All the members of our committee were impressed with the community meeting and all agreed that the weakness in our report was that it did not provide for the "human touch," the need of the elderly not simply for housing and financial assistance but for love and kindness and affection. Mrs. Redford and I were asked to re-work the plan and present it to the community group the next week, June 24.

This we did by indicating at appropriate points the need for visits, for friendship groups, for elderly people to have close human contacts with other elderly persons, with middle-aged adults and with youth and children.

The June 24 meeting was well attended with lively discussion and enthusiastic endorsement of the report. The only point of controversy centered on implementation. Mrs. Redford indicated that the report should now go to the Welfare Council for approval, and then to the Chest for funds for some of the recommendations made. There was some grumbling about the slowness of both Chest and Council, but Mrs. Redford was able to carry the day by illustrating some of the difficulties of moving without proper clearances. And so it was agreed to present the report to the Welfare Council.

Mrs. Redford had reported regularly to the executive of the Council, and the latter had planned that the June meeting would give primary attention to the report of the Committee on Elderly Persons. In fact the meeting of the Council had been set for June 29 so that the committee would have adequate time for preparation.

Our committee's report had three major recommendations, each with several parts. Briefly the plan approved by both our committee and the community group called for:

1. The establishment of a social and recreation center for elderly persons. While a professional worker would be necessary, great stress was laid on the need to use volunteers in operating the club. The renting of an old home, and an annual budget of $13,500 were recommended.

2. The establishment of a home for chronically ill persons. This would relieve the hospitals and also provide for ill persons confined to rooms in private homes. The city, with provincial help, should erect this building. It was estimated that this building would cost about $300,000. Again the importance of kindly supervision and help by both staff and volunteers was emphasized in this operation.

3. The establishment of a department of the Welfare Council to give primary attention to elderly persons. This department would be concerned with coördinating the work of existing groups, such as visitation and outings, encouraging new developments such as employment opportunities at home and in industry, planning new services such as a Sheltered Workshop, and pressing for new legislation such as that which would provide for supplementary financial assistance where necessary. It was estimated that the half of one worker's time would be necessary to staff the department (Mrs. Redford and I had in mind a well-trained and experienced social worker we knew to be available on a part-time basis), and that an annual budget of $6,500 would be necessary.

The Council meeting was impressed with both our statement of need, our report of community feeling, and our recommendations. However, they pressed Mrs. Redford on questions which the committee had not thoroughly investigated: Who is to head and finance the Social and Recreation Club? If, for example, the Chest is to provide the bulk of the annual budget for this club, who is the responsible group who will present the budget to the Chest and accept responsibility for the wise operation of the club? To these questions, Mrs. Redford replied that we had anticipated that an autonomous agency would be set up for this purpose (although this had not been worked through in committee). What then was the proposal, asked Mr. Harrold, Council president—was the recommendation that the Council approve the establishment of such an agency, that the Council now ask the Chest to approve the proposed budget before the agency was set up, or was it simply a matter of informal exploration with both Chest and Council?

They posed a series of questions on the proposed Home for the Chronically Ill: How many beds were required? How many rooms? For what age group was it to be planned, e.g., could a person 61 years of age be admitted? What would be the design of the home, e.g., would there be two floors or three? etc. Again Mr. Harrold put the difficult question: Did the committee wish the Council to urge this action on the city before we knew in detail precisely what was required, or was it simply a matter of informal approval of the idea in general?

On the third proposal, there were equally difficult questions: How would this new department relate to other departments which were in some instances concerned with the same services and the same people? Would this proposed department for elderly people become an operating department, e.g., would it be asking service clubs each week to take Mrs. Jones or Mrs. Robbins, or Mrs. So-and-So, for a drive? Would it begin to function as liaison between the servers and those served? Would it become, in fact, an employment agency?

Mrs. Redford's committee had not been unmindful of these questions but, as she and I agreed later, we had not worked out our plan in sufficient detail. When confronted with these questions, Mrs. Redford said quite frankly: "It is obvious that some of these matters have to be worked through further. However, I think we all know in general what we want and that there is approval here in the Council for our recommendations. Further, the community is interested and, I am afraid, impatient. Any issue before the Council, many feel, is unnecessarily delayed. I wonder if we could not: (1) approve the report in general terms; (2) instruct our committee to set up a board of directors for the recreational club which will submit a budget to the Chest in the fall; (3) give notice of motion to the City Council that we wish to meet with them in the fall to dis-

cuss the provision of a home for the chronically ill in Henshaw; and
(4) approach the board of the Community Chest immediately for
a budget for a department of the Council on elderly persons, and
at the same time, ask the Chest to be prepared to receive sympa-
thetically the budget request of the new social club for the aged in
the fall.

These four points were discussed in detail. With the exception of
the fourth point, they were approved. The latter was reworded to
indicate that the officers of the Chest would be asked immediately
to consider the budget requests in the fall for both a new Council
department and for a new social club for elderly persons. With this
modification, there was unanimous agreement to the proposal.

Mrs. Redford and I, indeed our whole committee and certainly
the community group, had hoped for action before summer. Now it
would be impossible to move much further until fall. Committee
activity during the summer would be at a minimum, and what was
to be done, Mrs. Redford and I would have to do. We did, however,
call an emergency meeting of our committee on June 30, and while
the committee was disappointed, they recognized a certain wisdom
in the Council's questions and asked Mrs. Redford and me to work
out details on each of our recommendations. I was to be away on
vacation in August, but Mrs. Redford and I spent a good deal of
time together in July working out the intricacies of our recommendations. By the end of July we were ready for the meeting of our
committee which we had already scheduled for September 6, the
day after Labor Day. We had selected 16 persons we were prepared
to recommend to the committee as board members for the new
agencies. We had drafted a tentative constitution and budget for
the consideration of this group and felt confident that if they agreed
to serve, the board could get underway quickly. We did a good deal
of work with Dr. Blight, a member of the committee, on the kind of
home Henshaw might build for the chronically ill, but we decided
we should suggest that the committee recommend that City Council
set up its own committee to study the problem which we would outline in detail with supporting data. As to the new department on

elderly persons, we developed a statement of policy showing its focus for work and its relation to other departments.

When I returned from my holidays on September 2, I found a note to call Mrs. Redford. When I phoned, her invitation to meet her as soon as possible sounded urgent, and I hurried over to her home even before looking at my accumulation of mail.

The burden of the conversation was that our whole elderly persons' project was in serious trouble and might be dropped by the Council. I was more than amazed and gradually the story came out. When the Council approached officers of the Chest in July regarding our budget requirements, there had been sympathetic interest and informal approval pending formal requests for budget allocations in the fall. Since that time, however, some of the Chest and Council board members had had conversations with Mr. Biford, who apparently was opposed to the whole project.

Mr. Samuel Biford (no one in Henshaw referred to him as Sam) was a fourth-generation resident of Henshaw, the owner of the farm implement factory, and a large shareholder in more than a dozen Henshaw business ventures, and a member of the board of directors of numerous companies of national importance. He was undoubtedly the most influential man in Henshaw. He was not a member of either the Chest or Council, or of any agency in Henshaw, but his influence in everything that happened was, or could be, apparent. He was a most generous man and usually gave the "first big gift" to start any new campaign—$100,000 to start a Y.M.C.A. building campaign, and comparable gifts to other such endeavors. Usually he took no active part in Henshaw health and welfare projects and was content to leave the initiation and development of such services to younger men who were pleased to go to him for advice and financial assistance.

Why he would oppose this project, I couldn't understand. I had met him only once but his record was one of generous and consistent support for almost every new venture the Welfare Council had initiated since I had come to Henshaw. I had come to regard him as a kindly and lovable old man anxious to do what good he could. Mrs. Redford, who knew him much better than I, indicated that his opposition might be due to any one of a dozen reasons, but that he was a little like this. Every once in a while, for some reason, he opposed a project—perhaps, she added, "just to show who is boss."

"But there's not much money involved," I said. "Wouldn't the Chest support it, if we work on them even though he opposes it?"

"Heavens, no!" Mrs. Redford exclaimed. "The Chest couldn't operate without his annual contribution. We have to recognize that he may be able to determine whether this project succeeds or not, and we must find some way to win him over to our side."

For a long time we talked about Mr. Samuel Biford, his likes and dislikes, his interests, moods, and weaknesses. We decided that perhaps we should not do more until after Labor Day and the September 6 meeting of the committee. At this meeting our revised proposals were quickly approved but the pressing question was raised as to whether it was of any use to proceed without Chest support. Finally, Mr. Samuel Biford's name was introduced and after long discussion and reminiscences, Mrs. Redford and I were asked to discuss the matter with him. In the meantime, it was decided, we would set up the board of the social club and pass on a recommendation to the City Council. "Let's operate on the assumption that Mr. Biford and the Chest Board will approve our requests."

Before we went to see Mr. Samuel Biford, Mrs. Redford and I had lunch with the president and secretary of the Chest. Both had been kept in touch with the work of our committee and had supported it throughout. We got down to business immediately. Why did Mr. Samuel Biford oppose this project? There was no clear answer. The president of the Chest had discussed it with him, but he had given no reasons—simply a flat rejection of the idea. This was of little help, and with some misgivings we arranged to see Mr. Samuel Biford. He would see us at 11 a.m., September 16.

Our interview with Mr. Samuel Biford was an impressive one, for me at least. He was a man in his early sixties, I would judge, tall, erect, and very handsome. He was most gracious to us, courteous, attentive, and not at all explosive on the subject we had come to discuss. Mrs. Redford told him of our investigation, our findings and our plans, and said she hoped he would be interested and support our efforts. We had not come to ask for money, merely to secure his support. He modestly disclaimed the fact that his support would make any difference, that he was sure we would go ahead anyway, but if he were completely honest he would have to confess to some reservations. "There is a very fine line between providing help to people in need and taking initiative away from them. I've been reading a book on the effect of certain welfare programs on the people in Denmark and Sweden. You would certainly know about that, Mr. Jenkins. I don't know how you feel about it but I feel they've sapped the initiative of those people. I don't want that to happen here. And I have the feeling that some of your plans lead us in that direction." We discussed the matter for about 20 minutes, when his secretary interrupted us to say Mr. Samuel Biford had another appointment.

We left realizing we had made no progress. He had a point, an important point, we conceded, but it was not relevant to our proposal. In discussing it later, Mrs. Redford and I concluded that he had just happened to read a book that stirred him in a certain direction and that he would have opposed any new project that came up following this experience. Perhaps in a year he would have forgotten all about it. But we didn't want to wait for a year. The old folks of Henshaw needed the program we planned now.

The next meeting of our committee was scheduled for September 23, and Mrs. Redford and I spent hours before that date speculating on what we would or could do about Mr. Samuel Biford. We listed 19 suggestions in all, but none of them seemed at all likely to succeed. On the morning of the 22nd I got an idea. According to the papers, President Earle Cameron from the university in the metropolitan center was to address a combined meeting of the Rotary and Kiwanis Clubs in Henshaw on September 30. President Cameron was known throughout the country as an educator, scholar, and statesman, and, I had heard, was a personal friend of Mr. Biford. I also knew that President Cameron was interested in welfare programs, that his daughter had been a social worker, and that he himself had served on the board of the Chest in the metropolitan center. Quickly, I put in a call for Bill Dixens, the secretary of the Chest in that city and a person I knew very well. I told him the whole story of our project for elderly persons, what was involved, and what the present status was. Then I explained about Cameron's visit and my guess that if President Cameron could tell about what was being done for elderly persons in the larger city and indirectly and cautiously, in private conversations with Mr. Biford, support the need for such work, it would help our cause immeasurably. Bill understood (bless him!) and promised to help. But he warned, "President Cameron is a difficult man to see but I'll do my best." I decided not to tell Mrs. Redford, in case the whole idea collapsed. But the day following, an hour before the meeting of our committee, Bill called to say he had talked on the phone with President Cameron, who had said he'd be delighted to help. "What's got into old Sam?" he had asked. With this I called Mrs. Redford, and she, of course, was delighted. It seemed the only way out. Our hopes rested on President Cameron, who, I am sure, never realized how desperately we counted on his help.

Our committee meeting heard first a report from Mrs. Redford on our conversation with Mr. Samuel Biford. She indicated that we had hopes that he would support the program but could not at the moment reveal the precise nature of our appeal to him. She suggested that we operate on the assumption that within a month we would have his support. With that in mind what would we do?

We had had a delaying letter from the Chest board concerning our new department, but now we decided that we would ask for a special meeting with their officers on October 20. By that time, also, we would have the board of the new social club set up and it could also meet to press for its requirements. The resolution to the City Council to set up a special meeting as planned was also forwarded to the mayor. Our line of endeavor now was clear.

However, at this point a member raised a question which had consistently bothered me. What about the community group? We had stirred their interest, whetted their appetite, encouraged them to believe they were partners, and now we seemed to have dropped them. Everyone agreed we should meet with them again. But when—before we met with the Chest board, when nothing new could be reported, or after, when hopefully we could report progress. We decided to meet the community group before the meeting with the Chest and to ask the community group to support our efforts before both the Chest and City Council. It was agreed that we call this group together for a meeting October 10.

September 30 came and went without any visible effect. I attended the dinner meeting at which President Cameron spoke. There was no mention in his address of the needs of the elderly nor was I able to get near him. But I heard he had stayed overnight at the home of Mr. Samuel Biford and I hoped he had an opportunity to talk with him about our project. Mrs. Redford and I both tried as discreetly as possible to get what information we could but there was little forthcoming beyond what we knew. As October 20 drew near, we tried in desperation to get an appointment with Mr. Biford but his secretary told us he was out of town and would not be back for three weeks. We never did have another conversation with him on this subject.

The community meeting October 10 was indignant and militant. Several people spoke about the "Chest routine" and about how "they never get anything done," but after a few such expressions they discussed our detailed recommendations and approved them. They were keen for action and appointed three members to go with us to meet with the Chest board and three to go to the meeting of the City Council at which our recommendation concerning a home for the chronically ill would be considered.

The October 20 meeting with the Chest officers was a revelation. We were three groups—our Council committee, the board of the new social club (the "Second-Mile Club" as they had decided to call themselves), and three persons from the community group. Each spoke briefly, and our requirements were put forward with clarity and urgency. The response was that this seemed like a very worthwhile program and would certainly be supported by the Chest. They could not, of course, commit the Chest board, but the requirements for the Second-Mile Club and for the Welfare Council Department on Elderly Citizens would be considered at the next meeting, and they were confident it would be approved. Further, if we wished, they would raise the question of officially supporting our recommendation to the City Council.

And sure enough, we had succeeded. Within a week our budgets were approved and we were assured of the support of the Chest in approaching the City Council.

What had happened? Had we overemphasized Mr. Samuel Biford's influence or had he changed his mind as a result of President Cameron's visit? We never did get the full story. What we heard was that one day shortly after President Cameron's visit, Mr. Samuel Biford had called the president of the Chest. After discussing a business matter (for Mr. Biford had a controlling hand in Jed Shaw's business), Mr. Biford had said, "How are things lining up for the Chest campaign? Are you going to need more money?—you probably are with that social club for the old folks. I'll be away when the campaign is on but you can increase my gift of last year by the same percentage the campaign goal is increased." Jed Shaw was in the process of thanking him when he was interrupted. "Mrs. Redford and that young man from the Council were over to see me—I like them—good people—we should encourage them—give them a hand, won't you?"

And that was that. And that brief telephone conversation was the reason our program was approved and fully supported by the Chest. Why Mr. Biford "gave the word" I never discovered. But both Mrs. Redford's, and my own, status rose considerably as a result of "the word."

From this point on, things moved smoothly. The new board of the Second-Mile Club was busy. It could not open the club until after January when the allocation from the Chest would be available. But they found a fine old home which they were to rent for $150 a month, they secured a trained social worker to begin work in July, and they began to enlist volunteers and members. By January 1, they had some 90 volunteer women ready to serve tea, arrange games, drive invalid members to the club, etc. Equipment and furnishings came in great quantities and the place, as Mrs. Redford said on opening day, looked wonderful. The membership was slow in coming, but as I write this one year later, I am aware of the fact that membership has been closed at the 400 mark and there is a waiting list of 80 persons who want to join. The board is now talking about enlarging its quarters.

Our appearance before the City Council was also a pleasant one. In addition to the endorsement of the Chest, the Welfare Council, and the community group, our recommendation was supported specifically by the two hospital boards and by the local medical society. The recommendation pointed out the assistance that would be forthcoming from the provincial government, and the whole was favorably considered. Not only was a committee appointed but it was given a grant of $3,000 to investigate what was being done in other cities, and was asked to recommend both the type of home that should be built and sites for its location. Alderman Richards, who was a member of our committee, was appointed chairman of the new committee and we felt this to be an excellent appointment. All in all we were well satisfied. Again after one year, I can report that the architects' plan for the new Home is almost ready and it is quite likely it will be approved by both the municipal and provincial governments and that the first sod on a modern home will be turned within a year. Alderman Richards' committee traveled widely, studying various types of homes for older people; the Henshaw Home will compare favorably with any of them.

As for the new department in the Council, it too is set up and functioning well. When we were given authorization to begin, the existing committee with Mrs. Redford as chairman was appointed to carry on. This committee decided, however, that all the persons in the community group should be asked to be members. An executive committee of ten should carry on the administrative duties of the department but the larger group, now over 60 members, should meet at least eight times a year. The new part-time secretary of the department began to work in May, 1954. Subcommittees to consider visitation and trips, employment opportunities, and increased financial aid were appointed and set immediately to work. One year later progress had been made in all three areas, but new problems have arisen and new work is being contemplated. Among the new concerns are the need for visiting nurses for old people who are in rooming or boarding houses and who are temporarily ill; the difficulties many aged persons have in passing the means test for supplementary financial assistance after they are 65 years of age; and the need for something like a sheltered workshop.

Mrs. Redford and I look back on this project with satisfaction. We made many mistakes, we know. But one year after Mrs. Redford had raised the matter with the Welfare Council, considerable movement was apparent. And two years afterwards, this movement had been extended and promised substantially improved services for the aged in Henshaw. Furthermore, the involvement of many volunteers has meant a considerable emphasis on the kindly and personal help we all came to believe essential in the operation of these services.

Questions for Discussion

1. What particular approach to the community was implicit in what Mrs. Redford and this worker said and did? Were they consistent in their philosophy and method?

2. What do you think of the Biford incident? Is it one which a worker should anticipate? How can such a "block" be handled?

3. What principles for community organization emerge from this experience?

Elmsville

As HIS train rattled into Elmsville, Jack Barnes squirmed in anticipation of the welcome he expected would be his. He was 27, with a master's degree in social work, and three years' experience in a settlement house in a large metropolitan center. He was going to Elmsville to be the first director of recreation in this town of 8000 people. He would, in fact, be the first trained social worker to be employed in Elmsville, and he could well imagine how excited both the adults and children would be to have him. He remembered a friend who went to a small town as the community doctor. He had been met by a band, welcomed by the mayor, escorted in a caravan of open cars to the office-home the town had prepared for him. Small towns were like that. They appreciate professional city folks who come to work for them.

As the train slowed and he gathered his bags, Jack urged himself not to expect too much. Elmsville might not have a band, and besides if he expected a lot he might be disappointed. Perhaps only the committee would be there to meet him.

Alas for our dreams! Alighting from the train, Barnes could see but a few stragglers hanging around the station. Even though he waited in his position near the train, not a person moved forward to greet him. Slowly, he reviewed the exchange of letters which led to his arrival. The chairman of the committee, Richard Wetmore, had been most cordial in his invitation, and while he had warned that Elmsville was unaccustomed to professional leadership in recreation, all were eagerly awaiting his arrival. His own letter giving the date and time of arrival had been acknowledged. There was no mistake in this, but perhaps there were reasons why the committee, or Wetmore at least, could not meet him.

Whatever else may be said of Barnes, he could adjust to a new situation. And this he did. Lugging his bags over to a taxi, he asked to be driven to Wetmore's office. According to the driver, Wetmore was a prominent lawyer and the location of his office well known. Soon he would make his first contact.

Wetmore, together with his office, was another disillusionment. He was a tall, shaggy, unimpressive man who occupied an office heaped with dusty documents and papers. He was pleasant and cordial but not excited or awed at meeting Barnes. The latter had two problems in mind: the state of his job, and where Wetmore planned he should live. Both these matters were quickly clarified for him.

"I know nothing about recreation," said Wetmore, "nor, if I am honest, am I very much interested. But for 20 years now we've had a trust fund which came into existence with money from the insurance on the old Y.M.C.A. building. I am chairman of the trustees of this fund and we came to the conclusion that we had to spend the money some way before all the trustees died. A Y.M.C.A. man from head-quarters wanted us to start a Y program but somehow we felt we didn't want an organization just for Protestants. Then he suggested a community recreation program and we thought that might work. He recommended you, so we hired you. Now, I know nothing about what you do or should do, but you do what you think best. You drop in every month and your salary will be here for you."

At this forthright statement, Barnes was flabbergasted. Wetmore must have noticed his disappointment for he added, "Now don't worry, you'll find people who are interested. I am just too old for things like recreation. And you'll get your salary every month for a year at least."

A few questions revealed that there were only three trustees living, that they never met and wouldn't likely meet, that the two other trustees were Judge Lawson and George Hamilton, and that Lawson was the chairman of a playground committee that hoped Barnes would help them.

As to where Barnes might live, Wetmore had no idea but undoubtedly the girl in the office could help. He was sorry but this was Tuesday and he must leave early today as he always went to his summer cottage on Tuesday and returned on Thursday. Barnes was later to learn that he also went to the cottage on Friday noon and returned on Tuesday morning.

The taxi driver who was waiting found Barnes a room, and he was soon unpacked and reflecting on his naïvete and the extent of his disillusionment. He was philosophic about it, at least to the extent of reflecting that "this is the way one learns" but he could not deceive himself. He was disappointed and the job was going to be more difficult than he had thought possible.

His second interview served to confirm this impression. He went to visit Judge Lawson later that day. While Wetmore was neutral, Lawson was openly hostile. Apparently "the deal" to hire Barnes had been made by the other two trustees and Lawson had not even been consulted. "As far as I am concerned, I didn't vote to bring you here and I am not interested in your being here," said Lawson flatly. To this outflow of anger, Barnes listened quietly. Gradually the edge left Lawson's voice and he answered more reasonably some of the questions Barnes asked about playgrounds. Toward the end of the conversation, Barnes asked if he could help in the playground program and Lawson said, "As long as you're here you might as well do what you can, but don't bother me." That was that.

That night, when Barnes reflected on his two interviews, he was less discouraged than perhaps he should have been. He liked both men, although they obviously disliked each other. Furthermore, he thought he could work with both, in spite of Wetmore's apathy and

Lawson's hostility. Both were essentially good men, he felt, and would probably give more to the community than they would ever admit. However, it was obvious that he had a difficult task ahead and that he would have to revise in a radical way his plan of work in Elmsville. He had looked forward to a community that was "ready" in the sense that most people were aware of what they wanted to do and how they wanted him to help. He had anticipated a community recreation council well organized and eager to work. To judge by reactions to date, not only was Elmsville not eager to have him, it was completely indifferent to him.

During the next few days, Barnes spent a good deal of time walking through the city. It was a beautiful community with broad tree-lined streets, a river running through the lower part of the city, and a small but well-designed campus on the hill at the back or north part of the community. On these excursions, Barnes discovered two large playground areas and two much smaller but useful play areas. All had been used, but such equipment as had been on these grounds was now battered or destroyed and less than a dozen children were to be found on all four playgrounds. In addition, there was a substantial football field and quarter-mile track. There was also a horse-racing track and a good sandy beach on the river. So, Barnes reflected, there were lots of recreational resources. But more important in appraising the community were the signs of vandalism, of fences ripped, of broken bottles on the beach, of playground equipment willfully destroyed. Obviously there was little discipline or what Barnes called "constructive leadership."

The smaller children whom Barnes met on the sidewalk and streets were shy and distant. Frequently Barnes would stop to speak to youngsters, but they would stand and stare at him or after a quick glance run away from him. The older boys he found aggressive and unfriendly. He stopped to talk to one group playing a scrub game of baseball. They were uncommunicative, but would gather in little groups away from him and laugh hilariously at the remarks of one or more of the boys. The reception of the children was hardly more cordial than that of their elders.

Another day he spent visiting the Roman Catholic priest and the Protestant ministers. Each member of the clergy received him with courtesy but hardly with warmth. When Barnes talked about a community program for either adults or children, it was pointed out by most of them that each of the churches had its own program and anything additional would not only be unnecessary but would detract from the churches' work. The playground program was considered to be different, since churches were largely inactive in the summer, but as the priest said, "the playgrounds have never amounted to much." Only the Baptist minister, a recent arrival in town, sounded a hopeful note. "We're desperate for leadership," he said. "The children here run completely wild—they're destructive and have no sense of fair play. Among the young adults there is a lot of drinking and sexual immorality, and among the older people, a great sense of indifference and apathy. I've never worked in a more difficult setting and if you can do anything to improve it, God bless you."

As he reflected on what he had seen and heard, Barnes was sure of where he must start. What he wanted was a council of the people themselves, working in programs and activities that they had organized themselves. This was the stereotype of a good recreation program, he knew, but he also knew it got results. It was clear that any such development was for the distant future. But the playgrounds gave him an opportunity both to demonstrate and to get acquainted. He would work with and through children.

With this in mind, he went to see Judge Lawson again. This time Lawson, having given vent to his feelings, was more reasonable, but far from friendly. His committee had a budget that permitted the employment of five university students; in fact, they had already been hired, to supervise the playgrounds. If he wished, Barnes could direct their work. There was considerable discussion of what Lawson saw as important in the operation of the playgrounds. "If we can keep them from breaking things and getting into fights, it will be an advance." Barnes did not press any other objective but moved on to a discussion of the five employed students—what could be expected of them ("Whatever they'll agree to do") and Barnes' own position relative to them. Judge Lawson agreed to speak to each of them and to tell them that Barnes was now the director and that they should work with him.

Barnes had some feeling that he might be moving too fast, for having been in the community less than ten days, he was labeled as a playground director and now, meeting with his staff, he was engaged in planning and directing a recreational program. He had wanted to wait and to encourage others to function; now he argued that this town could be moved only if they were shown how. And thus a summer playground program began.

The five students who composed Barnes staff were all residents of Elmsville and themselves a product of the very culture which Barnes was convinced must be changed. The three men were all good football and baseball players but knew little else about recreation. The two young ladies were pleasant but had little idea of sports, games, or hobbies. Again, Barnes became convinced that he himself must develop the plans for the playgrounds. He would work it out with the staff, but if anything was to be accomplished, he would have to stimulate and nourish it along. To some of his ideas there was resistance, and these he had to drop, but a surprising number of his ideas were accepted by the staff group.

And so a program was developed on paper. It called for a regular schedule at each of the four playgrounds, with evening programs as well as daytime activities. There were to be four classes of participants by age and sex, and regular activities were to be planned for every group, morning and evening, five days a week. Afternoons were for special events. The staff was to meet every Monday afternoon for planning and clearance. The program was to begin July 10, one week hence, and during the week the staff were to walk the streets, talking to children about the program, and providing those interested with playground membership cards. Barnes threw himself into preparations for the opening with great energy. Not only did he purchase and organize equipment and plan schedules, he taught himself and his staff some simple crafts: soap carving, leather work, bead work, wood work. The staff group actually enjoyed this and some *esprit de corps* developed immediately as they experimented with various small projects. Barnes' enthusiasm and his ineptitude with knife or hammer were a source of enjoyment to all. The program called for some game periods and Barnes undertook to teach all the staff various games that could be played during this period.

During the week he visited Judge Lawson, Mr. Wetmore, and Mr. Hamilton (the third "living trustee"), the editor of the local paper (the *Listener*), and the superintendent of public works. With all five, he just dropped in to chat, and gauged what he would talk about and the length of his visit by the attitude of his host. But he hoped, and indeed in all cases found it possible, to interpret what they planned to do on the playgrounds. In all cases, there were smiles at his boyish enthusiasm, and if there was some cynicism, there was also some interest. The newspaper editor, Mr. Pidgeon, a huge man of some 300 pounds, warned him against his optimism. "We're different here, we move slow, we don't want to be pushed. And most of you young fellers aren't any better than you think you are." Barnes had hoped for a write-up in the paper announcing the opening of playgrounds and inquired about this, but while Pidgeon said he'd see, no such news item appeared in the paper. From the superintendent of public works he hoped to secure a promise to grade and level a baseball diamond and a volleyball court, but while the superintendent, Mr. Morrison, was overtly sympathetic he said frankly, "There'll be a hell of a fuss if we put men to work fixing up those lots when we're supposed to be working on the streets."

The opening of the playgrounds on July 10 was not the historic event that Mr. Barnes expected. None the less, 167 children turned up, were organized in groups, and engaged in activities of various kinds. While there were no indications of great excitement about the new program, the children did seem to enjoy the activities, there were no serious fights, and even the hardball game for senior boys was kept under control. At one point Barnes saw Judge Lawson drive swiftly by one of the playgrounds and he wondered if this were interest in what was going on or other business that took him past this particular spot.

The remainder of the first week passed with attendance increasing slightly but without a major incident of any kind. Barnes spent part of Sunday writing a news release of some 1,000 words on the activities during the week, and early Monday morning he started his rounds by visiting Mr. Pidgeon at his newspaper office. Pidgeon was interested but, on the whole, unimpressed by Barnes' account of his activities. However, he promised to use his news release "if possible." That afternoon, a two-inch item appeared which used the first paragraph of Barnes' release.

Barnes called again on Judge Lawson, Messrs. Wetmore, Hamilton, and Morrison. With all he exchanged gossip about the weather, how he liked Elmsville, and what was happening at the playgrounds. The visits were somewhat more relaxed, and only with Lawson did he feel the need to get out of the office quickly.

The summer moved on. Each week new activities at the playground were organized: hikes for girls in the afternoon, swimming classes at the beach, bicycle races for boys at the horse-racing track, a track and field meet, and so on. Barnes himself organized these special events and taught the swimming classes. He found working with the children difficult. They were not used to listening to a group leader and inclined to go off on their own. It was with the greatest difficulty that he kept control of his swimming classes or lined up children for bicycle or running races. But he felt progress was being made. Children were learning to play and work together. They were coming in steadily increasing numbers. There were no fights.

In the town he was becoming established. The *Listener* was using more and more of the news releases he took to Mr. Pidgeon every Monday morning. Each week he visited his key men and gradually he extended his calls to include other people who he thought were leaders of groups in the city. It was clear that people were interested, even though skeptical about what was happening at the playgrounds.

During the first week in August, Barnes had an idea that a

campfire on the beach would be a fitting celebration for the completion of the first month of playground program. All the children at the playgrounds were invited. One businessman promised to give a chocolate bar to every boy or girl in attendance. Judge Lawson was to say a few words. Barnes was to lead a sing-song. One of the playground staff was to lead some games. One of the senior baseball teams was to set up the fire.

A grand bonfire it was, blazing and shooting sparks high into the air. But that was the only pleasant part of the night for Barnes. Some 500 children turned out and the fire seemed to act upon them in such a way as to stimulate their wildest urges. They shouted, ran, danced, threw whatever they could lay their hands on, and in general caused bedlam. Judge Lawson was hit in the head with a cushion and was bumped by running boys, the chocolate bars were grabbed and almost caused a riot, and Barnes himself had more than one bruise. The campfire program never had a beginning or an end and it was fortunate that no one was seriously hurt.

Barnes slept poorly that night, for this event had been planned to demonstrate how children would respond to a good recreation program. Now he felt all was lost. Oddly enough it was not so. He had on more than one occasion talked with Judge Lawson and others about the difficulty of discipline in dealing with children in Elmsville. And when he dropped in to see Lawson the day following the bonfire, he found the judge in a more sober and thoughtful mood than ever before. "I never realized until last night how these children have got out of hand. I've been around and I've seen what you've been doing in the playgrounds. It's good! Very good! And you can't be expected to change in one month what we've been doing, or not doing, to those kids for years. By God, it has to change. You know I didn't want you here in the beginning, but that's all changed. You can count on me 100 percent now." Among the adults who had gone to the bonfire, there was a similar reaction. Barnes was the recipient of considerable sympathy. A feeling of guilt about the behavior of their children seemed to develop, especially as this behavior affected a man who had generously tried to help these children. The great fiasco of the bonfire, far from ruining Barnes' work, seemed to make adults more aware of the difficult problem that had grown up in their community almost without their knowledge.

The second month, from August 10 to September 10, was indeed a different experience. Attendance at the playgrounds continued to increase, and toward the end of the period ran close to 600 children daily. Mr. Morrison, the public works superintendent, called Barnes and offered, because he "had a little breather," to "put the playgrounds in shape." Excellent ball diamonds, volleyball courts, and horseshoe pits were laid out. Activities for adults were organized in the evening and volleyball, crafts, and horseshoes were popular. Barnes, in his travels through the community, discovered people with various talents, and these were all used. An ex-boxing champion was enlisted as a volunteer to teach boxing one afternoon a week, a professor at the university was induced to lead a "summer fiction" club of adults which Barnes organized, a gymnast was enlisted to teach boys tumbling, a musician to lead a music appreciation group, etc. Most impressive, perhaps, were two other developments. The first was the "settling down" of boys who played in the hardball league. Prior to this sumer, games were inevitably marked by squabbles and umpire baiting, and seldom was a game completed without a fight. What caused the change Barnes was unable to say. He had insisted on good equipment, on the diamond being properly marked off (on more than one occasion early in the season he had himself chalked the lines), and on one of the staff serving as umpire of all games. Once when he had been "ump," he had had a showdown with the players. There was vigorous protesting on the part of one team of one of his decisions. The protesting team gathered around Barnes in a threatening manner but he had stood his ground firmly and said, "You have five seconds to get back in your positions or the game goes to the other side. One . . ." Quickly the boys resumed the game with the exception of one boy— the largest in the group. Again Barnes acted quickly with the command, "You're out of the game and don't come back for two days."

The fates were kind to Barnes this day, for what surely would have resulted in physical combat was halted before it began when a man who had been watching the game stepped forward and slapped the boy on the face. "Do what you're told, you squealer," bellowed the man, who proved to be the boy's father. The latter, who worked as a night watchman, often came to watch the activities at the playgrounds, and while Barnes had spoken to him and knew him as Walter Service, he had not known he had children in the activities. At this point, Service and Barnes became friends—a friendship which lasted throughout Barnes' stay in Elmsville. After this incident, however, there was never any serious trouble in the playground ball league and the success of this league became a matter of pride in the community. Its effect in establishing Barnes cannot be underestimated. A considerable group of adults for whom baseball was very important developed respect for Barnes which they showed in many ways that supported the playground work.

The other major development, surprisingly enough, was in the area of arts and crafts. Barnes himself had exhausted his ideas and skills at the end of the first week, but the two girl staff members both developed tremendous interest and skill and worked with groups on many of the suggestions in books which Barnes supplied for them. The result was a considerable flow of arts and crafts from the playground into the homes of Elmsville. Later, when Barnes reviewed his work, he concluded that the arts and craft program did more to win the interest and support of parents than almost anything else at the playgrounds.

The climax of the season was "Playground Day," an open house when parents and visitors were invited to see what was being done at the playgrounds. An all-day program of activities was planned, arts and crafts were on display, and the day was concluded with short speeches, lemonade and cookies, and the awarding of prizes and trophies. Over 3000 adults attended. An indication of the change in attitudes and practices was the fact that there was not one hitch in the whole program. The children, without being inhibited, were friendly and coöperative, and carried through their program with ease and skill.

If Barnes' entrance into the community was not spectacular, the degree of his acceptance in Elmsville was indeed reassuring. Literally, hundreds of adults came to greet him and thank him for his part in the playground effort. But, oddly enough, it was not a "one-man show." Barnes himself did not speak, nor did the speakers, Judge Lawson, Mr. Hamilton, or Mayor Moore, refer to him in anything but mildly appreciative terms. Barnes knew what they thought of his effort and he was glad not to have the speeches turn into a back-slapping session for him.

It was a great day for Elmsville, and this fact was reflected in the next edition of the *Listener*. On the front page was an editorial reviewing the work at the playgrounds during the summer and commending the efforts of Judge Lawson, Barnes, the staff, volunteer leaders, and others who helped. On page 3 was a photo of Lawson, another of the playground staff, and a long two-column item written by a staff reporter about Playground Day. There was little question that the playground program had sold itself and that it was widely appreciated by both children and adults. It was clear that Barnes had made many friends among both young and old and that he had established a place for himself in the community. He had come with rather different ideas of what a community recreation director should do, but he adjusted when necessary, and above all had established contacts which now permitted him to move into another phase of his work.

Mr. Barnes had carefully considered strategy for doing what he considered a "community job," and his summer was devoted to providing a base for the implementation of this strategy. He did not consider himself a playground director, or a recreational leader, or a teacher of swimming. These things he did as a way of both rendering a useful service and beginning a larger job. This larger task he saw as helping the community of Elmsville develop ability to pull itself out of its apathy and to do something as a community to improve itself.

To accomplish this, Barnes was aware that he must know well the community, its groups, leaders, and culture. A good deal of time during the summer was spent collecting data pertaining to them. He did not make a survey or spend extra time building up his knowledge of Elmsville. But he was observant—a careful questioner and a good listener. At one point, for example, he wanted to find out a little more about George Wetmore's place in the community. During three successive conversations, he received a whole history of Wetmore and his family, simply by commenting "George Wetmore is a most interesting fellow . . . "

Barnes found that the community was divided in a variety of ways and that all the divisions of people required consideration. There was a major division by religion, for Elmsville was a "church town" and few families were not closely aligned with a church. There were divisions by income and wealth, by family tradition, and by location of residence. There were not uniform groups in the social classes. Of the three wealthiest men of high status in the community, one was a Roman Catholic, one an Anglican, and one a Baptist. Further, these three men lived in quite different parts of the community. All were Anglo-Saxons but the family of one had lived in Elmsville for generations, one had come to Elmsville as a boy with his father, and the other had been in Elmsville less than ten years. There were other divisions—the intellectuals, the educated, the uneducated, the sports-minded, the nonsports-minded, the heavy drinkers, the social drinkers, the nondrinkers. All such divisions had some rationale, yet none of these was adequate.

Elmsville had few of the organizations with which Barnes was accustomed to working. There were no social agencies, no Community Chest or Welfare Council, no Home-and-School or Parent-Teachers association. None the less, as he worked through this problem he began to develop the following division of people:

1. The older and weathier business and professional men. All but three of these persons were members of the Rotary Club. This club he felt to be a key group and of stragetic importance. Howard Kitchen he marked especially, as he was not only a Rotarian but a

wealthy man with close contact with the three wealthiest men mentioned, none of whom was a Rotarian.

2. The middle-age group of business and professional men. These men were mostly in the Lions and Kiwanis clubs. They did not have either the status or wealth of the Rotarians but they were more numerous and of considerable influence and capacity.

3. The young businessmen. These were the young junior executives. Many of them belonged to the Y's Men and Kinsmen clubs. Many were also associated with young people's church groups, and some were executives of the ball club.

All of the above groups were linked in some way with the Board of Trade, the Golf Club, and the Yacht Club, but Barnes felt these latter were loose organizations and that the three service club groupings had a degree of cohesiveness which required consideration in any community organization project.

4. Another group he called the "intellectuals." This was a loose-knit group which was not formally organized but which had much in common, recognized this common identity, and fraternized at small house parties. It included many of the faculty members of the university. Among these, he discovered that the leader was probably Professor Burr Johnson, a brilliant young English professor who was much admired at the university and in Elmsville.

5. Another group were the socially prominent women. This group was composed of women from all denominations, though they were mostly Protestant, and while not formally organized were none the less easily identifiable as a group. Most of them were associated with the Golf Club and the Yacht Club, but their cohesiveness was most notable when one of them ran a garden party or a reception of some kind.

6. A second group of women were mostly Protestant but lacked the social prominence of the first group. These were the women who served at suppers for the ball team or similar "banquet occasions," who played at the Friday Night Euchre, who belonged to the Honta Club, a local club whose origin was lost in history but whose primary purpose now was to operate a rummage sale each year and to give

the proceeds for various worthy causes, such as gowns for a school choir, Christmas baskets for the poor, a flag pole and flag for the public park, etc. The leader of this group was clearly Mrs. Bert Purdy, the wife of a local minor public official, a woman of good humor, charm, and ability.

7. The other group of women were those Roman Catholic women not in either of the groups above. They were, on the whole, women in families of low-income, and while largely unorganized did come together occasionally for church socials. Barnes noted several women in this group who were obvious leaders, accepted by both the priest and the women, but he felt the outstanding representative would be Mrs. Ruby Jones, a widow living on a small pension, a woman of strong loyalty and conviction.

In some ways these groupings might be considered representative of the population as a whole, but Barnes was quite aware that in fact this might be a false assumption. He recognized that the small residential area near the east-end playground would not be represented in such a selection. Here, Barnes was sure that a resident of this area, in the person of Walter Service, was essential in any community-wide planning operation. Then there was the senior baseball team, a kind of institution in Elmsville, with its players, directors, and followers. If the major parts of the community were to be included, this institution must be represented. Walter Service would represent it, in part, but Jim Rivers, the manager, a rough and profane man with the traditional "heart-of-gold," was undoubtedly the key to the baseball operation. One must also consider, Barnes concluded, a small residential section across the river. Here, there was a small property-owners association, and Charles Ronson, the president, highly regarded by the people there, would undoubtedly be a good representative of that section of the city. There were only seven Jewish families and 11 Negro families in Elmsville, and Barnes was uncertain whether such a small group required representation on a community council, but as part of his job he became acquainted with both groups and could readily identify a Jewish and Negro leader if necessary. Another segment of the population was, perhaps, the hard-drinking youth group among whom Bus Hawes, the catcher on the ball team, was a natural leader.

Barnes felt reasonably confident after a summer of careful searching that he had identified the major groups and leaders in the community. If he could just get them together, he was confident that they could make Elmsville a city to be proud of. He himself saw dozens of things that needed to be done in the community, but he was ready to start whenever the people were and to move with them. He was not going to impose a community program as he had done in recreation through the playgrounds.

But Barnes could not help being disturbed by what he saw around him. Apathy with respect to community matters seemed widely characteristic. Groups were not merely separate but actively hostile to one another. Gossip was not friendly and jovial but bitter and often vicious. Heavy drinking was common. There was little questioning of what went on in the civic government and little awareness of what the community lacked. For example, Barnes was appalled by the fact that there was no public library, no garbage collection, no public concerts or lectures, no regular street cleaning—to mention only a few of the deficiencies he noted. More depressing was that in this university city, no one seemed disturbed by these shortcomings. The intellectuals were concerned with international affairs, with the cold war and such great issues, and were quite indifferent to local affairs. Even in Mrs. Jackson and Mrs. Purdy, women with relatively progressive views, he found indifference. Mrs. Purdy said of garbage collection, "We manage pretty well now. Besides it would simply increase taxes." Barnes was shocked but not discouraged.

When he discussed with Judge Lawson and Mr. Wetmore his idea of a community council, he met firm negative attitudes. "Look," said Judge Lawson, "you've done a great job for us here; be content with that. Don't tempt the fates. Stick to recreation. You don't undertsand this community. Why, you couldn't get some of the people you've mentioned sitting down at the same table. And to talk about things like a library. Can you imagine Jim Rivers or Bus Hawes sitting in a meeting planning how to raise money for a library? No! No! It's not realistic."

"You may be right," Barnes replied, "but I'd like to try. See what has happened so far, what you and I and a few others did. We did it for the kids and adults. Sure, they had a good time, but it's only a little better than giving ice cream out at a Sunday School picnic. What I want to see is these people doing something for themselves, learning that if they work together they can do something more important than what we did. They'll learn to do by doing. Their whole attitude about themselves and this community will change."

"Look, Barnes," said the Judge, "you know I like you and believe in you, and I'll go along with you. I think this idea is crazy but then I've thought a lot of the things you tried were crazy, and most of them have worked. I'll help."

Most of the interviews Barnes had were of the same order. The people were frankly skeptical but were willing to try for Barnes' sake. As he thought about this afterwards, Barnes felt a tightness in his stomach. "Lord, they trust me," he thought. "What if the whole thing turns out to be a mess?" He disliked building an organization around himself but he thought that perhaps he could gradually shift the focus to some real community problem.

So a first meeting of a community council was set up. Judge Lawson agreed to act as interim chairman and sent out invitations to the organized groups Barnes had identified, with a suggestion that perhaps Mrs. So-and-So (a person in each case who Barnes felt was a real leader in the group) would be able to represent the group. In the case of unorganized groups, an invitation was sent to the person Barnes suggested. A representative from every group or section in the population identified by Barnes, including the Negro and Jewish groups, was invited.

Before the meeting, Barnes visited every one of the persons invited. All agreed to come although few could see what could be accomplished. Barnes pressed each for his view of community problems, but when the interviews were concluded, he was appalled at the lack of any common problems. Each had a few things his group wanted (a baseball stadium, an indoor swimming pool, etc.) but no two persons agreed. Barnes had counted on something emerging. Now he felt he was in trouble.

True to their word, everyone invited to the meeting turned up on the night of September 27 in the City Hall. This was more a tribute to Barnes than interest in the meeting, but the gathering was indeed a cross section of the city and even Judge Lawson was impressed. Lawson, in the chair, welcomed the group and called upon Barnes to explain the purpose of the meeting. This Barnes did, perhaps too briefly, explaining how such councils operated in other cities, some of the projects they undertook, some of the things that might be done in Elmsville, and the value of this kind of procedure in a democracy. The group then discussed what might be done in Elmsville. As Barnes feared, the meeting was not without suggestions, but there was no common ground and for every suggestion put forward there was a counter-suggestion or a reason why it was not possible. In conversation afterward, Barnes said to Judge Lawson, "They had a difficulty for every solution." The meeting was inconclusive. But as Judge Lawson remarked, "There were no open fights—it really went a lot better than I expected." Perhaps it did, Barnes reflected, for while Mr. Roberts, the Negro leader, and Bus Hawes, the baseball catcher, seemed very quiet and a little ill at ease, most of the others took part in a fairly animated discussion. Howard Kitchen, representing the wealthy businessmen, was the one impatient member, and only his loyalty to Barnes kept him from casting "a plague on all your houses." On the whole, the meeting was friendly and cordial and it was agreed to meet again in two weeks' time.

Barnes had hoped they would work on some of the obvious problems he saw—the lack of garbage collection, the lack of a library, etc.—but it was evident that these were not considered deficiencies. The problems identified at the meeting were 26 in number, ranging from the need for a war memorial in the park to the need for imports for the ball team if it were to maintain its winning streak. Not one of the items in the list would, Barnes guessed, win the support of as many as 50 percent of those attending. One of the interesting aspects of the meeting was the resistance to any community-wide recreational activities such as hockey, or square dancing, or gym programs. It was pointed out by Mrs. Ruby Jones that the churches looked after such programs for their own members and anything else was unnecessary and wouldn't be supported. Both Walter Service and Charlie Ronson glared at this, the latter muttering, "They don't do much of a job."

This provided Barnes with the only lead he could get for the second meeting, at which he proposed that the council sponsor a leaders' training program that would help the various churches and clubs do better whatever they were doing in the way of recreation. This would not compete with the churches but would help them. The proposal was discussed at great length and in considerable detail. It was soon apparent that everyone agreed that this would be a useful thing to do, although it was obvious that a number of persons, such as Howard Kitchen, Charles Maxwell from Kiwanis, Charles Ronson, Bus Hawes, Samuel Cohen, and a few others, were merely going along with the idea without any enthusiasm. A leaders' course was agreed upon, and each member was asked to clear it informally in the groups to which he belonged.

The third meeting was, Barnes realized, "the payoff." Only half of the council members attended; not all had discussed the idea with others; and while they would continue on the leaders' training program (to which they were now committed), they would do so without conviction.

In the ensuing months, the leaders' program was planned, organized, and conducted. It was a success. Over 100 leaders from various clubs and churches attended three all-day Saturday sessions, they enjoyed it, learned a lot, and the *Listener* publicized it well. The council which had raised the money and promoted it found considerable satisfaction in this success, but Barnes felt they had learned less from this project than they should have. The council meeting had never, after the first two meetings, had more than half the members present. Some members like Professor Johnson had never come a second time, but the group who came had worked faithfully at the task although Barnes felt each had to force himself somewhat. There was not the spontaneity and enthusiasm he had expected. None the less, it was a start. Now if they could only get hold of a real project, they might make progress. Barnes had been so engrossed in this present project that he failed to realize that fate had taken a hand and was to sweep his ideas into the background.

Early in the fall, a local boy who had made good in England was invited to come to Fall Convocation to receive an honorary degree at the university. He had come to Elmsville for three days prior to Convocation "to visit around." Evidently he was disillusioned, for his Convocation address dealt with the responsibility of the university to stimulate and influence the larger community in which it existed. More directly, he had referred to Elmsville as "smug, complacent, apathetic," "decayed and dying" and "unaffected by the trends of modern life and indifferent to its responsibilities and opportunities." This address had been fully reported in the *Listener* although not commented upon editorially. It was evident, however, that it had hurt many people; the result, however, was not self-examination but bitter criticism of the speaker as one who "went away and got big ideas."

Another shock in the same vein came later in the fall when a world-renowned figure stopped off in Elmsville to visit the grave of a poet, some 50 years dead, who had lived and written his best work in Elmsville. In an interview published in the *Listener,* the celebrity had been openly critical of folks in Elmsville who had left the grave of this great poet unattended and almost unmarked. "What kind of people live here anyway?" he was reported to have asked. "Have they no sensitivity or pride?" This also was a blow which was to be part of a cumulative wallop.

Shortly after New Year's the Baptist minister, perhaps encouraged by the reactions he felt to the two above incidents, let loose with a blistering sermon on alcoholism and sexual immorality in Elmsville. He told in dramatic fashion of one young man who "passed out" and was found in the gutter of one of the main streets, of young girls

who became pregnant, of drinking at dances and in parked auto-
mobiles. This sermon was considered by people in Elmsville to be
"in very bad taste" and the minister had an extremely difficult time
with his Board of Elders. But the sermon was not without its effect,
which whispered comments at service clubs and ladies' groups indicated. Elmsville people were slightly disturbed.

The climax of this series of events was twofold and both incidents
happened on the same night. Jack Fraser, the youngest member of
the Rotary Club and a man highly respected in the Anglican Church,
a lawyer of influence and wealth, the husband of a prominent woman
and the father of a teen-aged girl, suddenly left town with Mrs. Jane
Murrow, the wife of a man prominent in the Roman Catholic
Church. No word of this was published in the *Listener*, but before
three days were past everyone in town seemed to know about it,
and its meaning and implications were widely discussed. This, perhaps more than any event, shook the people of Elmsville.

The second event, which was featured in the front page of the
Listener, was a fight which broke out at a local basketball game during which the referee was badly beaten up and one of the local
players was so seriously hurt that for two weeks it was feared he
would lose the sight of one eye. In all, four people were confined
to the hospital as a result of the fight, and many others were bruised
or had their clothes torn or damaged. On this episode, the *Listener*
ran one of its rare front-page editorials in which it condemned the
behavior of people in Elmsville, concluding with: "We had hoped
that the new Community Council organized last fall would begin
to change the unfortunate, but apparently all too accurate, reputation Elmsville has achieved. To this date, we see few signs of
progress in this direction."

The day this article appeared, Barnes' phone rang constantly. At
the end of the day, he realized that every member of the council
with the exception of Cohen and Roberts had called him. The burden of all the conversations was, "We've got to do something before
this town falls apart." Judge Lawson called to ask him to his home
that evening. When he arrived, Barnes found not only Lawson but

Howard Kitchen and Charles Maxwell as well. It was apparent that
they were deeply concerned and were ready for action, and their
plan was soon revealed. Kitchen took the lead when he said, "You
did a job on the playgrounds for us, and we figure you can do the
same thing in the city. Now we're prepared to pay. You get the
assistants you require and go to work. But do it well. We want this
to be a decent town, and by God, we'll do it if we have to bring in
an opera company."

The discussion was long and heated but it is to Barnes' credit that
he carried the day. Basically he argued that no outside persons were
going to change the city. The people themselves had to change, they
had to want to improve the city, and now that they recognized what
must be done, they could do it. "Give the council another chance,"
he pleaded. With some reluctance this was agreed but Kitchen's
final word was, "If they don't produce in a month, watch out."

The next meeting did, indeed, mark a new era in the council's
history. After six months of indifferent attendance and spasmodic
effort, all the members were present and, perhaps more important,
were determined to develop a program that would "make a difference" in the community. Whereas the early meetings had been
marked by a harmony which Barnes now realized was only super-
ficial, feelings were bared at this April meeting. All were convinced
that something was wrong in Elmsville and they were determined
to right it. But the diagnosis of what was wrong differed with various
members. While not openly stated, it was implied by Charles Maxwell that the "underprivileged" were at the root of the trouble, Mrs.
Jackson referred to "cocktail parties" with some scorn, Mrs. Purdy to
"drunken riff-raff," and Bus Hawes muttered something about
"people who live in glass houses." Howard Kitchen grew red in the
face and looked as if he would again put "a plague on all your
houses," and Judge Lawson rapped the table and said, "Now! Now!"

At this point, Barnes stepped in. He himself was stirred by the evidence of feeling and it was only with great restraint that he was able
to control his own impulse to "get in the fight" on one side or the
other. He realized that this would not help the work of the council

but he was determined to be more frank than he had been at any time. When he got the floor, he said as calmly and as deliberately as possible: "I think we all feel bad about some of the things that have happened in this town. I believe we recognize that we are the ones who have to take the lead in improving the situation. It won't be the Kiwanis Club or the Honta Club or the Catholic Church that will do it—it will be all of us working together. The council is made up of the leaders of these groups and if we can't work together, other people in these groups won't either. We have to show the way or I will predict with considerable assurance that the situation in Elmsville will get worse.

"Now, if you don't mind, I'd like to say what I think is wrong with Elmsville. I've been here long enough so that you know what I say is not criticism but an attempt to get us to look at the problem we have to tackle. As I see it, there has developed here almost a tradition, an attitude that people's responsibility ends with their own families, or certainly does not extend beyond their own neighbors or their own little group. Not many care about the community as a whole. You can see this attiude in the way the children treat public property, the way adults look at city government, the way people support the city ball team, the way people "don't give a damn" about community recreation, library facilities, or what not. It is this attitude which I think is wrong. And if it isn't changed, it will get worse. Kids will grow up as irresponsible brats and not as responsible citizens. And we're not going to change this attitude by bringing in leaders to educate our children. Kids get their attitudes and beliefs from the homes and neighbors more than from leaders. We had a good program at the playground but the effects of that will disappear overnight if we don't change the attitude of adults about this community."

Barnes could see as he was speaking that heads were nodding in assent. He felt he was getting the meeting focused, and he continued; "The difficult question is, what do we do? How do we change such a difficult thing as an attitude? I know only one thing, that is, that it won't happen overnight. But it can be done and we can do it gradually. How? By beginning to encourage the whole community to work on practical problems in the community. What those problems are I don't think is important as long as people in the community feel they are problems. It may be garbage collection, it may be a new library, it may be a program for the kids, it may be a Youth Center, or any one of 50 things. What is important is that all of us—and by all, I mean as many as possible of the people in the groups or sections of the city which we represent—work together to get these things. It's learning to accept responsibility, to work together, to improve our community. Not someone else doing something for us, but we ourselves feeling we are responsible and *accepting* this responsibility."

Barnes, in spite of himself, had allowed his emotions to flow into the latter part of this statement which he delivered with great force and conviction. When he finished, there was a pause and then spontaneous applause! Judge Lawson's voice when he spoke next wavered with emotion. While Barnes had not been very specific, Lawson said, "I believe we all know what we have to do." Heads nodded. The meeting got down to work.

Late into the night the council struggled with the development of its program. There were frequent disagreements but these were worked through and gradually the following program was formulated:

1. A program for children which would provide for sports and handicrafts, which would stress sportsmanship and responsibility, and which would have the approval and support of the churches. A committee of Charles Ronson as chairman, Bus Hawes, and Mrs. Jones was appointed to bring in detailed plans.

2. A youth or teen-age program which would provide sports, trips, and dances and would encourage youth to participate in the organization and operation of these activities. A committee of Mrs. Purdy as chairman, Jim Rivers, and Ernest Van DeMan, was appointed to work further in this area.

3. The organization of a Parent-Teachers Association which would attempt to develop a consistent approach with school children in

both home and school. Mrs. Jackson and Charles Maxwell were appointed to explore this possibility.

4. The development of certain community projects, specifically a community concert series and a public library, the latter with sections for both youth and children. A committee of Howard Kitchen as chairman, Professor Burr Johnson, and Mr. Cohen was appointed to carry these matters further.

As to procedure, it was decided that the committee should go to work immediately. Mr. Barnes was to make arrangements for the council in two weeks to travel as a group and spend a whole day in Maples, a city of comparable size some 150 miles away that had a considerable reputation for its progressive community. The committees would then work on final plans to bring before the council three weeks hence. Mr. Barnes suggested that before putting the program into operation the council should get a mandate from the people, and it was decided to hold a public meeting to be announced immediately and held one month from the present meeting.

The committees worked hard and enthusiastically. The trip to Maples proved to be a great stimulant, and the contrast in the character of life in the two communities was sufficiently striking to impress all council members. When the various committees reported, there were not only practical plans but ways of implementing these plans. For example, the Kiwanis Club had been consulted and were prepared to put up the money to support the children's program, the Lions and Kinsmen would provide the money for the youth program, and the Rotary Club wound underwrite the community concert series. Schoolteachers had met in various groups with Mrs. Jackson and Mr. Maxwell, and far from resisting the idea of a P.T.A., they were most anxious to help organize one. Mr. Kitchen had taken several city council members aside, and he felt a substational city grant could be secured to make a start on the library. Almost all the people whom the members of the council had met and talked with offered to help, and it was obvious that the problem now was to move efficiently and in such a way as to build good will and broad solid support.

It was agreed that the next steps for the council were: (1) to build up attendance at the public meeting (each member pledged an active campaign among his colleagues); (2) to recommend that the present council members together with 12 others carefully chosen from approximately the same groups as Barnes had identified and including the Roman Catholic priest and the Baptist minister, serve as council members for the next year and appoint their own officers; (3) to present for approval a plan in each of the program areas identified by the council; (4) to recommend the general principle that while some programs might require financial support from one of the service clubs, every program sponsored by the council should seek to pay its own way as far as possible (in other words, as Walter Service said, "No charity programs"); and (5) to ask Mr. Barnes to work out with Judge Lawson details and arrangements of the public meeting, including the securing of the high school band. The public meeting was to be held, it was decided, in the university gym, as the council felt no hall in town could hold the crowd they expected.

And indeed, this was true. Over 2000 citizens of Elmsville crowded the gym to launch the council formally. It was an enthusiastic meeting but not a passive one. Mr. Barnes had persuaded Judge Lawson, much against the latter's will, ("Damn it, Barnes, you get me involved in the worst messes!") to use buzz sessions for discussion. These were organized by Barnes and involved dividing the huge meeting into groups of 12 or 15 persons for a seven-minute discussion of each committee report. Groups reported briefly, e.g., "We're for it 100%," "It's good, but don't forget the kids under five," "Don't forget the need for leaders," etc. Longer comments were written out by a secretary in each group. Not all groups reported each time but most groups during the evening had a chance to say something. And the sample chosen for each report gave "a sense of the meeting." Certainly the audience enjoyed it and even Judge Lawson admitted, "It's really something. I never thought it would work."

The result of the evening was enthusiastic approval of the plans of the council, its membership, and its statement of objectives. There was little question that if the 2000 present were at all representative, the council and its new program was fully endorsed by the citizens of Elmsville.

The months which followed were difficult ones for Barnes. As secretary of the council, he felt an obligation to keep each committee moving smoothly, to help pick up and handle little details which the committees in their enthusiasm overlooked, and to keep stressing the fact that there should be no short-cutting of the fundamental objective of learning to work together, i.e., minority opinion should not be ignored or by-passed, integration and consensus should be sought. Most members joked and teased Barnes about this, but his counsel apparently had some effect, for there was a noticeable effort on the part of all to make the meetings congenial affairs, where "everyone had his say," but where agreement was important, if not essential, before action.

There were other difficulties which would make another record, but most were overcome, and within two years substantial progress had been made in each of the items in the council's program. Two new staff members had been added, the programs for children were well developed in coöperation with both church and school, a new library was being constructed, a series of five concerts had been oversubscribed, the P.T.A. was an active and effective group. The first annual meeting had endorsed the work of the council and had suggested new projects. Among the new members elected to the council was Richard Wetmore, and at the following meeting he was elected to succeed Judge Lawson as president of the council. Barnes chuckled to himself as he saw these men shake hands after each had made a little speech praising the other. Perhaps, he thought, this is symbolic of what has really happened in this town. Hatchets have been buried, people are thinking positively rather than negatively, they're working together for the same goals, the whole town is moving forward together.

At the end of the third year, Mr. Barnes left Elmsville to take another position. At a banquet in his honor, Barnes was given, when he was less expectant than when he arrived, the key to the city.

Wetmore, the presiding officer, said, "This is not simply the key to the city, it's the key to our hearts, and John Barnes has had this key, even though we didn't know it, for the past three years. The greatest thing he's done in Elmsville has been to help us understand and appreciate one another. It's a wonderful thing that's happened here, and Barnes is more responsible than anyone."

Judge Lawson, who gave the formal speech, speculated, "I am only just beginning to understand this fellow, and he is leaving before I really have hold of it. What has he done here? A fine job that first year with children, we all agree. But that was just shock treatment to show us what could be done. It wasn't his real work. His primary work was with adults. But again, ask what he did with adults? We feel that *we* ourselves have got the library, that *we* run the P.T.A., that *we* started and still operate the community concert series, that *committees* run the children and youth programs, that *we* got garbage collection in this city, that *we* changed the traffic regulations, and so on. Barnes didn't do these things; *we* did. And here is the secret, I believe, of his work and of his effectiveness here. He was able to get *us* to be aware of what was going on, he got *us* interested, he got *us* doing things. And now that he is going, the greatest tribute to his work is that he can go knowing that we realize our responsibilities and that we'll carry on."

Questions for Discussion

1. Which approach to community work does Barnes use? Illustrate. Are there inconsistencies in his philosophy and method? If so, illustrate.

2. What would you say were the important contributing factors in the success of Barnes' work in Elmsville? What particular discipline, insight, and skill did he bring to the job? What helpful personality characteristics?

3. What do you think of Barnes' leadership on the playground job? Should he have taken the initiative as he did? What are the dangers for a worker in the community becoming a specialist as he did in this situation?

Centertown[*]

I. THE SOCIETY FOR DEMOCRACY
HOLDS A MEETING

THE SOCIETY AND CENTERTOWN

ABOUT A year ago, a small group of social and political liberals in Centertown formed an organization. They named it "The Society for Democracy." [†] Centertown is a center for trading and small industry with a population of about 50,000. There are many ways in which statisticians might slice this population and its social and economic life in order to represent it in graphs and tables. And it may be that members of the Society should know more of these ways than they do. But these are some of the perceptions they do have of Centertown. At any rate these were the things the President of the Society, Mr. Briggs, told Professor Lenford from the State University on a Tuesday afternoon just before Lenford was to visit a meeting of the Society that evening.

The industries now in Centertown came in during the war years. The men and women who came to work in these industries brought

[*] Kenneth D. Benne, Leland P. Bradford, and Ronald Lippitt, *Group Dynamics and Social Action*, Anti-Defamation League of B'Nai B'Rith, 1950, pp. 7–56. Reprinted by permission of the publisher.

[†] Authors' Note: We will call it "the Society" from here on.

with them C.I.O. unions and a sprinkling of Negro families. The leaders of the old-line A.F. of L. craft unions and the Railway Brotherhoods, which have been established for many years, have little or nothing to do with the new union leadership. There are many clubs and organizations in the city—over two hundred of them—but most of these avoid even the discussion of controversial issues, not to mention active campaigns to inform or to shape public opinion with respect to these. There are individual teachers in the school system and individual members in the social agencies who very much want to find and use ways of building an enlightened and active public opinion with respect to current issues and problems. In fact, about half of the membership of the Society is drawn from these two sources. In general, however, the schools and the social agencies avoid publicity which might antagonize several strong and very vocal "patriotic" organizations which thrive in Centertown.

Centertown people are predominantly Protestant in their religious afficiations—5% of the population are Jewish and 20% Roman Catholic. There is some latent hostility and suspicion toward each other among religious groups, but church leadership maintains a public front of friendly tolerance and coöperation, with joint statements of mutual goodwill on ceremonial occasions. The Society membership includes two Protestant ministers and a Rabbi. So far, one Catholic—a layman—has joined.

Centertown has one daily newspaper which gives most of its editorial space to nationally syndicated columnists with a conservative slant on current affairs. One of its editorial writers, however, is of a liberal cast of mind and is a member of the Society.

It is the apathy of Centertown toward the issues of the day, local, national and international, which mainly concerns the Society. In fact, it was a deep sense of the dangers in this apathy which brought the original membership together. Mr. Briggs recalled to Professor Lenford the incident which actually had led to the formation of the Society. Fifteen months ago, Mr. Fisher, a social studies teacher in the senior high school, had been attacked by an influential "patriotic" organization in the community for teaching a factual unit on the history of the Soviet Union in his classes. Sermons were preached in several churches questioning the right of the schools to impose Russian ideas upon the young people of the community. A number of angry letters protesting such teaching appeared in the public letter column of the newspaper. A petition to the Board of Education requesting the dismissal of the teacher was circulated.

It was at this point that Mr. Briggs and a number of other liberals circulated a counter-petition asking that the Board of Education resist unreasonable pressures to dismiss a good teacher and that a public meeting to discuss freedom of teaching be held. Many people approached by this group said they were sympathetic with Mr. Fisher but they didn't see how they could afford to sign any petition. Most people said they didn't know enough about the issue to make a judgment either way. Only about seventy-five names were obtained. When the meeting on freedom of teaching was held in the high school auditorium, one hundred fifty people came. Hecklers from several organizations interfered with the meeting and a strongly-worded resolution to the Board of Education affirming freedom of teaching was voted down by a small majority. Mr. Fisher was dismissed. About thirty liberals who had helped with this unsuccessful campaign decided to form an organization to work against public apathy toward current issues and to counter reactionary movements in Centertown. It was in this way that the Society was born.

During its year of life the Society has circulated petitions to Centertown's representatives in Congress and in the state legislature on four or five legislative issues. They have encouraged the sending of letters and wires on these same issues. They have written letters to the editor of the local newspaper urging the liberal viewpoint on various questions. And they have sponsored one public meeting which they considered quite successful—a forum on the report of the President's Committee on Civil Rights. The Society's membership numbers about thirty—some have dropped out and others have come in since its organization. About twenty members come to most monthly meetings.

Mr. Briggs also told Professor Lenford how he happened to be invited to tonight's meeting. One member Mr. Stokes, the high school supervisor knew that Professor Lenford was to be in town working with the Curriculum Council of the public schools. Mr. Stokes had told the Society's Executive Committee that Professor Lenford was a student of "group dynamics" and of methods by which organizations might be made to work more effectively. Mr. Briggs told Professor Lenford that the Executive Committee hoped that, if he had a chance to observe one of their meetings, he might be able to make some suggestions on improving the program of the Society. Mr. Briggs said that there had been some informal talk in the Society about how their program might be improved but he for his part thought they had been doing about as well as could be expected. Mr. Briggs cordially accepted Professor Lenford's suggestion that two graduate students who had come with him to work in the schools also attend the meeting.

Readers are invited to join Professor Lenford and his graduate students in observing this meeting of the Society and to help them afterward in analyzing what happened and in formulating tentative suggestions concerning the improvement of the Society. Professor Lenford learned one other fact about tonight's meeting which reader-observers should also know.

Recently there has been increasing talk in Centertown about redistricting elementary school units. Those who favor redistricting probably do so for a variety of reasons. The completion of a federal housing project within the last year in an upper middle-class neighborhood seems, however, to have highlighted one of these motives. For this project brought Negro children along with sizable numbers of factory workers' children, into the elementary school of this neighborhood for the first time. There were some complaints to the Board of Education from the old residents at first but these seemed to have died down. Now, in the last month, a Citizens' Committee for Better Schools has been formed and is pressing for a definite program of redistricting. Several public meetings have been held. Petitions are being circulated backing the program. As the Executive Committee of the Society studied this proposed program, it became apparent that the program would take the housing project area out of its present district and join it, rather awkwardly, into a new school district with an area outside the city limits but within the city school jurisdiction, an area with a considerable number of Negro and white factory workers' families. The program as outlined includes a fine new school building for this new district. Petitions and publicity have made much of this and other school building needs. The Executive Committee of the Society concluded, after its study of the publicity of the Citizens' Committee for Better Schools, that the intent (as well as the effect) of this redistricting program is to accomplish some measure of segregation along race and class lines in the public schools of Centertown. The meeting of the Society tonight has been called to discuss what to do about the situation and more particularly to plan counter moves.

THE MEETING

Twenty-five came to the meeting. Mr. Briggs called the meeting to order and asked Mr. Stokes to introduce the Society's guests, Professor Lenford and his two associates, Harry Stewart and Jim Barnes. Then the meeting got underway.

Mr. Briggs: Friends, some of you know what your Executive Committee has decided we should discuss tonight. Those of you whom we had a chance to talk with before the meeting thought our idea was a good one. I'm sorry we didn't have a chance to discuss it with all of you. But here's the idea in a nutshell. Some folks, calling themselves the Citizens' Committee for Better Schools, are circulating petitions to the Board of Education asking them to redistrict the elementary schools in Centertown. When the proposed redistricting plan is studied carefully, it becomes apparent that its effect would be to segregate Negro children and factory workers' children in one or two schools. Whether or not this was the intention of the Citizens'

Committee, we thought this raised an issue that our Society ought to meet. And we're proposing that the Society sponsor a public meeting to air this thing and get a strong resolution opposing any redistricting move which would promote class or race segregation in our schools. What do you think about this?

Miss Foltz: (Of the Y.W.C.A.) I think that's a swell idea, Mr. Briggs. I don't think there's any argument about whether we ought to get into this thing. The only question is how. Let's start planning the meeting now.

Mr. Green: (Of the Brotherhood of Trainmen) Now wait a minute, Miss Foltz. There are only so many things we have the time and energy to do. And I think we ought to think pretty carefully whether this is the most important thing we can find to work on. I happen to live out in the neighborhood where the housing project is located. And I know some of the people who are working for this redistricting plan. They're my neighbors. I think we ought to see their side of things too. After all, whether it's right or wrong, the property value of their homes depends partly on the kind of schools they have in the neighborhood. And another thing—we claim to stand for democracy in this Society. And is it democratic to deny parents the right to decide what kinds of schools their children will go to? I think we need to discuss that kind of question before we decide.

Miss Foltz: Mr. Green, I can't understand why you fall for that kind of tommyrot. The only democratic attitude toward segregation is to oppose. People who take any other attitude are simply not democratic. And I think they ought to think very seriously about whether or not they belong in an organization like this one.

Mr. Hatfield: (Of the Centertown newspaper) Now wait a minute, Miss Foltz, it isn't as easy as you're making it. After all, the Committee for Better Schools is trying to get better school buildings for our town. Many of them are among our heaviest taxpayers. And they are willing to tax themselves heavily to get new buildings, not for their own children, but for children from the housing project and the rest of the new district. Do we want to oppose a move for better school buildings and more adequate support for schools? What is the "democratic" position to take in a situation like this? I frankly don't know.

Miss Runner: (Of the high school faculty and member of the Executive Committee) I think all of these arguments are just red herrings to get us off the track. We're a liberal club, aren't we? We're opposed to segregation, aren't we? If we aren't, I don't think we ought to pretend to be liberals. The real question is whether we want to be a liberal action group or not. Here is a community problem we can really go to town on. The Executive Committee went into it very thoroughly. But some of our members seem always to want to think and think until the chance for action is past. I for one don't like that attitude.

Mr. Briggs: Now, Miss Runner. I'm sure, if we stop and think, we will all agree that Mr. Green and Mr. Hatfield have as much right to their opinions as any one else has. Any more ideas?

Mr. Henry: (Y.M.C.A. secretary) I don't know whether I dare to say so, with Miss Runner feeling the way she does, but I'm inclined to agree with Mr. Green that we ought to take more time to think this over. I don't think too much of the arguments Mr. Hatfield suggests. We could go on record as favoring better and more school buildings and more adequate school support and still oppose segregation through redistricting. But I do have other questions which trouble me. Just what do we hope to accomplish by trying to stop this move toward redistricting which may well be in part a move toward segregation? Is our purpose to build the membership and influence of our Society in the community? Is it to educate our own members in ways of training others with respect to social action? Or are we primarily interested in accomplishing something positive with respect to inter-group relations in Centertown? I don't think we've ever clarified our aims as a Society and, if we're going to rush into action all of the time, I don't think we'll ever get our goals cleared up. And don't we need to take time to educate ourselves to do a good job on whatever we do undertake? Can I say one more thing? Most of us are paid workers in various organizations. I have to think out how the actions of this Society affect my relations to my organization and its controlling board. I won't get help on this problem from deciding impulsively to act and then thinking afterward.

Miss Runner: Of course, Mr. Henry, all of us have jobs to think about. I surely have in the school system. But if we started to think of other people's attitudes and reactions toward our action, we never would act at all. And, meanwhile, the problem is there, getting worse while we sit around and worry about ourselves.

Mr. Briggs: (interrupting) I think we have Mr. Henry's point of view—and Miss Runner's. Shouldn't we move on now to other people's ideas? After all, our time is limited.

(The discussion moved on from here with most members pointing up their remarks to support either Miss Runner's or Mr. Henry's position. Two novel elements were introduced along the way which Professor Lenford and the readers may want to analyze later. The first occurred when Dr. Gordon, a clergyman, came into the discussion)—

Dr. Gordon: I would like to make an observation which possibly might help the group. We seem to have become divided over an issue which isn't clear to me. Some of us seem to be saying that we want to act and others that we want to think. Surely these two emphases aren't as opposed as we seem to be making them out to be. I'd like for us to stop for a while to see why our group discussion got slanted this way and how we can get out of the dead-end we've run into.

Mr. Stokes: That's a good idea, isn't it? Let's look at the process of our discussion so far. Is that the idea, Dr. Gordon? (Dr. Gordon nods his agreement.)

Mr. Green: That would probably be all right if we had all of the time in the world. But we're reasonable people—at least I hope all of us are. I think the thing to do is to get back and think hard about whether the project which the Executive Committee thinks is so good is really what the Society should undertake at this time.

Miss Runner: I'm happy to be able to agree partly with Mr. Green at last. It's bad enough to want to talk and talk about what we might do, if we had all of the time in the world. But now we are asked to talk about how well we've been talking. If you'll pardon me, Mr. Stokes, that reminds me too much of our curriculum committees at school. It doesn't get us anywhere.

Mr. Briggs: There seems to be some disagreement on Dr. Gordon's suggestion. Shall we vote on it?

(Dr. Gordon's suggestion was voted down 10 to 3, with about half of the members abstaining. A little later in the discussion, Mr. Hettinger, Executive Secretary of the Council of Social Agencies, brought in a suggestion)—

Mr. Hetinger: I think part of our trouble here is that we don't have enough facts to go on. We don't really know, for example, how the people of Centertown feel about segregation for educational purposes. Couldn't we do a better job of deciding which groups to work on because they're undecided, which ones are already on our side, which ones are hopeless from our point of view, if we did some research on this question? I can't help feeling that some of our arguments are about alleged "matters of fact," where on one really knows what the facts are.

Miss Foltz: I wish I could agree with Mr. Hettinger. It would be nice to know more facts. But this is an action organization, isn't it? The truth is people always have to act without knowing all of the facts. I think we know enough now to act on, if we only have the will to act. I can't see taking time out to do research. The same old arguments will come up again after the facts are in. I wonder if we're not agreed on that much. We are an action organization, aren't we? (General nodding of agreement.)

Mr. Briggs: Yes, we seem to be agreed on that. Mr. Hettinger, I think your idea is an excellent one but apparently not for our Society. Perhaps the research division of your Council could carry out such a study.

(After a few more minutes of discussion, Miss Runner made a motion that the Society accept a campaign against the move for redistricting in the schools, insofar as its effect is racial or class segregation, as their principal annual project and that a mass meeting be planned as the principal effort in this campaign. Mr. Eckert, of the C.I.O. United Auto Workers, seconded the motion and it was passed by a vote of 16 to 5 with 4 abstaining.)

Mr. Briggs: Well, we made that decision by a clear majority, didn't we, and I'm sure we'll all be glad to go along with it. Now, in our remaining time, I suggest we get ideas out for the meeting and make a decision as to who is to carry on with detailed plans for the meeting. Mr. Green, what ideas do you have?

Mr. Green: I'm sure all of the members of this group have better ideas than I have.

Mr. Eckert: The main idea, I think, is to get people out to the meeting. Can't we talk it up in the meetings of our own organizations? And maybe Mr. Hatfield can get us some free publicity in his paper.

Mr. Hettinger: I agree with Mr. Eckert, of course, about getting people out. But doesn't it make a lot of difference what we do at the meeting? If we can get big names on the program representing various points of view, I think we'll get more people there and we'll also have a better educational experience for the people at the meeting.

Miss Foltz: Don't we have to be very careful about getting wrong points of view represented? After all, we do stand for a liberal position in this affair.

Dr. Gordon: Of course, we want our own position effectively represented at the meeting, Miss Foltz. But on this issue I'm sure we can get agreement and help from people and organizations with points of view very much different from ours on other issues. And I suppose we want all of the help we can get in making people aware of what this move may mean to Centertown, and more widely too, and in working toward more constructive goals in the same area. I've been wondering if the meeting shouldn't have constructive goals as well as a protest character; let's say, better school facilities for all of our children and qualified Negro teachers on the faculties of various schools, as well as spelling out the dangers of slipping back toward segregated schools under the guise of redistricting.

Miss Runner: I agree with you, Dr. Gordon, in principle, but we all know that people respond more to the dramatic than to hard constructive thinking. And protest is dramatic. You really can't get constructive thinking done in a very large meeting, can you?

Mr. Stokes: Aren't both Miss Runner and Dr. Gordon partly right? Couldn't we get people thinking in their various clubs and organizations ahead of the meeting about the dangers of segregation through redistricting and about constructive moves to reduce this danger? Then we could ask these organizations to send representatives to the meeting to try to put the recommendations and ideas of various organizations into a common set of goals to work for.

Miss Foltz: I think that's too complicated, Mr. Stokes. We don't have time to work out all of that before the meeting. And, besides, how do we know what ideas these different organizations are going to come out with if they start thinking without help? Our meeting might come out with some ideas that we couldn't go along with at all. I really think it would be safer to stick to the idea of our own mass meeting which we've already voted for.

Mr. Briggs: All of these ideas should prove very helpful to the program committee which I'm sure we'll need in order to make detailed plans for the meeting. How shall we get that committee? Shall I appoint it? (General agreement.) All right, Mr. Green, Miss Runner, Mr. Henry, and Miss Foltz, will you serve on the committee? And Dr. Gordon, will you serve as chairman? If you'll keep us posted as plans shape up, I'm sure we'll all be glad to help. Meeting adjourned.

Mr. Briggs, Dr. Gordon and Mr. Stokes came to Professor Lenford immediately after adjournment and urged that he write out his suggestions for the improvement of the Society and its meetings and send them to Mr. Briggs. Professor Lenford agreed to do this and to send another copy to Dr. Gordon as chairman of the committee to plan the campaign.

(Before Professor Lenford left the meeting room, Miss Runner came over to him and commented in a low voice—"Professor Lenford, you've seen tonight what happens every time. About five people really don't want to act at all. You saw when the vote was taken that they don't really think like the rest of us do. Sometimes I think we'd be a lot better off if they weren't in the Society at all. And I didn't really mean our curriculum meetings are so bad. I just had to put Mr. Stokes in his place. He seemed to be playing along with the stalling five at times tonight."

In the hall a little later, Mr. Green said half jokingly to Professor Lenford, "Well, Professor, if you can give us ideas as to how to control flighty, aggressive females in a meeting, you'll help us out a lot.")

II. PROFESSOR LENFORD AND HIS STUDENTS DIAGNOSE THE MEETING

The next morning Professor Lenford and the graduate students who attended the meeting met at his office to discuss the meeting and to formulate suggestions to the Society.

Professor Lenford: I'm glad you're willing to help me analyze this meeting which we looked at together. We threshed over our general feelings about the meeting driving home last night. I believe you asked me then to suggest a framework for our more systematic analysis this morning. I would like to suggest two ways of analyzing what we saw. *First,* how productively did the group function as a group? We will probably want to look at both the leader and member functions before we're through. *Second,* how effectively was the group thinking concerning ways by which they might produce changes in their wider social environment in Centertown? For example, what changes do they want to make in what people and groups of Centertown through the meeting they are planning? And how well do you think the plans for the meeting to date will accomplish these changes? Does this seem a satisfactory way to get at our problem?

Jim: It sounds good to me.

Harry: Let's try it that way.

Jim: I found myself sympathizing deeply with this group of liberals who are really trying to get the attention of an apathetic and fearful public focused on important social problems and issues. But I found myself very bothered about the size of the job they have undertaken and their difficulties in finding united ways of defining required steps in doing the job and in organizing themselves to carry these steps out.

Harry: I think we all sympathize with the Society and recognize the importance of the kind of thing its members are trying to do, Jim. And isn't our job now to analyze their ways of working and thinking as a help to the Society in training itself to be more productive and efficient as an organization?

Professor Lenford: I'll buy that way of looking at our job. (Jim agrees.) Isn't it very important that we approach our diagnosis as objectively as possible, not to praise or blame the group or some part of it, but to understand why the group and its parts behaved as they did?

Harry: I'd like to start with the leader's role. I didn't think it was very effective in terms of what the group needed last night. He did let a lot of people talk. But I was waiting for him to help the group find some common problems to talk to *as a group.* He didn't. He just kept getting ideas out with little or no relation to any group goal or to the building of such a goal. He took a vote on issues, sometimes before they were very clear. He didn't try to clarify these and help the group reach some sort of consensus as the best solution.

Professor Lenford: I think I agree with you, Harry, about the leadership. It's probably not only the leader, though. I'm inclined to think that the Society has never formulated any very clear common goals or any very conscious ways of working as a group. And, in the meeting last night, most of the thinking seemed to be faction-centered or individual-centered thinking rather than group-centered.

Jim: You're probably right, Professor Lenford. But does the responsibility for getting a more common direction in the group deliberation belong entirely to Mr. Briggs?

Harry: I don't think it does. Members in a mature group share many of the functions of leadership. Did you notice that a few of the members were trying to perform leadership roles on functions which the group needed in their thinking together? For example, I noticed Dr. Gordon trying to suggest to the group that they weren't discussing the real issues that divided them, that they had built up a straw man issue under emotional stress. He tried to get on to one of these "real" issues. Wasn't he playing something of a clarifier role?

Professor Lenford: I think he was trying to supply one of the roles that the group needed, though they didn't see it the way he did. And Mr. Stokes tried also when he suggested that Miss Runner's and Dr. Gordon's ideas and values could both be served. He was doing a job which groups require and which leaders often do perform in harmonizing two points of view and suggesting a synthesis.

Jim: Are you saying that improving this group would require training members as well as the leader in what productive group functioning requires? That's a new idea to me.

Professor Lenford: But it is a logical one, isn't it, Jim? A productive mechanism as complicated as a group certainly requires insight by all members into how it works and skill in making it work well, if the group is really going to produce efficiently at all. Until all group members see the group's need for certain kinds of help from different group members, the group won't improve much in producing common solutions, except by accident, will it?

Jim: Then wasn't Dr. Gordon's and Mr. Stokes' idea of having the group stop and examine its processes and decide why it had got into an unproductive jam a good one from this point of view?

Harry: I guess it was a good idea but I don't see how Mr. Briggs could have got the group to accept it at the time. There was a lot of resistance to it, wasn't there?

Professor Lenford: I suppose there are many reasons for the resistance. I can't answer precisely for this group. But most groups show some resistance to accepting self-observation and self-evaluation. And there seem to be several reasons why. One is surely that most people don't see *groups* or think in terms of *group* factors or forces. They see and think in terms of a collection of individuals. As a result, the suggestion of an analysis of their *group* processes seems like much ado about nothing to them. They are more likely to attribute group inefficiency to personal factors in some members, e.g., members will blame each other as reasons for the group's unproductiveness, or to impersonal factors in the environment, (e.g., we just don't have time enough to do a good job), even where the difficulties are at least partly in group and member factors and forces. Then too, some of the resistance to accepting a new way of working comes from the fact that it actually demands some changes in member behavior. It is not too different from "therapeutic" situations, where the "patient," in this case the group, tends to resist accepting interpretation of its own needs and difficulties where such interpretation challenges accustomed patterns of adjustment. This resistance is often strongest toward observation and probing of certain of the group's sorest spots, which might reveal some of the needed readjustments in member and group behavior.

Harry: I wonder if part of the resistance doesn't come from the fact that they just didn't want to waste time with discussion of procedures when so much content remained to be discussed. I mean that's the way it looked to them. And, until they see some benefit from time spent in self-evaluation of procedures, until they see that they could work more efficiently as a result of it, it just isn't "reasonable" for them to spend time that way, is it?

Jim: I think you're right, Harry, in this sense. Just telling the group that self-evaluation would be a good thing to do isn't going to do the job. They have to be helped to see for themselves that they need to study themselves as a group and change practices and procedures which interfere with their productivity, if they are going to improve. And that's not an easy hurdle to get over, is it? Is that what you meant?

Harry: Yes, I guess that follows all right from what I said. And it just occurred to me that they won't see much need for improving unless they see that they are not using their human resources nearly up to potential capacity. They're going to have to be helped to see how productive and mutually satisfactory group thinking can be before they raise their sights for themselves very much, won't they?

Professor Lenford: We seem to be getting at some of the very real difficulties involved in anyone's trying to help a group improve itself. And we'll have to face these difficulties ourselves in deciding what suggestions we should make to the Society. I wonder if we might not sort out some of these as we go along. We will probably find some observations about the Society's procedures which we believe the Society is now ready to accept and about which they might make some constructive decisions. Other observations of ours might do more harm than good. If we reported them at this time they would increase resistance in the Society to self-examination and to change in inefficient procedures. Let's see what ought to be reported to the Society from what we've already discussed.

Jim: I think we ought to report our sympathy with the effort they are making and our recognition of the very real difficulties an organization like theirs faces.

Harry: I wonder too if we shouldn't mention that we are not praising or blaming people in what we say but trying to understand objectively why the meeting probably went as it did. I think we should also stress that our ideas are only hypotheses for them to think about and that we don't have data enough to prove or disprove any of them.

Professor Lenford: Couldn't we mention further that the meeting seemed to have genuine difficulty in reaching common agreements on what the Society's job was and how it should go about it? We could also mention some of the kinds of contributions and procedures which tended to keep the group divided into factions. We might note some of the functions needed to get issues clear and encourage the building of a common view. We could note that these latter functions tended to be missing when needed most or disregarded when some members tried to supply them. And we might mention that sensitivity on the part of leader and members to kinds of contributions needed at different times and skill in supplying these is often an important factor in making groups more productive and efficient in their thinking and planning. Does that seem about right so far? (Harry and Jim agree.)

Now I wonder if we shouldn't get back to the way the Society actually functioned as we saw them working last night. I wonder if you were as much impressed as I was by the lack of confidence in the group that they could work through differences among various members and sub-groups of members to any genuinely common plan or program. The implicit tactic on both sides seemed to be to get group action by either demobilizing or eliminating the opposition.

Jim: Say that's right, isn't it? Miss Foltz tried to shove Mr. Green into line, didn't she, by implying he really wasn't a "liberal" and didn't really belong in the Society.

Harry: And Miss Runner took cracks at Mr. Stokes' curriculum meetings to silence him.

Professor Lenford: But this same tactic wasn't limited to Miss Foltz and Miss Runner, was it? Mr. Green questioned the "democracy" of Miss Foltz's position, you'll remember. And Mr. Henry implied that the opposition was "irresponsible" in deciding before thinking. I saw it as part of the general atmosphere of the meeting, probably reflecting a group standard concerning deliberation which has become established in the Society. And I wonder also if this same attitude toward "the opposition" didn't characterize the Society's thinking about the "general public" of Centertown too. But we'll come back to that later.

Jim: Of course, Mr. Stokes and Dr. Gordon did try to get more of a spirit of discussion instead of debate into the meeting at times, to change this group standard, I suppose you'd say. We agreed on that already.

Harry: I wonder how much of this we should report to the Society. I feel personally we can be pretty direct about this. Could we point to the tendency in the group to get a group goal and group efficiency by each side to a controversy's trying to eliminate the opposition from the discussion or even, by implication, from the Society. This tendency of groups to get unity by "purging" the opposition, if carried to an extreme, would reduce the group to one individual. And, if that individual was ambivalent, he would have to eliminate part of himself. I think they could take this, don't you?

Jim: I think we could interpret rather directly here, if we could point out objectively that this "strategy" of meeting opposition by beating it down came from both "sides" in the meeting last night. I think the dangerous effect of this strategy in reducing the Society's strength, which is already too small, would impress them. (Prof. Lenford agrees.)

Harry: To get back to the meeting. If the Society can't think and act in terms of reaching a consensus in their own group, how can they ever succeed in building consensus in Centertown at large? You know, I wonder how much they were really thinking in terms of what they could accomplish in Centertown in improving intergroup relations. Most of the time they were trying to win points against each other, weren't they? Just how carefully did they think about what changes they are in a position to make, have the power to accomplish, in the wider community? And did they really know what forces in the community would support them and which would oppose them? I wonder if different factions weren't making different assumptions about these things too. Maybe that's one reason they didn't get together more.

Professor Lenford: Aren't there really two points there, Harry? And I suspect they're both important. Couldn't the first point be stated something like this? Group thinking won't be realistic—it will fly off at tangents—it will be directed toward different goals—it will break down into faction thinking and name calling—unless the group assesses its *power field* pretty thoroughly and agrees on the assessment. As you put it, a group needs to think through just what it has power to do in its present situation. And I don't think the Society did a very good job of doing that in planning its program last night.

Jim: And maybe that's why some members wanted to make big gestures while others seemed to feel they should do little or nothing. But shouldn't a group not only study its power field but also try to increase it? Maybe that's where more of its thinking should have gone last night. How can we strengthen our position in the community so we can do more to improve intergroup relations there? I think that could be reported, don't you? I mean the apparent differences among members with respect to what the Society had the power to accomplish now in Centertown and the need to get a common view here, so that all members might agree on steps needed to increase the influence of the Society beyond its present limits. (The three agree.)

Harry: What's the other point, Professor Lenford?

Professor Lenford: You've already said it, Harry. You doubted whether the Society really recognized its lack of needed information at certain important points. Did the members really know what Centertown people—different groups of them or people in general— feel about intergroup relations? I don't think they did. For example, I wonder if they tried to understand the motivation of the "Committee for Better Schools." Or did they stereotype it as "the opposition"? Mr. Green could have been a resource person here, I suppose. I'm afraid they don't understand the human forces they are trying to change very well.

Jim: And yet they rejected Mr. Hettinger's suggestion that they find out more relevant facts of this sort, didn't they? I wonder why.

Harry: Wasn't that related to the factional type of thinking in the Society which we mentioned earlier? Mr. Hettinger's suggestion of fact-gathering looked like a delaying tactic to Miss Foltz and Miss Runner and their followers and so like just another aid to "the enemy." And Mr. Green and Mr. Hatfield had been pretty well silenced by that time so they didn't take it up as a help to their side. I don't mean that Mr. Hettinger meant it as a delaying tactic but those who were trying to block the proposed action might have used his suggestion that way, if they hadn't already given up in actively advancing their point of view.

Jim: I agree. And I seem now to see another angle to this failure to recognize their need for information which I didn't see earlier. Wasn't there a tendency for some members to use their ideology, their beliefs about what ought to be, as a substitute for the facts they needed in planning ways to advance their beliefs effectively in Centertown? Miss Foltz, for example, used the idea that the "will to act" in liberal causes was the main thing, that facts wouldn't make much difference in the program after they were collected anyway. And most of the members seemed to agree. Doesn't that show that they may have thought that holding "the right ideology" made facts rather unnecessary? (Harry and Professor Lenford nod agreement.)

Professor Lenford: Those observations help us in analyzing this particular disease of the Society, I think. And yet we must not in any sense blame them for not seeing that research can be done to get facts needed for improving the strategy of a program of action or in answering questions about which of several lines of strategy best promises to be successful. So many "surveys" have been made with no thought of a program of action in mind or as no part of any effort to map more successful strategies for action. And "the facts" which such surveys reveal very often don't mean much in terms of action-thinking, do they? The Society will have to see for themselves that research can help an action program to be more successful before they feel the need for doing any research for themselves. But, if we agree that the Society needs to become more "research-minded" for its own good and for the good of Centertown, that sets an important self-training job for the Society, doesn't it? Shouldn't we point out in our report some of the lacks of information that seemed to be present in the meeting, suggest that surveys often are used as delaying tactics and that they often don't help action-planning, but also suggest the experiences some groups have had in gearing survey research directly to getting the facts which they needed for intelligent action?

Harry: Couldn't we point out also that the Society might plan and carry out its own research, with the help of technical experts, and so keep the research geared to its own action concerns? (The others nod agreement.)

Professor Lenford: Another line of thinking about the Society's meeting may help us in assessing further their needs as an action group. I'm thinking of the way in which the committee named to plan the public meeting was formed. One test of a group's maturity is its ability to use the resources of its parts—members and subgroups—to the best advantage. How do you think this committee will work out?

Harry: Well, they have the leaders of both sides on the committee, haven't they? And Dr. Gordon is there as a kind of mediator. Anything they work out and agree upon should be accepted pretty well by the whole Society. If they can agree upon a plan, it should be genuinely representative of the Society.

Jim: But isn't that a very big "if"? I don't see how they can agree upon very much, unless they have a change in outlook and ways of working together. And I don't see now anything happening which might cause such a change, do you? I'm afraid they have just transplanted the cleavages in the Society into the Committee. And I wonder too if they picked members who represent the best resources of the Society in terms of knowledge and skill in planning large meetings. Feeling strongly on an issue doesn't guarantee that a person knows much about a job he is asked to do. I'm afraid Dr. Gordon is in for a rough time as chairman.

Professor Lenford: I wonder if we couldn't look at it this way and agree. As Harry suggests, conflicting points of view are a resource to a group if they have the group skills to use this conflict constructively, to make a plan which incorporates values from both points of view and so is better than the plan either side could have worked out by itself. But we've also agreed that the members of the Society seem to be deficient in such skills. So I wonder if the Committee will be able to make an advantage out of this conflict. A lot depends on Dr. Gordon, of course an insider with good intentions but probably with limited skills in training groups and group members. I wonder whether he will be able to shock the two factions into seeing the ill effects of their battle-tactics and into seeing alternative ways of working in which the two viewpoints could furnish complementary resources in building a better common plan. I'm inclined to agree with Jim that he won't be able to swing it.

Predicting how a group or how members in it will behave depends on analyzing the forces that will be operating on the group and on its members as they work. As we try to predict how this committee will behave at its first meeting, I wonder if we can analyze what forces will be operating on the different members. Our analysis will be very hypothetical, of course, because we have limited data to work with. Let's take Mr. Green and Mr. Henry first. They're out of sympathy with the project with which they've been asked to help. They will have the pressure of the Society's action to make them go along with the job. But Mr. Green's neighbors will be pressing on him (in his mind, of course) and Mr. Henry's colleagues and board members on him to make the Society's public meeting as inconspicuous, as nearly invisible as possible. They will also feel pressed to maintain the interests of the three others who voted with them in the meeting against the project. Are there any other forces or pressures which will be working on them to influence their behavior? Any that we have data about, of course?

Jim: Won't they be motivated to do a good job on the meeting in the interests of the Society? They're members of it and they will want its project to succeed.

Harry: I think you're right, Jim. But isn't the difficulty here something we mentioned earlier? The Society has never formulated any very clear common goals for itself. And Mr. Green and Mr. Henry may, as a result, very honestly think they are serving the best interests of the Society by making what they consider one of its particular, ill-advised actions as uninfluential as possible. Do you accept that, Jim? (Jim nods agreement.) I'd guess one other thing about their behavior in the Committee. They will tend to put a "loose construction" on the mandate of the Society, feeling that the Committee can change the very general instructions which the Society has given to the Committee. And I think Miss Foltz and Miss Runner will be "strict constructionists" with respect to the Society's action, trying to keep the opposition from "watering down" the action.

I wonder if I could try my hand at identifying forces operating on Miss Runner and Miss Foltz. They must maintain face by being very consistent with the stand they took in the Society's meeting. Any compromise on their part will seem to them as weakness and letting down the fourteen who voted with them. They have "succeeded" with their tactics in the meeting and they will resist any hint that these tactics be changed. They have spoken publicly against attempt to involve other organizations in planning the meeting, against constructive as well as protest objectives for the meeting, and against fact-finding as a basis for further planning. They will tend to see the reopening of any of these issues as stalling tactics designed to thwart the majority will of the Society.

Professor Lenford: I'll accept Harry's prediction. What about you, Jim? And will you try your hand at predicting Dr. Gordon's behavior in the Committee?

Jim: I guess you and Harry are right about the behavior of the two factions. Dr. Gordon will try to get compromises but he won't get too far. He will see that the internal warfare will lead the Committee to forget the social environment of Centertown which they should be trying to analyze, in order to change it. The factions may work harder on each other than on trying to check the action of the Citizens' Committee for Better Schools or in communicating better intergroup practices to the public in Centertown. He will feel his inadequacy to change the attitudes and behavior of the two factions and I'll bet he will try to get some help from the outside—maybe from you, Professor Lenford.

Professor Lenford: How much of our predictions about the working of the Committee do you think we should report to the Society?

Harry: I'm inclined to think these predictions should be reported pretty completely. They can be introduced at the right time in the committee meeting by Dr. Gordon. If the Committee is very dissatisfied with their productivity at the end of their first meeting, as we predict they will be, they may be ready to listen to suggestions for improvement. And, if our predictions on the basis of forces and factors which they haven't recognized is correct, I think they will be impressed by their need to look into the kinds of things we have tried to observe and to use such observations in becoming more efficient.

Jim: I think I agree.

Professor Lenford: And so do I. O.K., I'll write up our report as we have outlined it and try to get copies for Mr. Briggs and Dr. Gordon into tomorrow's mail.

III. THE COMMITTEE GOES TO WORK

Dr. Gordon, the Chairman, arrived at the Committee meeting a few minutes late. As he entered, Mr. Green and Mr. Henry were lined up on one side of the table and Miss Foltz and Miss Runner on the other. It was obvious that the tensions of the last meeting were to be carried into the Subcommittee, and that the two factions had dug in for a determined battle.

The meeting opened with some questioning by both Mr. Green and Mr. Henry of the Society's decision to move ahead on the issue of school redistricting. Both Mr. Green and Mr. Henry raised this point somewhat indirectly. Miss Foltz rather tartly said she thought the Committee had a very clear mandate to move ahead in developing plans for action on the subject of redistricting and the camouflaged issue of segregation. She went on to say that for her part, and she was sure Miss Runner would agree with her, the issue was very clear. At all costs, they should fight to maintain non-segregation in the schools. The only other answer, she said, would be weakly permitting the conservative forces to put the community back hundreds of years.

As the discussion developed, it became clear to Dr. Gordon that the members of the Committee saw and accepted only two alternatives—either enforced non-segregation or a *laissez-faire*, hands-off policy on the whole issue. Both Mr. Green and Mr. Henry seemed convinced that the Society's mandate to the Committee made impossible the second alternative, at least on the surface, so they sought to obstruct and soften the other alternative as far as possible.

Gradually the battle lines developed over a question of the strategy to employ. Miss Foltz and Miss Runner vehemently advanced plans for a counter-petition and a general mass meeting in which the issue could be "aired." Both Mr. Green and Mr. Henry joined in urging that it would be much better to make a more "private" appeal to members of the Board of Education, or to the key leaders of the Citizens Committee for Better Schools. In this way, they said, no one would get really emotional, and the community wouldn't split wide open. Neither faction made any effort to seek an alternative path of action, or, more important, to develop any common criteria for the selection of effective courses of action. Each faction was promoting a point of view rather than attempting to analyze short-term and long-term consequences of any plan proposed.

Up to this time, Dr. Gordon had entered into the discussion very little. Neither side seemed quite sure which point of view he would take, and so neither Miss Foltz and Miss Runner, nor, on the other hand, Mr. Green and Mr. Henry, pushed any question to a vote. Finally, Dr. Gordon broke in, in an effort to turn the group's attention to what they had been doing to date. He suggested that it might be profitable if they were to read over Professor Lenford's comments about the larger meeting and his predictions concerning what would happen in their own committee meeting. Rather reluctantly, the members accepted this, but, after Dr. Gordon read Professor Lenford's statements, they were obviously both impressed and concerned. Some discussion developed rather spontaneously about the problem of working together. The group seemed to have sufficient insight to see that the Committee's problem was also the problem of the larger Society. Merely by appointing a small committee with the same stresses and strains as those in the Society, there is no assurance that good thinking and good solutions will be made by the committee. Someone said that the small committee may have been badly selected. The members were picked merely because they were vociferous and represented opposite sides. After the expression of this point of view, however, the group went little further in its self-analysis. They didn't look at all at the mistakes of their own methods of working, but pushed ahead again in an effort to come to some conclusion of the meeting. In looking back to the larger meeting, they failed also to analyze the need for the Society to learn ways of improving meetings.

As the Committee meeting wore on, however, it became obvious that they weren't getting anywhere. No real decisions were being made, and the Committee was really no further ahead than before it met. Dr. Gordon again suggested that there must be some way around their stalemate, that perhaps this way lay in determining better ways of working as a committee. This stimulated a little discussion, and the group finally did decide (about the first successful unanimous decision reached) to ask Dr. Gordon to see if he could induce Professor Lenford to come to their next Committee meeting to help them out.

Professor Lenford came with Dr. Gordon a week later to the second meeting of the Committee. He brought along Harry Stewart, one of his graduate students. When the Committee assembled, Dr. Gordon said that Professor Lenford had been kind enough to join with them, and had asked permission for one of his colleagues to sit in, too, and observe. The group nodded agreement, and Miss Foltz immediately turned to Professor Lenford and asked him to tell them what to do so that they could carry out the mandate of their Committee to devise a plan of action to block the efforts of the group seeking redistricting. Professor Lenford quietly suggested that perhaps the best thing would be for the group to review with him what had happened at their previous meeting. This was done by Miss Runner, with some contributions from both Mr. Green and Mr. Henry.

Professor Lenford: That is an extremely interesting account. I have a number of questions that are bothering me. It seems to me you people have not asked yourselves enough questions about the consequences of carrying out the plans you proposed. What will happen, for example, if you do hold a big mass meeting? Might that build up antagonisms which could possibly be of greater harm than good to your cause? Are you basing your plan on a psychology of protest only? Are there more constructive approaches which might possibly be made?

Mr. Green: Just what I've been saying. All we would do would be to stir up emotions and make the whole situation worse.

Miss Foltz: That's all very well, but we must act. This is a real issue, and we can't wait.

Mr. Henry: We could still act, as you say, Miss Foltz, by talking quietly and privately to the leaders of the other group.

Professor Lenford: Even if you carried out this alternative plan, do you feel that this would bring about the most successful results? Would you perhaps have merely blocked this one move, only to have the same kind of move come out in some other way? I wonder if you don't really need to work out some definite criteria which will help you to develop and test the kind of plan the Society should adopt.

Mr. Green: That sounds like a good idea. Maybe that's what we do need to work on.

Miss Runner: You mean that's a good way not to have to act, don't you, Mr. Green? If we spend all of our time discussing criteria, the issue will have passed by. That's the trouble with liberals—we just talk, and never act. This is a time when we really ought to do something.

(This issue was discussed rather heatedly for a few moments. Both Mr. Green and Mr. Henry seemed to accept Professor Lenford's suggestion as primarily a way of delaying action, while Miss Foltz and Miss Runner saw it as the same thing, and consequently fought against it. Dr. Gordon endeavored to put in a compromise by suggesting that they might set a definite time limit for trying out Professor Lenford's proposal. If it didn't work, Dr. Gordon suggested, they could go back to their previous question and thus not hold up action unduly. Rather reluctantly, Miss Foltz and Miss Runner accepted this compromise proposal, and Dr. Gordon brought the discussion back to Professor Lenford with the request that he illustrate the kind of criteria he had in mind.)

Professor Lenford: One criterion that occurs to me immediately, and one I think you have been following in part, is, "what are the consequences of our plan in terms of reaching the goal we want and at the same time not damaging relations in the community, if that is possible?" Is occurs to me also that perhaps we need to look at our goal again—do we really want to *enforce* non-segregation, or do we want to build increased intergroup cohesion and friendliness? In other words, do we wish only to block something, or do we wish to build better human relations in our community?

Mr. Green: Those are good points. I wonder if this isn't another one—shouldn't we ask ourselves whether any given plan lies within our ability to carry it out? After all, we're only one group in the community.

Miss Foltz: That's another good way to excuse ourselves from acting. We can always say that the job was too big for us to tackle.

Dr. Gordon: I think we can accept that idea, however, Miss Foltz, without keeping ourselves from doing something. We wouldn't want to tackle something that is bound to fail, would we?

Miss Runner: As long as we're considering such points, it seems to me we ought to ask ourselves whether any plan we accept really creates more liberal attitudes in our town.

Professor Lenford: Fine. Certainly your Society would want each thing it tackled to have a long-time democratic effect in the growth of your community.

Mr. Henry: At the same time, we might ask ourselves whether any suggested plan might wreck our organization.

Miss Foltz: Apathy will wreck our organization, as well as ill-advised action, won't it?

(There was general argument at this point, but the majority had become intrigued with the criteria discussed. The discussion led back to further criteria, and Miss Runner herself suggested the criterion that Mr. Green gave earlier—boundaries to the power field of the organization. Someone reminded her that this had already been mentioned, and this enabled Professor Lenford to suggest both that the group might need a recorder, and that it might be a good idea if the group picked someone to write the criteria down on a blackboard. A very brief discussion brought the selection of Miss Runner to keep notes on the meeting's production without ruling out her participation in the discussion. Dr. Gordon volunteered to go to the blackboard. He went and wrote down the criteria which various members of the group recalled to him. Further criteria were given which pointed more and more toward an agreement by the group that they would really like to build intergroup cohesion rather than merely block the plans of the other group. At this point, the discussion rushed back to a consideration of the action required, and the group split once again between Mr. Green and Mr. Henry on the one side, and Miss Foltz and Miss Runner on the other, over what they should do to build intergroup cohesion.

The split into two sides stalemated the group again and Mr. Henry then asked Professor Lenford to tell them which side was right.)

Professor Lenford: Rather than try to answer that question, I'd like to ask you people what happened to us. We decided that we needed criteria to determine the effectiveness of any action we planned, and we spent some time in listing some criteria on which we seemed to agree. Then we turned to the discussion of action plans again and totally disregarded all of the criteria we had established. No one stopped to examine proposed actions in the ways we had said would be desirable. We merely divided again into two sides, each side trying to push its plan through. Why do you think that happened?

Miss Foltz: I think it just proves that we wasted time on thinking about those criteria. After all, our job is to come out with a plan of action and we haven't too much time.

Mr. Henry: We never seem to get anywhere when we try to make a decision, though. We certainly wasted all of last meeting in trying to make a plan.

Against the background of Miss Foltz's *sotto voce* comments that "some people just want to block action," Professor Lenford and Dr. Gordon helped the group to think more seriously than they had to date about their problems of working together. Gradually, with

Dr. Gordon doing a masterly job of leadership while working at the blackboard, a number of rather basic insights began to appear. Dr. Gordon wrote them down as follows:

1. Creating a plan for social action is difficult and complex.

2. We lack understanding of what is required for planning effective action.

3. We approach action-planning haphazardly instead of scientifically.

4. We need to know how to analyze forces affecting desired changes.

As these points developed, the Committee became aware that planning action in any community is a serious proposition and should be approached with every bit of knowledge and help possible. This led into a fifth point that Dr. Gordon wrote on the blackboard.

5. We lack skill in working as a group in planning action.

As these points made more and more of an impact on the members of the group, they turned back to the criteria they had listed and thought about them again. With Professor Lenford's help they categorized them and then discussed those dealing with the goals of the Society. They came to an agreement that its goal in the present setting was to bring about improved intergroup relations and that any plan for action should be in that direction. This meant that the strategy of any action should not be merely toward blocking or defeating another group, or toward bringing about non-segregation by force, but toward planning action that would improve the willingness and ability of people in various groups to work productively with others. Following this, the group examined and agreed upon a criterion that all people concerned should be involved in any action planned.

Professor Lenford, at this point, suggested that perhaps they needed to analyze the forces in the community which were working against good intergroup relations or would serve as blocks if a definite program were started. In the same way, he added, the group might analyze the forces in the community favorable to developing good intergroup relations. The Committee accepted this suggestion and tackled the problem vigorously. They listed quite a few pro and con forces. One of the most important difficulties growing out of their analysis was the obvious lack of knowledge the Committee had as to how the people of Centertown actually felt about intergroup problems. More and more, as the Committee discussed its steps of action, it became clear that this information was vitally necessary. The group felt completely blocked here until Professor Lenford said that he thought it wouldn't be too difficult to develop a survey that would not only produce this information but would also involve and interest many more people in the problem. He suggested, however, that it probably would be better to find out people's present active interests in intergroup coöperation rather than to ask people whether they want to work with other groups. If the latter were tried, it might merely reinforce attitudes and stereotypes against such coöperation.

The Committee became more and more involved in this step but also more and more certain that they wouldn't know how to go about it. Professor Lenford said that he thought he could interest Professor Brown, one of his colleagues at the University, who was something of an expert in the field of interviewing and community surveying, to consult with them. Professor Lenford cautioned the group that the job would still be theirs but that Professor Brown might provide some help. After some discussion, it was decided that, if Professor Lenford would get this help, they would start planning this action step at their next meeting. The entire Committee joined in this conclusion.

Miss Runner put the satisfaction of the group into words when she said, "Well, believe it or not, we finally really did decide something together."

Dr. Gordon: You certainly said what we all feel, Miss Runner. It was a great relief to get somewhere, and I wonder if that doesn't lead us to the need to analyze what was wrong with us before. Perhaps we should ask Professor Lenford to discuss with us some of the things we had been doing wrong.

Miss Foltz: Need we go back over all of that again? It seems to me if we spend so much time arguing about how we work that we will never get down to work. I agree we have to know how to work together, but can't there be too much of a good thing?

Dr. Gordon: I think we would all agree that the purpose of analyzing how we work is to learn to work together more efficiently. By looking briefly at where we made mistakes today we may be able to learn how to prevent these mistakes another time. (The values of an evaluation of the Committee meeting were discussed. With some qualifications on the part of two members of the Committee, it now decided to go ahead, and Dr. Gordon asked Professor Lenford to start it off.)

Professor Lenford: I could get us started with what I observed, but you will remember that I played a fairly active part today and so I undoubtedly missed observing some very crucial points. Consequently, my observations may be inaccurate. On the other hand, Harry Steward has been sitting here all afternoon watching what has been happening. Why don't we ask him to mention one or two points he thinks are of most importance in our afternoon's work? (One or two questions from the group indicated that some members feel Professor Lenford has tended to make observation of groups needlessly complicated and almost artificial. But the others indicated their readiness for Stewart to go ahead. Yet obviously they didn't expect much. And there was evidence of a little defensiveness on the part of some group members.)

Stewart: It's been extremely interesting to observe this group today and I find it difficult to decide what is the most important to you of all that I have observed. I think, though, that I was most influenced by the need the group had for its missing members.

(Stewart paused here and Professor Lenford noticed that the group was suddenly interested.)

Stewart: For example, if someone in the group had been aware, at certain points, that the Committee had become a collection of individuals each trying to argue others into an acceptance of his own point of view rather than a group analyzing and evaluating various contributed ideas, that person could have called the group's attention to what it was doing to itself, and much valuable time would not have been lost.

Perhaps others of you can think of other missing members. Professor Lenford mentioned a couple of times when the group seemed to need someone to integrate what looked like very divergent ideas but which were really not so far apart. Dr. Gordon and Mr. Henry also suggested several needed member roles which, if played at the right time, would have helped the group.

With this start the group warmed up to a fairly thorough analysis of what had happened. From this discussion, Dr. Gordon listed the following major points on the board:

1. Several missing member roles prevented good group productivity.
2. Group was unclear concerning how to reach decisions. It acted as if decisions were to be reached only by one side's winning over the other or by compromise rather than by the group accepting a goal of common production of the best possible decision.
3. Group was satisfied by a relatively low level of production.
4. Group was confused over what the leader should be—chairman, arbitrator, or what?
5. Group scapegoated its own inadequacy on larger meetings of the Society. It failed to analyze ways in which the Committee could improve in spite of the way it was appointed; in fact, the sub-committee might find ways to help the Society work more productively as a larger group.
6. Group was overly dependent on consultant at times and yet resentful of him at the same time.

All these points served as a considerable shock to the group. All the previous lack of interest in self-observation and self-evaluation was now gone. In fact, quite an excited discussion was held about how each member could improve his own awareness of what was happening in groups, of the effect of his own behavior on the group, and of how each could improve in the skills required by an effective group member. They began to see that, by becoming skilled themselves in group observation, they might be able to help in the improvement of the meetings of the Society as well as those of the Committee, and probably in other groups outside of the Society. The upshot of the discussion was that Professor Lenford and Harry Stewart promised to spend one meeting period later in giving them training as group observers. And the Committee put on the agenda for its future meetings further discussion of ways they might help the rest of the Society improve its meetings.

IV. A SURVEY OF INTERGROUP RELATIONS TAKES SHAPE

Professor Lenford and Professor Brown, the consultant in surveying and interviewing, came to the third meeting of the Committee. It was interesting to Professor Lenford to see how much change had taken place in the group. Now Mr. Green and Mr. Henry didn't seem to line up on one side of the table against Miss Foltz and Miss Runner. A feeling of common, group concern seemed to be present. When Dr. Gordon raised the question of selecting a recorder and observer, the group had little trouble in selecting two of its members to serve in these capacities. It was decided that because of the smallness of the Committee, the observer, Mr. Henry, would also participate. He agreed to take soundings, as an observer, during ten minute periods near the beginning, the middle and the end of the meeting.

Professor Lenford was impressed, also, with the evidence of increased ability of the Committee to make wise use of an outside consultant. Following Dr. Gordon's suggestion, the group, with one member doing the major part while the others contributed, described concisely to Professor Brown the previous thinking of the Committee concerning needed facts and their specific need for his help in planning their fact-finding survey.

Professor Brown suggested that he didn't feel at all capable of giving answers about what their survey should be, that he would be glad to help them to define the problems which they would encounter in planning an appropriate survey and to work out ways of solving these. The group, with the help of Professor Brown and Professor Lenford, listed on a blackboard the major dimensions of their survey problem.

1. What should the survey accomplish?
2. How prepare the interview instrument?
3. What groups in the community should be interviewed?
4. What samples from these groups will be necessary?
5. How could these groups be interested in supporting the survey?
6. Who should do the interviewing?
7. How should the interviewers be trained?
8. How should prospective interviewers be informed about the purposes of the survey?
9. Who should code and tabulate the data from the interviews and how can they be trained to do this job?
10. How should the results of the survey be presented and to whom?
11. Who else (in addition to the Society members) should be involved in planning and carrying out the survey?

These eleven problems presented quite an imposing agenda and the Committee realized that much work would need to be done. They first discussed briefly how thoroughly each point should be dealt with at this meeting and made a rough allocation of their time so that they wouldn't spend all their time on one problem.

The first problem listed obviously needed to be cleared up at this meeting. After fairly thorough discussion, the group listed the following basic purposes of the survey:

1. It should secure information as to: the attitudes of various groups toward working with other groups; the perceptions each group has of the problems and purposes of other groups; the perceptions each group has of the barriers to intergroup coöperation which must be removed. It should secure information concerning the intensity of the desire to bring about better intergroup relations on the part of those interviewed.

2. It should, if possible, and without affecting the objective collection of information, influence interviewees toward wanting better intergroup relations. (This point was discussed at length. It was the final decision that the group could be forthright in standing for improved group relations without making the collection of information any less objective or accurate.)

3. It should secure information as to whether interviewees think their responses are like those others would make.

4. It should find out for each group what the effective sources of influence on that group are. These were seen as providing help in later efforts to induce changes in different groups in the community.

5. It should so interest the interviewee that he will attend any future community meeting connected with the project and become more active in interesting other people in the project.

The Committee realized that all these purposes could not be completely realized in many cases, but that they certainly provided desirable goals for the survey.

The second major problem was passed over fairly rapidly. Professor Brown promised his own services and those of his assistant in giving technical help in the preparation of the interview schedule. The one major decision made by the Committee in this area was that, as much as possible, most questions in the interview should be so worded that those interviewed could express their feelings and opinions in their own way. This called for the use of "open-ended" questions, as Professor Brown expressed it.

The third and fourth major problems called for considerable discussion. Lists were made of the groups in the community where most differences in intergroup attitudes could be predicted. Plans were laid for getting other people to check this listing to suggest additional groups. It was decided to make every effort to get a random sample in each of the groups chosen for survey.

This discussion led easily to a number of further decisions—that the Society committee ought to be enlarged into a Survey Team to bring representatives from each group to be sampled into the further planning for the interviewing (this, as Miss Foltz pointed out, took care of question 11); that interviewers in each case be chosen from the group to be interviewed so that people would speak in the interviews with more freedom (answer to question 6); that interviewers selected be willing to undergo brief but intensive training to eliminate, as much as possible, bias and to secure more reliability among the results from the many interviewers (partial answer to question 7); and that judicious publicity in the newspapers and through announcements in the meetings of various organizations be given to the entire project, both to prepare interviewees for visits by interviewers, to check the development of false rumors about the survey, and to interest as many members of the community as possible in this scientific effort of the Society and cooperating individuals and groups to get needed factual help in solving a crucial community problem (answer to question 8).

During the discussion of what groups in Centertown should be sampled, a list of twenty such groups had been written down. The name of a likely "representative" from each group as a member of the enlarged Survey Team had also been listed. Before the Committee ended its meeting, each committee member agreed to see four of these during the next week in order to interest them in the project and to try to get them to join the Survey Team at its next meeting. At this point, Dr. Gordon said he thought he understood what he was supposed to accomplish in talking with the four people on his list but he didn't know whether he knew how to do it. The other four members admitted that they too felt somewhat insecure in the job they had accepted. Professor Lenford made the suggestion that they try out right now one of these "involvement" interviews and see how it worked. Mr. Green said he knew Mr. Togliatti, one of the men on Dr. Gordon's list, quite well and agreed to be "Mr. Togliatti" while Dr. Gordon tried to involve him in becoming a member of the Survey Team.

The practice conversation between Dr. Gordon and "Mr. Togliatti" went on for about six or seven minutes. "Mr. Togliatti" was becoming even more cagey and "resistant" concerning Dr. Gordon's idea than he had seemed at first. Professor Lenford cut the practice session at this point and suggested that they discuss why the conversation had gone as it did. Mr. Green said that, as "Mr. Togliatti," he had felt that Dr. Gordon was being over-simple in his explanations of the survey project, that he had felt that Dr. Gordon was "talking down" to him. Miss Runner observed that Dr. Gordon had seemed to become defensive when "Mr. Togliatti" made slightly slurring remarks about the "Society." Dr. Gordon admitted that these things had happened and asked for suggestions as to how he could improve his technique. After several suggestions had been agreed upon, the conversation was tried again and went much better. "Mr. Togliatti" agreed to be at the meeting next week.

All the members of the Committee started talking at once. All agreed they felt more secure now but wished that each of them could have a chance to try his or her hand at practicing, if only time permitted. Miss Foltz observed that really we have been getting training as interviewers right here and wondered if the same method wouldn't be used in training the fact-finding interviewers later. Professor Brown said he thought the idea was a fine one, that he himself hadn't used "role-playing" much in training interviewers, but that his assistant, Bill Sheldon, who was coming to help with the survey, had used this method successfully elsewhere and that he was sure that Bill would want to use it in Centertown too.

Everyone was anxious to hear from Mr. Henry, the observer, as to how he had seen the meeting today. Mr. Henry reported that he was so interested in the planning that he had had some difficulty in taking time out from participation to observe. He noticed how common the goal of the Committee now seemed to be, how general the participation had been, and how the "factions" in the group had seemed to disappear. He did wonder if the group hadn't tried to depend at times on Professor Brown for "answers." He noticed that often Professor Brown had refused to "decide" for the group by throwing the question for decision back to the group. A few times however, he felt Professor Brown had yielded to this demand for "answers." Professor Brown admitted that he had been "seduced" a few times and thanked Mr. Henry for pointing this out. The group then discussed the "use of experts" for a short time.

Mr. Henry pointed out further that they would have a real test of what they had learned about working in a group next week when a number of new members of the Survey Team would be meeting with them. He wondered if they shouldn't make some plans for that time. After brief discussion, the group decided on a plan for the next meeting to orient the new members to the purposes of the survey as planned to date and to the ways of working as a group which they had found useful, including the use of an observer and a recorder.

The next four weeks were a busy time for the Society Committee and for the other new members of the Survey Team. The Committee presented its suggested plan for the survey to the Society and told how they had come to agree on this plan. The Society, after discussion, was enthusiastic too. Several members volunteered to help with the interviewing; several volunteered to help code and tabulate data; others agreed to help plan the reporting of data to the public of Centertown.

Several training sessions were held for the interviewers, in which they used role-playing to develop "objectivity" and to eliminate their "biases" from the way they asked the questions and recorded the answers. A few sample interviews were recorded mechanically and the group listened to these and analyzed and criticized them. The interview schedule was revised in the light of this discussion. Another training session was held after the first round of interviews in which the interviewers reported the problems which they had encountered and discussed and practiced ways of solving these. Other "research" workers were trained in coding and classifying the data from the recorded interviews and in tabulating the results. Warned in advance by Professor Lenford, the Society did not make the mistake of rushing into the survey without preparation. At every step in the long, complicated process of survey research, the "researchers" were supervised by Professor Brown or his assistants.

After the tabulations were completed, the professor gave his help in the job of analyzing the results. Thanks to the long training and careful supervision, the survey, though conducted largely by "amateurs," was comparable in validity to a professional job.

As preliminary survey results began to be assembled, it seemed clear that the best way to present these results to the public was to hold a large open meeting at which results of the survey would be reported and decisions about what to do on the basis of these facts carried through. Thus, eight weeks after the initial meeting of the Society on the problem of segregation through redistricting, a Society-sponsored mass meeting was held.

V. THE CENTERTOWN COMMUNITY MEETING

It has become increasingly apparent to Dr. Gordon and the other members of the Committee that the community meeting they had been delegated to plan for should be focused on the results of the group relations survey rather than on the one specific issue of school redistricting. The Committee, now thoroughly involved in the survey, felt that the Society could render a more important community service than had originally been intended by utilizing the rather widespread expressions of interest in the survey and its results. Dr. Gordon obtained the approval of the executive committee of the Society to make this change in the emphasis of the meeting, and to add other members of the Survey Team to the planning and steering committee for the community meeting. Mr. Hettinger, Executive Secretary of the Council of Social Agencies, who was now taking active leadership in the Survey Team, and Professor Lenford were among the five added to the planning committee. Mr. Briggs raised the question as to whether it would be better to have the community meeting sponsored by a "representative group of citizens" rather than by the Society. After some discussion of this point, it was agreed that it would be more appropriate for the Society to assume definite sponsorship of the meeting, making a special effort to clarify publicly the wider participation of the community in the survey and the role of the Society as a stimulator of the enterprise rather than as having a "vested interest" in a particular line of action to be taken following the meeting.

Mr. Hatfield did an excellent job in getting the local newspaper to carry stories about the progress of the survey, the role of non-Society members in the project, and the plans for the community reporting meeting. The steering committee had a number of planning sessions at which Professor Lenford helped them to think more deeply than any of them had ever done before about the problems and techniques of large meetings, with all their difficulties of communication and audience participation. The committee came to see how helpful various principles of social psychology could be in guiding the planning for a large public meeting. Rather than take the time now to go through the various steps of planning, let's attend the meeting and see what happened as a result of these plans.

When Mr. Briggs opened the meeting, about three hundred persons had assembled. He spent ten minutes describing clearly and rather humbly how the Society for Democracy had originally appointed a committee to look into the question of how action might be taken on a problem of school redistricting which had come to the attention of the Society. But, as the committee had attempted to carry out their job, they had discovered that many unavailable facts were needed to do intelligent thinking about the issue, and that the issue itself was just one aspect of the larger problem of effective working and living relations between various groups that made up the community of Centertown. Therefore, it had appeared necessary that the Society should engage in an objective fact-finding expedition. This expedition sought to discover just what the community actually thought about the relations which do exist and should exist among the diverse cultural, religious, economic, and other groups that had to adjust to each other and learn to work together in order to make Centertown a better place in which to live. Mr. Briggs related how the committee had found members of most of these groups interested in the idea of such a survey, so that a Survey Team had been formed, representing diverse community outlooks, to work with social scientist consultants from the University on this fact-finding venture. He hoped that those present would agree that this had helped the community to do some thinking about this problem, rather than just the members of one organization, the Society. Tonight the members of all community groups had been invited to share in a first look at the survey results and to help make decisions as to what further steps of fact-finding or other types of action seemed to be called for.

Mr. Briggs then called on Professor Lenford who, as a member of the Survey Team and a social scientist, is ready to help us get a clear picture of the survey results and work together in thinking about next steps.

Professor Lenford explained that after a presentation of survey findings by members of the survey team everyone would be asked to work in small groups on the meaning of the findings and as consultants on what next steps should be taken, if any, by the community or various groups in the community. He did his best to challenge everyone to prepare for an active role in the events of the evening.

"Obviously," said Lenford, "it's natural that certain groups should disagree with other groups. It is also true that many conflicts are due to misunderstandings and lack of knowledge of one group about another. Until we clarify what our differences and misunderstandings are, we are sure to have continuing difficulty in living with each other. So our survey interviews sought to discover the attitudes Centertown groups have toward each other and some of the knowledge they have about each other. Here is a sample of how this information was gathered. This is a section of a recorded interview with a fifteen-year-old girl from a family that has lived many years in Centertown. Several recordings like this were made with the permission of the interviewees so that we would have illustrations of interviewing technique." A recorded interview excerpt was then played over the public address system in the auditorium. Everybody suddenly found himself "sitting in" on an interview.

The recording illustrated clearly the nature of the survey interview—and the answers given by this girl to the several questions clearly revealed hostile intergroup attitudes and irrational reasons for holding these attitudes. It was important that everyone in the audience see and accept those facts—in the interview example and in themselves. To help get this idea across Professor Lenford became a "clarifier" or "interpreter" to the audience. Several times during the playing of the ten minute recording he turned off the machine to point out the meaning of a specific remark. For example—"You notice in that remark she shows us that she feels persons who were born in foreign countries are a 'different group' from those born in this country, and are inferior in some undefined way—she can't quite explain how—but that doesn't deter her from holding this attitude. This is certainly very natural for her and for all of us . . ."

Professor Lenford then raised an important question with the audience. "Just how adequate a picture of the thinking of the major groups in the community do we have from the analysis of the relatively small number of interviews made during the survey? And just how valid are the interview results from these interviews done by fellow-citizens with their own particular sets of biases?"

Dr. Gordon as chairman of the Survey group quickly reviewed the concern of the Committee about these two questions and asked Professor Brown from the University to explain the basis for the sampling of group members which had been taken. Mr. Hettinger then described the way in which the interviewers had participated in an intensive training program to locate their problems of bias and to standardize their interviewing techniques. With these two points clarified, it was time for the Survey Committee to report their findings.

Mimeographed tabulations of the analysis of the interviews were now handed out to the whole audience and Dr. Gordon took the total audience through the reading of the first tabulation by point-ing to a copy of it projected on a screen. "Now," said Dr. Gordon, "rather than read through all of these other summary tabulations at this time, let's listen together to a carefully prepared summary and you can examine the written details later at your leisure. As you see, these chairs that are being placed on the stage are labeled to represent each of the groups from which answers have been summarized—you see this chair represents the Jewish group, this one the Italian-Catholic group, this one the businessmen, etc. The representatives of the Survey Team who are now taking these seats are thoroughly familiar with all of the statistics concerning the answers from their particular group. Each group representative in turn will summarize the thinking and point of view of that group as reflected in the data. He will not be speaking as himself, but as a statistical summary of the data from all the questions answered by members of that group. As these summaries proceed, one after the other, Professor Lenford has been asked to feel free to step in and point out to us any observations he has been able to make about the differences, similarities, misunderstandings, etc., which we may be able to find in these group outlooks."

In short clear statements, these personalized summaries of group outlook came through the loudspeakers. From time to time Professor Lenford stepped in to push thinking a little deeper. For example, "You notice how each of the last three groups—the white Protestants, the Negroes, and the Jewish group have expressed the same basic desire to have Centertown provide the best possible facilities for bringing up healthy children—but none of the groups has seen the other two groups as thinking seriously about this problem and as partners in solving it. Now, if we look at the way in which each group sees these goals, we note that . . ."

It was clear to the committee members as they watched that there was intense interest and thoughtful reflection in the audience as the summaries continued. Without slowing up to allow the tension to die down, Professor Lenford moved the group into a more active phase of participation.

"Well, you see the kinds of facts we have about ourselves here in Centertown. Now let's all put our heads together for a little while in doing some thinking about what these facts might suggest as to next steps that might be taken, and by whom. You all need a stretch, so, when I give the signal, will you stand up and each five of you in the first row, third row, etc., turn around to your five neighbors in the row behind and form yourselves into a committee of ten. Your chairs are movable so make a little circle so you can hear yourselves above the buzz of the rest of us. Will each group appoint a record keeper to jot down the bright ideas your group has as to next steps you think would be valuable? In ten minutes I'll interrupt you for one last assignment before we meet together again to share our thinking. O.K. let's go."

In less than a minute all "stretching and getting organized" was over and thirty buzz groups, including two on the stage composed of members of the Survey Team on the program, were actively underway. At the end of the ten minutes Professor Lenford called for attention and requested, "Now would each committee do two things before we reconvene in general session—first, would you each elect a member whom you would like to have represent you? Clearly, we will not be able to go over all the ideas of all groups here tonight, so we want to suggest that a smaller group of one representative from each group be delegated to meet and go over the many ideas that have been developed, to report back to you at a later date. Second, we would like you to decide what one or two of the ideas you have developed are most important for sharing with all of us here tonight. We will ask the elected representative from each group to join us on the stage for a short reporting session. Let's take about two minutes now to get these two items of business finished up."

The reporting session on the stage seemed to be of great interest to everyone. Each member of the audience was now also a member of a specific subgroup. He was eager to see his group well represented in the discussion, and to hear how the thinking of the other groups compared with and differed from his own. Many common ideas emerged from the various reports which Professor Lenford summarized as the reports followed one another. It was clear, for example, that a number of the buzz groups were anxious to have the survey report made available for discussion in various community groups. It was also agreed that a printed report, though needed, would not be enough. One suggestion was that a team from each group, including a member of the survey team, receive training in reporting the findings and leading the discussion in their own organization or social group. The need for committee development of specific projects was stressed several times. Two groups proposed a representative community committee on human relations. Another community interpretation session to which other citizens should be stimulated to attend by those here at this meeting was recommended. An impressive array of other concrete action ideas was listed. A date for a next meeting of the elected buzz group representatives was set for them to go over the total list of group suggestions and to arrive at recommendations. Everyone was invited to indicate his name and address on one of the cards which were passed out, if he wanted to be kept informed, and to indicate also whether he was ready to volunteer to help carry the survey report to his own group or groups. There were one hundred twenty-five such volunteers and nearly everyone left his name and address to receive further reports.

"And now before we adjourn," said Professor Lenford, "let's be sure that we profit in one very important way by the experience of our working together here tonight. Every such meeting has many potentialities for creative production which go unrealized. We need to learn to plan our meetings, large and small, in such a way that these production possibilities can be more fully realized. Each of us can help now by checking on the slip that has been distributed to you, your experience with this meeting, and your ideas for improvements. These will be analyzed by the steering committee as a basis for thinking about future meetings. To me we have clearly demonstrated tonight that a group of citizens with many different backgrounds and viewpoints can think intelligently and constructively together about common problems."

The post-meeting evaluation sheets, as the steering committee looked through them after the auditorium had emptied, showed a great majority feeling very enthusiastic about the meeting and indicating a desire to push ahead in further participation rather than regarding the meeting as "over." Quite a number suggested a longer period for buzz committee work next time. Many expressed their appreciation for the role Professor Lenford had taken as commentator at various points during the evening. Dr. Gordon noticed that the other Committee members, like himself, seemed to feel eager to push ahead rather than regard this as the official end of their job. A first successful venture in community research, training and action seemed to call for more.

NOTE: This is evaluation form used at the meeting:

POST-MEETING EVALUATION

Name ....

1. Check on the line below at the point which best indicates your feeling about this meeting:

....

Swell   Good   All Right   Mediocre   No Good

2. What were the main strengths of the meeting?:
3. What were its main weaknesses?:
4. Suggestions and comments:

VI. SPREAD AND CONTAGION

The enthusiasm of Dr. Gordon's Committee for the help they had received from Professor Lenford was contagious. At the monthly meeting of the Society following the community meeting one of the members not on the Committee said they had all been impressed by the work of the Committee in planning the survey and the community meeting. They had heard a little about the ways in which Professor Lenford had helped the Committee improve its ways of working together and in thinking about changes in the community. He wondered if they might not all be interested in hearing more about the ways the Committee had used in improving its working and thinking together. Dr. Gordon explained the idea of the group observer and group self-training sessions as best he could. There seemed to be considerable interest which crystallized around approval of Mr. Briggs' suggestion that Dr. Gordon plan to act as observer at the next meeting of the Society. Dr. Gordon agreed, although he felt quite insecure about what he might be able to do. He talked over the whole job of the observer with Professor Lenford during the month. He did an excellent job at the next meeting and received a good deal of support from members of the subcommittee. The Society agreed on the value of continuing the observer function, rotating it among the various members. They agreed with Dr. Gordon's suggestion that Harry Stewart might be invited in for a meeting to be devoted to training every Society member in the elements of the observer's job. This was worked out at the next meeting.

In the meantime the success of the community meeting and the widening activities growing from it was resulting in a changed perception of the Society by other community groups and individual citizens. This was reflected in the addition of a number of valuable new members, and also in approaches from other groups with invitations to collaborate or requests for help. For example, two weeks after the community meeting, Dr. Gordon received a call from the Federation of Women's Clubs asking if he would come to the monthly meeting of committee chairmen and give them a talk on "improving committee chairmanship." Someone from their group had been on the Survey Team and so had worked with the Committee of the Society. Dr. Gordon was wise enough to make clear that he was not an expert who could give a talk on chairmanship but that he would be glad to share the experiences of his Committee with the group.

The increase in such requests by organizations to members of the Society led to a conviction that the Society might sponsor a community wide training institute of two days length for committee leaders and members from various organizations. Mr. Hettinger and Dr. Gordon were asked to discuss the idea of such an institute with Professor Lenford. Professor Lenford approved the idea but made it clear that he could not continue to give as much time as he had been giving to training activities in Centertown. A core of local "trainers" would need to be developed who could furnish leadership in such activities as the training institute for committees.

During this discussion, an idea struck Dr. Gordon which led him

to call on Mr. Briggs that evening. Since the main purpose of the
Society has always been to stimulate more intelligent and active
citizenship in Centertown, wasn't one of their most effective approaches that of training local leadership in the skills of efficient and
democratic group functioning? Couldn't the members of the Society,
or at least one team of them concentrate on training themselves to
do such jobs as this proposed community training institute? Mr.
Briggs was enthusiastic about the idea and suggested they go over
to the university for lunch with Professor Lenford to discuss ways in
which this "training of trainers" might be accomplished, if the members of the Society wanted to go ahead with it. It was clear that the
Society was on its way to becoming an energizing source in spread-
ing the understandings and skills of democratic and scientific
methodology throughout Centertown. It was finding its place as a
strategic agency of social change through stimulating training and
research dedicated to the improvement of human relations.

Questions for Discussion

1. There are some who feel that this is a record of "group dynamics"
and not "community organization." Others say it is "group dynamics or
social science" but not "social work." What do you think? Why?

2. What other ways do you think the Society might have secured its
objectives? List these and compare them. What are the particular values
of each method?

3. Identify the philosophy and list the methods of Professor Lenford.
What is his "approach"? Compare his work with that of some of the
workers in the other records in this section. How would you rate them in
terms of effectiveness? Why?

4. Would you say Centertown "has more capacity to deal with its
common problems" after this experience than before it? If so, why? List
the areas or items in which it has grown in capacity. What specifically
contributed to this development?

South Haven

Every group develops its own traditions, sense of perspective, and ways of evaluating what is "good" and "bad." In the project described below, three groups are involved, and the different view of each in the same situation is perhaps the essence of this record. Since action is taken on a matter of common interest, either agreement between the groups must be reached or the dominance of one group or combination of groups will determine what is to be done. The group with power is often able to call the tune but the effort of the community organization worker is often to secure agreement, if not consensus, so that some of the interests of all concerned may be protected. The latter is far more difficult than it seems. Often, for example, pressure is exerted and what seems like agreement is secured, but the vitality and initiative of one of the interested groups or individuals are thereby sacrificed. The effort to work through the maze of interests of different groups is well illustrated in this record. The degree of success of the worker in this case is left to the reader to judge.

South Haven is the fastest growing suburb in a large metropolitan area. In 1941, the population was a mere 21,000; by 1951 it had grown to 86,000; and by 1953, the time this record begins, the population was 135,736. On the whole, there are few industries in the area. South Haven grew as a middle-class residential area for workers who were employed in other parts of the city. Large farms were sub-divided, streets laid out, and rows of relatively low-cost houses were speedily erected. There were the inevitable difficulties of adequate sewage, schools, streets, and transportation which plague such new residential areas, especially those without industry or other sources of substantial tax payments. These problems were far from being solved in South Haven, but at the time this record begins, the most difficult aspects of the problem had been overcome by means of a unique fiscal arrangement with the state government which pro-vided sufficient funds to permit the construction of sewers, roads, and schools.

But in 1953, aside from the South Haven Public Welfare Depart-ment, there were no established welfare agencies in this munici-pality. What services were available came from established agencies in the central city. Some of these latter agencies were being called upon by South Haven residents, and a number of agencies felt they should establish branches in South Haven. The previous year, several of them had submitted to the Community Chest budgets which provided for extension of services to South Haven and similar new communities, but because of lack of funds none of these ex-tensions was approved or provided for.

In preparation for the 1953 campaign, however, the Community Chest decided to organize South Haven and other municipalities in the metropolitan area in an effort to increase the amount of money raised. In other words, the Chest now planned a metropolitan cam-paign on the assumption that the welfare agencies supported by the Chest served all the separate municipalities in the metropolitan area. When, however, the Chest began to organize campaign teams in South Haven, it met resistance. A crucial call came from the mayor to the director of the Chest. Quite sharply, the mayor stated that none of the Chest agencies operated in South Haven, that he was flatly opposed to raising money in South Haven for downtown agen-cies, and that he would not support the Chest campaign and would advise against it until such time as "some of the money raised in

South Haven is spent in South Haven—goodness knows, we need it here."

When this matter was discussed in the executive committee of the Chest, it was obvious that the group were anxious to placate the South Haven folks. The mayor of South Haven was not specific in what was required, and the executive itself had few ideas about what services should be provided. To put it crudely, they were concerned about raising money and felt that in order to do this in South Haven, they would have to give something in exchange. After some discussion, it was decided to ask the Welfare Council to recommend what welfare services were required immediately in South Haven and to state what these services would cost. This request was made in early June, 1953, and since the campaign was scheduled for the fall, an immediate report was required in the hope that during the summer some services could be provided and thus serve as a "selling point" in South Haven.

The Welfare Council executive was in somewhat of a dilemma when confronted with this request. It recognized the need to help the Chest in this situation (if only because it was in its interest for the Chest to secure as large a fund as possible) and it knew that any community of this kind could probably use such services as a family service agency, a recreational agency like the Y.M.C.A., etc. But the policy of the Council, established after much painful experience, was to (1) study a local situation before recommendation, and (2) consult local leaders in developing recommendations. The Council, therefore, explained its position to the Chest and asked for $5,000 to provide for a worker who would do a study in both South Haven and a comparable suburb named Westville.

The reaction of the Chest was heated, if not outright hostile. It refused to provide the grant of $5,000 and repeated its request. The assumption was that if the Council knew its business, it would know without "one of those long, drawn out surveys" exactly what was required. It appeared as if the power and will of the Chest were to be exerted. The Council with more understanding of the Chest's position than the Chest of the Council's, sought a compromise. The chairman of the Council board, Mr. Sidney Hall, who was also a member of the Chest board, suggested that an immediate and rapid survey be made of all Council agencies to see if a fairly accurate count could be made of services rendered by these agencies in the past year to residents of South Haven. Such data, he felt, might provide the Chest with the ammunition it required for the immediate campaign, and in the meantime, the long term strategy of the study might proceed. This was agreeable to the Council board, and Mr. Hall and the Council secretary, Miss Roberts, arranged to lunch with the Chest president, Ora Callum, and the Chest director, Robert Jones, to discuss the matter. The view of the Council was clarified, understood, and agreed upon. It was decided that the Council members on the Chest board should be given an opportunity of presenting this new proposal at the next meeting of the Chest executive. At this meeting, Hall was able to present not only the proposal but also data indicating the extent of the services rendered by "downtown" agencies to residents of South Haven. There was immediate agreement that these data were adequate for the present, and that there would be some advantage to developing a plan of welfare services in coöperation with residents of South Haven and Westville. A budget of $5,000 for this latter purpose was approved, and the Council asked to proceed immediately with the two studies.

In August, 1954, the Council board decided to release Miss Betty Perry, one of its regular staff members, for a six months' period in order to conduct the two studies mentioned. (Unforeseen difficulties arose in respect to Westville, and this record is confined to a report of South Haven). Miss Perry was an experienced social worker and had served for five years in the Child and Family Welfare Department. She undertook this task with interest and with a conviction that the study should pave the way for the development of an indigenous plan for welfare services in South Haven. A committee of the Welfare Council was appointed to consult with her on the study; she was aware that she must work not only with this committee but with officers of the Community Chest and the community of South Haven as well.

At the first meeting of the consultative committee of the Welfare Council, Miss Perry confronted her first difficulty. In spite of the commitment of the Welfare Council to work with local citizens in developing plans, the committee was sharply divided on one aspect of this policy. Miss Perry had recommended the immediate organization of a citizens' committee in South Haven to serve as a consultative group and to help on some aspects of the study. Her point was that if these people were involved in this study, they would be more adequately prepared to develop plans when the time for planning of services arose. At least half of the committee supported this view. Other members of the committee felt that the organization of such a committee at this time would be a time consuming task that would interfere with the study and its effectiveness. Time enough, they argued, to consult South Haven people when the study is made— both the Council and Chest require an early plan in a "Let's get this done first" fashion. This matter was discussed throughout one meeting without resolution.

At the next meeting of the consultative committee, Miss Perry introduced her plan for the study. This called for (1) the collection of statistical information on South Haven, including distribution of population by age, sex, religion, the social organization of the community (including formal and informal groups), etc.; (2) a more detailed and accurate list of needs or wants of South Haven as revealed by calls to the Information and Referral Bureau and to agencies in the downtown area during a six weeks' period; and (3) a list of needs and wants as revealed by residents of South Haven as the result of 200 sample door-to-door interviews. The details of this plan were approved, and Miss Perry was able to suggest rather effectively that both the first and third parts of her plan required the coöperation of citizens in South Haven. Would it not facilitate the study to have a committee in South Haven to help her in this respect? It was finally agreed that this would be feasible, especially if it speeded up the plan which the Council had promised to provide the Chest.

Following this meeting, Miss Perry developed a memo outlining the proposed procedure for the study which she sent to each of the members of the executive committee of the Chest. At the conclusion of the memo, she emphasized her conviction that this was not simply a study "but a method of developing a plan for South Haven which its residents approve and support. The use of such procedure may be more time consuming than the development of a plan in the Welfare Council office, but it should result in a plan that is more lasting and effective."

A good deal of the material for the study was readily accessible. The most difficult part of the study was getting to know the people of South Haven, their pattern of life, what they wished to see in the way of welfare services in their community. The organization of a citizens' committee was to be the step which would lead to this goal. This proved much more difficult than Miss Perry had anticipated. To begin with, there were not the clearly organized groups which one found in the average suburban community. Several new churches were being built but many churchgoers still went to "downtown churches," and this was true for many other relationships. It was necessary, therefore, not only to discover what groups existed and secure representation from them but to try to get individuals that would be known by, and representative of, large groups of other people. Miss Perry spent much time during her first weeks in South Haven "pounding the pavement," talking to municipal officials, real estate men, storekeepers, schoolteachers, doctors, women she would meet on the street, policemen, etc. She drove through the whole area noting subdivisions and other areas that seemed to be relatively isolated and communities in themselves. She kept asking constantly about groups and about individuals; she told one and all about the proposal for a committee of citizens to plan for things the community needed.

She discovered a list of groups which should be represented on the committee: there were Community Councils in each of the major subdivisions, one large Roman Catholic Church and four Protestant churches, a Kiwanis Club in process of organization, a State Street

Businessmen's Association, there were Parent-Teachers Associations connected with three schools, Community Improvement Associations in two areas, and, of course, the Municipal Council. There were certain groups largely unorganized but with a sense of identity which should be represented. This was true of a fairly large Jewish group on the north side and a somewhat smaller Danish group on the west side. In addition, Miss Perry had secured the names of 12 persons who she felt would represent various other interests and groups in the community. Counting 2 representatives from each of the groups, she had a list of 48 persons as prospective members of her consultative committee.

During her period of exploration, she had been keeping an eye open for a chairman of the consultative committee. She felt James Hickman was the man and the more she discussed this possibility with various members of the community, the more sure she became that he was the person for the job. Hickman owned a large shopping center which had just opened the previous year, he was wealthy and influential, but more important, he was interested in civic affairs and was very active in almost every constructive enterprise in the community. Moreover, he was an intelligent, sensitive man who, while quiet, was well liked and, for a new community, widely respected. Miss Perry one day made the decision to ask him and went to see him. He accepted immediately saying, "I believe what you propose could do a lot for South Haven."

Hickman went over Miss Perry's list of possible committee members with approval. He added only two other names. "It's a wonderful list of representative persons in this community," he said. They agreed on a date for the first meeting, and Hickman agreed to secure one of the schools for the meeting and to send out personal invitations on his own stationery to those on the list. They also agreed to meet for an hour to go over the agenda for this first meeting.

In preparation for this meeting, Miss Perry developed a questionnaire which she thought might tap the feelings of those who answered it in respect to welfare needs and services. She also developed a rough sampling procedure: five selected homes on 40 representative streets in the area. She proposed that the wife or woman in each of these homes be interviewed, and she hoped the committee would help with this task. Hickman thought this a good idea but confessed he had no idea about such studies. "What concerns me most," he said as they discussed the meeting, "is how we are to get everyone interested. What problem will we bite into? Will it be your questionnaire?" This matter they discussed for some time, finally agreeing that after each made a statement about the purpose of the meeting and about Miss Perry's role, they would explore as a group some of the common problems in the whole community and gradually move on to the study, which presumably would be a more systematic way of doing that about which the committee had been speculating.

Twenty-nine persons turned up for the first meeting of the Citizens' Committee. Mr. Hickman, in opening the meeting, explained that while South Haven had made considerable progress in respect to schools and transportation, little had been done about welfare services. He went on to tell about several families he knew who were in difficulty and who had no idea where they could get help. This meeting was called, he explained, to see what services were required and how they could be secured. He then introduced Miss Perry, who told about the interest of both the Chest and the Council, and their desire to work with the people of South Haven. Her responsibility was to help the group, if they were interested, to identify what was required and to plan ways to secure it. At this point, the meeting was opened for questions and discussion. The questions came rapidly but not in an orderly fashion. Was this a "gimmick of the Chest to get more money in South Haven?" "What was the Welfare Council?" "What did Miss Perry consider as welfare services?" "Was this a way of getting community support for certain agencies like the Y.M.C.A.?" etc. The meeting was frankly suspicious, and it was some time before these suspicions were allayed and discussion moved to the topic of what was required in South Haven. By this time, adjournment time had been reached. More positive interest was being shown, however, and the group agreed to meet one week hence to go over Miss Perry's plan for a study. Mr. Hickman again agreed to arrange a meeting place and to send out notices.

Only 22 attended the second meeting but interest was considerable. There was a freshness and enthusiasm in the group that Miss Perry missed in many of the downtown committees. The group made innumerable valuable suggestions about sources of data in the community. They changed the questionnaire, broadening it and adding questions about neighborliness, etc., which Miss Perry did not feel relevant but about which she did not want to argue. Fifteen of those present agreed to do five interviews at homes and on streets specified by Miss Perry, and two women promised they could easily secure additional interviewers if desired. It was agreed to try to get 40 interviewers—one for each street—and they would meet for a brief training session at a date set by Miss Perry. (Thirty-five turned up for this session. Miss Perry covered the other five streets herself, and the whole interviewing process was completed in two weeks.)

The Citizens' Committee agreed to meet in one month's time to consider the tentative results of all aspects of the survey and to make a special effort to have present other members of the committee who were unable to attend the first two meetings. At this meeting, 41 attended and there was deep interest in Miss Perry's report of the study, especially the summary of the 200 interviews. There was lively discussion on these matters, and before the evening was over the committee was quite sure of what must be provided in South Haven. These in order of priority were (1) a well-developed recreational program, especially for children five to nine years of age; (2) a center where people could get advice or help on small problems or at least information of where to go if specialized help were required; (3) a nursery school; (4) a juvenile court with well-trained officials in charge; and then (5) the following services, all to be of equal importance; home nursing service, case work and recreational services for the aged, and child guidance and adoption services. These needs or wants were stated in lay terms but it was quite clear what the committee meant by each. As the next step,

Mr. Hickman suggested five small committees to explore what was required in each area, how it could be secured, and how much money would be needed.

While working with the Citizens' Committee, Miss Perry had several meetings with her consultative committee and reported through them to both the Welfare Council and the Chest. At first, the consultative committee heard with approval of the interest of the Citizens' Committee of South Haven and the help they provided in completing various parts of the study. But they viewed with some concern the list of priorities established by the South Haven committee. The consultative committee had been particularly concerned with that part of the study dealing with requests to established downtown agencies from people in South Haven. For the most part, there were agency people on the consultative committee and they were impressed with the agencies' report. This report showed pressure on agencies for service in South Haven in the following order of frequency: (1) visiting nurses, (2) homemaker services, (3) Y.M.C.A., (4) Family Service Agency, (5) probation services, (6) a Big Brothers organization, (7) Mental Health Clinic, (8) Society for Crippled Children. The list trailed off with a small number of requests from a wide variety of agencies.

Although it had never been voiced in the consultative committee, it was assumed that the way to deal with South Haven was to provide branch offices of those agencies most frequently in demand in South Haven. The list of needs developed by the Citizens' Committee sounded strange and inconsistent with what the consultative committee considered to be the "real needs." Obviously, there were difficulties ahead.

It was now mid-January, 1954, the Chest campaign had been completed (with only modest success in South Haven), and some of the Chest men were now beginning to inquire how things were going in South Haven. Further, in a few weeks, requests would be going out for agencies to submit their proposed budgets for 1955, and some resolution of what was to be done in South Haven was required.

Miss Perry had a long session with Mrs. Jasper Ridley, the chairman of her consultative committee. Mrs. Ridley was a former chairman of the Welfare Council, was at present a member of the Chest board, and was considered a mature, competent, and influential woman. They agreed that the situation was difficult, and could become much more so if the two committees moved in different directions. "As you know," said Mrs. Ridley, "the Visiting Homemakers and the Y.M.C.A. have wanted to move into South Haven for years. If we come in with a recommendation that does not support their desire, we will be in trouble. Both those groups have influence in the Chest, and they can stir up a lot of trouble. No, I think we have to support at least the move of Visiting Homemakers and the Y.M.C.A. And why not? Both those agencies are needed in South Haven whether the community recognizes this or not."

Sitting in a downtown restaurant, Miss Perry was inclined to agree. She had been enthusiastic at the way the Citizens' Committee in South Haven had taken hold of its work, and it appeared that it might demonstrate citizen planning at its best. Now, she could see she had not taken into account all the forces at work in the situation and might well be headed toward a serious problem. She was now completely on Mrs. Ridley's side and raised the question of how the situation could be handled. Could Mrs. Ridley come to the next meeting of the Citizens' Committee? She could and would.

At the next meeting of the Citizens' Committee, all the committees reported. It was evident they had been talking all over South Haven about their plans, and while some of the proposals seemed naïve to Mrs. Ridley, there was enthusiasm.

Mrs. Ridley was introduced and expressed her interest in the work of the committee but played a waiting game, planning to come in at an appropriate time. As the meeting progressed, she became, however, increasingly concerned. For the group, in considering all the separte recommendations, was discussing the possibility of one central organization to which one could come for any kind of help and from which would come all kinds of services. There would be a recreational department, a nursing school staff, a mental health clinic, and visiting nurses. But central to the whole operation would be an information and counseling center. Here anyone could come for information and advice. If possible, help would be given directly, but if not, the person would be referred not to four different departments but to the appropriate person in the same building. In other words, all who asked for help would be seen by a person skilled in appraising needs and able to make kindly and intelligent referrals.

As this idea developed, Mrs. Ridley felt forced to step in. She congratulated the group on its work and original thinking but felt she must remind them of the experience of many of the individual agencies. Each had years of experience in a particular area, and it would be impossible for any one agency to accumulate the knowledge and skill of all these separate agencies. Each had its own particular service and each performed this service effectively. To think of one agency would be to lose the advantage of these years of experience. Further, would it not be excessively expensive? For example, each agency trains and supervises its own workers. Who would be able to supervise a visiting homemaker, a family case worker, a nursery school teacher, and a recreational leader? The committee listened with interest, and probably with some understanding and appreciation, but as she worked through her arguments, she concluded with a sentence which immediately aroused hostility: "I doubt very much," said Mrs. Ridley, "if our committee would be prepared to recommend the single agency you suggest."

Mr. Hickman asked politely for an explanation of the relationship between the two committees and Mrs. Ridley explained the request from the Chest to the Council and the appointment of her committee which had responsibility for recommending what should be done in South Haven "Why, then, this committee?" asked Mr. Hickman. Mrs. Ridley did not do well on this question but suggested that there should be coöperation between the two groups. Mr. Hickman seemed to swallow and said, "Of course, we recognize that the Welfare Council has a great deal more experience than we have in these matters, and we want your advice and help. Perhaps your committee would be willing to meet with us when we are clear what we feel would be a good plan for South Haven." To this Mrs. Ridley readily agreed and the meeting was adjourned before some of the anger that had been developing was expressed openly in the meeting.

Following this meeting, Miss Perry gave some careful thought to her own position and role. True, she had been swayed by Mrs. Ridley almost to the point of wishing the Citizens' Committee did not exist. For things would be so much simpler. She could have reported on her study to the consultative committee, recommendations would be drafted, everyone would be happy, and she would return to her old position with increased status. But her job was to work through difficult situations—it was not to look for an easy way out. Her job was not to decide what a "good plan" for South Haven was. Her job was to help those responsible people who thought they knew what was "good" to come to some sort of agreement and to get the plan implemented. With a new sense of mission she began the next phase of her work.

At the next meeting of the Citizens' Committee, she apologized for not having clarified the role of Mrs. Ridley's committee. Actually, she confessed, she expected both committees to arrive at about the same conclusions. Obviously that was not to be the case, and the Citizens' Committee must now consider whether it would be adamant about its general plan or recognize that, however difficult it would be, there might be value in having the experience of the Council people and the support of the Chest from which some of the money must come—in which case working with these latter groups would be important. While there was general acceptance of Miss Perry, there was no agreement with her idea of "working things out" with the "downtown commitees." As one member said, "What we want to avoid is all those separate organizations each with a vested interest to protect." But as the meeting wore on, especially with the help of Mr. Hickman, the committee moved to the position of developing a plan and discussing it with the Council committee.

In the three meetings that followed, the general plan of the Citizens' Committee itself underwent some change as inevitable difficulties arose. The municipality would support a public recreation department, would house it in a "central building" but the workers would be on the city payroll and would have to be responsible to the municipal council. A mental health clinic with a government grant was possible, but it would be difficult to integrate it into a general social agency. There were other complications. The plan as it finally emerged was for (1) a central health and welfare building in which various agencies would be housed; (2) the first services to be recreation, visiting nurses, a mental health clinic, and the Big Brothers Association; (3) a central counseling and information bureau, and (4) a separate nursery school and a recreation club for the older people.

Meanwhile, Miss Perry had been working with her consultative committee. With this group she took the position that of course the Citizens' Committee could be ignored but it would be at the cost of good will in South Haven. The Citizens' Committee might actually set up its own organization in opposition to the Council and/or the Chest. Further, there was need for experimentation in social work and it might be that new patterns of organization were required in new communities. This had its effect even though most members influenced by Mrs. Ridley's report felt the Citizens' Committee was far "out of line." But there seemed to be a determination to work out the issue together in some way. It was decided, however, that in meeting representatives from the Citizens' Committee, representatives from the Chest executive should be included. The joint meeting of ten representatives from the Citizens' Committee, the six members of the consultative committee, and three members from the Chest executive committee was set for March 14, 1954.

This meeting was a long and difficult one. It was implicitly recognized that it would be all but impossible to get these groups together for further meetings and there was a determination to settle the matter on this occasion. Mrs. Ridley served as chairman of the committee and opened the meeting by suggesting its purpose be to develop a plan for welfare services in South Haven that would be consistent with the needs of the people of South Haven, the best knowledge of the Welfare Council, and the financial resources of the Community Chest. A representative from each group then spoke. Mr. Hickman outlined the revised plan of his group; Mrs. Judd, Mrs. Ridley's associate and a member of the board of Visiting Home-makers, reported for the Council consultative committee, and Mr. Roger Banks for the Community Chest. The latter was geniality itself, emphasizing that "we must get together not for ourselves but for those people who need our services." Banks was the head of an old firm of stockbrokers, wealthy, influential, and much more shrewd and intelligent than he appeared.

As they reported, it appeared that what was requested, in order of desirability, was approximately as follows:

Citizens' Committee	Consultative Committee
1. A central building for health and welfare services	1. Visiting nurses association
2. A central counseling and information center	2. Visiting homemakers association
	3. Y.M.C.A.
3. A public recreation program	4. Family welfare association
4. Visiting nurses association	5. Catholic welfare bureau
5. Mental health clinic	6. Big Brothers organization
6. Nursery school	7. Society for crippled children
7. A Sunset Club (for older people)	

There was, therefore, considerable discrepancy between what the two committees felt was needed in South Haven. Mr. Banks, speaking for the Chest, said its members were less interested in the specifics of the plan than in giving the best possible services at the lowest possible cost.

Here one of the South Haven committee developed at considerable length the reason for the central counseling and information center as a way of saving money and giving better services, because instead of having "agencies tripping over each other" there would be one agency to which all people could go. Ninety percent of their problems could be solved in this agency and the other 10 percent could be referred to the proper agency—downtown if necessary. There was no need to bring in "all these agencies." The meeting moved gradually from this point into a heated argument, the members of the consulative committee challenging the South Haven people on the basis of the judgments they were making. The study in South Haven came under sharp attack: How good was the sample of 200? Was it at all reliable? Could a few interviews secured by untrained interviewers be considered of any value? Soon the study was the subject of heated discussion. Miss Perry tried to shift the focus by pointing out the "common agreements," but without success. The battle waged on.

Mr. Banks then interrupted to recount at considerable length an experience he had had in his business with several research men. The story had no point or relation to the discussion, but because he was Mr. Banks no one would interrupt. This interlude did serve, however, to cool tempers, and while those present were impatient with Mr. Banks, they began to relax a bit. No one knew whether it was deliberate or not, but soon Mr. Banks went into a discussion of the issues and the plans. He was not very articulate and he mumbled a lot but what he had in mind soon began to come out clearly and all those present were listening carefully. It was clear, he said, that some of the recommendations of the Citizens' Committee did not require decision here. The central building for welfare service—"something I've always felt was needed in this city"—was a good idea but was the exclusive concern of people in South Haven. The Chest could not provide funds but if the folks in South Haven erected such a building, he was sure the Chest would support the idea and encourage its agencies to rent offices in such a building. The public recreation program was, of course, also the sole concern of South Haven and he was pleased that they had already moved on this matter. The mental health clinic was obviously important but a separate board should be set up and should apply to the government for a grant. This grant, if possible, would be supplemented with Chest funds, but the Chest policy was not to carry the full costs of such a clinic when government funds were available for this purpose. The nursery school, he understood, would have to be worked out also with both the local and state governments, for if this was developed in a manner consistent with government standards a considerable grant would be available. Further work on all these matters would undoubtedly be carried on by South Haven people. As to the common concerns, he personally approved the central counseling service and congratulated the South Haven folks for developing the idea. But no one knew how this would work out—it should be a great success but we couldn't be sure. Therefore, instead of two or three workers for this center, why not try the idea for a year on an experimental basis with one worker? If it proved itself, it could be expanded; if not, only a modest investment would be lost. As to agencies to extend their work in South Haven, he felt a visiting nurses association, a visiting homemakers organization, the Y.M.C.A., a Catholic welfare bureau, and a family welfare association should be given the same opportunity to try a year on an experimental basis with branch offices in South Haven. He was sure such a plan would be supported by the Council and the Chest. Banks had spoken for 40 minutes without a note and without referring to any of the details of the plans of either committee. He seemed in some way to capture the whole group and if Mrs. Ridley had put the matter to a vote, it would probably have been approved unanimously. However, she allowed time for discussion, and after a long pause and a few questions, some opposition began to emerge, particularly on the part of one of the Citizens' Committee as to why only one worker was to be appointed in the counseling center.

Mr. Banks then spoke again. It was as if no one had spoken since he finished his statement, "In light of what I've said, Madam Chairman, I would like to make a motion." He then summarized his major points in the form of a motion. This was seconded by one of the other Chest representatives. Before bringing it to a vote, Mrs. Ridley said she felt the motion provided a good plan but that she would like to feel Mr. Hickman agreed with this. The latter agreed, especially because of the "one year trial basis" of *all* the services to be supported by Chest funds. On the basis of the approval of key persons, the motion was passed with 16 in favor and 2 (from South Haven) opposing. In closing the meeting, Mrs. Ridley thanked all those present for their work, particularly Miss Perry for her continued hard work.

It was, of course, impossible for the Citizens' Committee to secure a central building in the first year of its operation. Thus, when the "approved agencies" moved in they took separate offices in various parts of South Haven. The central counseling and information center secured an experienced worker and suitable headquarters in the central part of the community. But the worker had a difficult problem. She had a large number of relatively simple questions to answer, but she was also the recipient of some "tough cases"—multiple-problem families with long records of difficulty (some of which she found out later were sent to her by other agencies) and it took a good deal of time to sort out the problems and the proper agencies to consult.

Most important was the trend in organization. The workers in the other agencies all organized South Haven boards or committees to guide their work. The Y.M.C.A., especially, secured a powerful board. At the end of the first year, these agencies were well established, each had its own work, its own program, and its local board or committee of interpretation and support, as well as encouragement from a downtown agency. The budget of each was approved without serious question for the second year, and it could be assumed they were now on a permanent basis.

On the other hand, the Citizens' Committee had difficulties. Miss Perry returned to her old job on the Welfare Council and the committee continued without professional advice or help of any kind. The burden proved to be considerable, there was confusion in several small details (such as the place of the next meeting), and seldom were there more than 12 in attendance. The committee did, however, get the public recreation program underway and did make approaches to the government regarding nursery schools and a mental health clinic. These projects, however, required a good deal of citizen action and the committee did not seem to have the energy or inclination to follow through. The committee had served also as the board of the central counseling and information service, but because of many other concerns, little attention was given to this project. A request was made for a budget for the second year, but after investigation it was turned down by the Chest and the agency was closed. This seemed to be a final blow for the Citizens' Committee and it did not meet again.

Questions for Discussion

1. Evaluate the professional work of Miss Perry. What were her strengths and weaknesses? Where was she effective and where ineffective?

2. Why did the Citizens' Committee gradually go out of existence? What gave it strength and enthusiasm? What sapped its strength? What were the factors in the situation that operated against it?

3. Evaluate the part played by Mr. Banks in this episode. What do you think he had in mind in approving so much of the Citizens' Committee plan?